Salesforce DevOps for Architects

Discover tools and techniques to optimize the delivery of your Salesforce projects

Rob Cowell

Lars Malmqvist

Salesforce DevOps for Architects

Group Product Manager: Alok Dhuri

Publishing Product Manager: Uzma Sheerin

Senior Editor: Nithya Sadanandan

Book Project Manager: Deeksha Thakkar

Technical Editor: Jubit Pincy

Copy Editor: Safis Editing

Indexer: Manju Arasan

Production Designer: Shankar Kalbhor

Developer Relations Marketing Executive: Deepak Kumar and Mayank Singh

Business Development Executive: Thilakh Rajavel

First published: January 2024

Production reference: 1190124

Published by
Packt Publishing Ltd.
Packt Publishing Ltd
Grosvenor House
11 St Paul's Square
Birmingham
B3 1RB

ISBN 978-1-83763-605-1

www.packtpub.com

To my wife and daughter, for patiently waiting for me as I disappeared every evening to my desk.
To my employer, for their support, encouragement and education.

– Rob Cowell

To Ada, Pino, and Damiana—without whom nothing else makes sense.

– Lars Malmqvist

Contributors

About the authors

Rob Cowell is a Salesforce DevOps Advocate at a leading platform provider in this space. He uses his wealth of experience as a Salesforce Dev and Architect to guide and advise on best practice for Salesforce DevOps. He has gained a unique insight into Salesforce trends and challenges over the years, and uses this to help organizations of all shapes and sizes to optimize their Salesforce processes. Alongside his day job, he is an active participant of the Salesforce community, providing support and sharing experiences to help others thrive.

I'd like to thank my beloved wife and daughter for enduring my long evenings at the desk with patience. Additionally, I extend my gratitude to my employer for their unwavering support, encouragement, and the educational opportunities provided

Lars Malmqvist is a 32x certified Salesforce CTA and has spent the past 15 years in the Salesforce ecosystem building advanced solutions on the platform. Currently, he works as a partner in the management consultancy, Implement Consulting Group, focusing on supporting large Nordic Salesforce clients in their transformation journeys. He has published two books, Architecting AI Solutions on Salesforce and Salesforce Anti-Patterns, both with Packt publishing.

To Ada, Pino, and Damiana—without whom nothing else makes sense.

About the reviewers

Andrew Barrick has been a part of the Salesforce ecosystem since 2015. He has worked at ISVs - firstly as a Scrum Master and Lead Engineer within product engineering teams, and then as a Technical Architect in Professional Services teams designing, building and implementing customisation projects. He is currently a DevOps Architect at Gearset, bringing experiences from across those years to help customers define modern, scalable and resilient Salesforce DevOps practices. Andy has spoken at events across the world on DevOps ideas and ideals, and their application across the software delivery process. He lives on the edge of the Yorkshire Dales with his wife Maria and children Matthew, Samuel and Daisy.

Aidan Harding is the Head of Platform Engineering – Salesforce at Mantra Tech. Before that, he spent 9 years at Nebula Consulting as Technology Director. He regularly speaks at Salesforce community events in the UK including London's Calling and DevOps Dreamin'. During his time at Nebula, Aidan created various open-source Apex packages including Nebula Core - a set of tools to empower developers to work in a fast and modular manner on Salesforce. Academically, Aidan gained a PhD in Computer Science in 2004 for his work on model-checking systems with game semantics.

Table of Contents

3

The Value of Source Control   21

4

Testing Your Changes   39

5

Day-to-Day Delivery with SFDX   55

6

Exploring Packaging   71

10

Monitoring for Changes   137

11

Data Seeding Your Development Environments   151

16

Other Salesforce DevOps Tools   207

17

Conclusion   217

Index   227

Other Books You May Enjoy   236

Preface

As the Salesforce Platform evolves into an increasingly complex landscape, architects face a growing demand for advanced solutions. The key to successful Salesforce projects lies in effective DevOps practice, and this book helps you achieve just that by offering strategic and practical insights into Salesforce components.

This book starts by cultivating a DevOps mindset, focusing on collaboration, coordination, and communication. It helps you learn how to efficiently demonstrate governance, visibility, and accountability. Building upon this architectural foundation, you'll delve into tools and techniques to plan your strategy using the capabilities of SFDX. Once you've gotten to grips with Salesforce packaging, you'll learn how to build a CI/CD stack with freely available software and configure it for automated change delivery. You'll then address the operational concerns of a mature DevOps process as you explore topics such as ticket management, backups, change monitoring, and data seeding. These are essential for maintaining a clean and healthy Salesforce org. Finally, you'll learn about the ecosystem of third-party solutions, which provide out-of-the-box capabilities to accelerate your Salesforce DevOps journey.

By the end of this book, you'll have demystified Salesforce DevOps, empowering you to deliver Salesforce projects with the expertise of a DevOps professional.

Who this book is for

If you are a Salesforce architect or senior developer looking to bring DevOps best practices to your projects, this book is for you. To learn from this book, you should have a strong familiarity with Salesforce platform development both in code and low-code, understand concepts such as metadata, JSON, and XML, and feel at ease with command-line operations.

What this book covers

Chapter 1, A Brief History of Deploying Salesforce Changes, discusses the unique challenges of developing on the Salesforce platform and looks at previous attempts to solve them.

Chapter 2, Developing a DevOps Culture, sets up a foundation for DevOps success by emphasizing the need to establish a cultural mindset ahead of technology.

Chapter 3, The Value of Source Control, explores the fundamental technology that enables a DevOps implementation – source control.

Chapter 4, Testing Your Changes, reiterates the importance of regular and early testing and explore methods for accomplishing it.

Chapter 5, Day-to-Day Delivery with SFDX, walks through a reasonably typical development and deployment scenario using Salesforce's SFDX toolset.

Chapter 6, Exploring Packaging, looks at the another change delivery method in Salesforce, as we visit the different types of Salesforce packaging.

Chapter 7, CI/CD Automation, dives into powerful DevOps automation techniques that make up a full CI/CD pipeline, with examples for popular platforms.

Chapter 8, Ticketing Systems, visits the ways in which a work ticketing system enhances your process and aids rapid delivery through manageable chunks.

Chapter 9, Backing Up Data and Metadata, reiterates the importance of backing up both your data and metadata, and explores the various methods for doing so.

Chapter 10, Monitoring for Changes, discusses the importance of tracking changes across your entire Salesforce estate, ensuring no change is missed.

Chapter 11, Data Seeding Your Development Environments, demonstrates the need for accurate test data in your Salesforce development lifecycle to aid accurate testing.

Chapter 12, Salesforce DevOps Tools – Gearset, begins our exploration of third-party Salesforce DevOps platforms with a look at Gearset.

Chapter 13, Copado, continues looking at the Salesforce DevOps ecosystem as we turn to Copado.

Chapter 14, Salesforce DevOps Tools – Flosum, moves on to the next major player in Salesforce DevOps, with an overview of Flosum.

Chapter 15, AutoRABIT, completes our evaluation of the most common third-party Salesforce DevOps tools as we run through AutoRABIT's capabilities.

Chapter 16, Other Salesforce DevOps Tools, catches up on other Salesforce DevOps solutions that are less common, but still an option.

Chapter 17, Conclusion, wraps things up with a summary of what we've learned and reiterate the important takeaways.

To get the most out of this book

The nature of this book assumes a knowledge of Salesforce development, which suggests you've likely deployed changes in some way. There is no assumption of existing DevOps knowledge, as this is covered in the book.

Software/hardware covered in the book	Operating system requirements
Salesforce	Windows, macOS, or Linux
Git	
Any other software of platform is covered on a per-chapter basis	

If you are using the digital version of this book, we advise you to type the code yourself or access the code from the book's GitHub repository (a link is available in the next section). Doing so will help you avoid any potential errors related to the copying and pasting of code.

Download the example code files

You can download the example code files for this book from GitHub at `https://github.com/PacktPublishing/Salesforce-DevOps-for-Architects` If there's an update to the code, it will be updated in the GitHub repository.

We also have other code bundles from our rich catalog of books and videos available at `https://github.com/PacktPublishing/`. Check them out!

Conventions used

There are a number of text conventions used throughout this book.

`Code in text`: Indicates code words in text, database table names, folder names, filenames, file extensions, pathnames, dummy URLs, user input, and Twitter handles. Here is an example: "The related `ContactId` and `OpportunityId` fields need to be populated correctly to link records."

A block of code is set as follows:

```
from salesforce_bulk import SalesforceBulk
import csv

# Salesforce credentials
username = 'your_username'
password = 'your_password'
security_token = 'your_security_token'
```

When we wish to draw your attention to a particular part of a code block, the relevant lines or items are set in bold:

```
from salesforce_bulk import SalesforceBulk
import csv

# Salesforce credentials
username = 'your_username'
password = 'your_password'
security_token = 'your_security_token'
```

Any command-line input or output is written as follows:

```
sf force package create -n "My Managed Package" -t Managed -r force-app
```

Bold: Indicates a new term, an important word, or words that you see onscreen. For instance, words in menus or dialog boxes appear in **bold**. Here is an example: "Installing the package by clicking the **Get It Now** button on the AppExchange listing, which initiates the installation process in the customer's Salesforce environment."

> **Tips or important notes**
> Appear like this.

Get in touch

Feedback from our readers is always welcome.

General feedback: If you have questions about any aspect of this book, email us at customercare@packtpub.com and mention the book title in the subject of your message.

Errata: Although we have taken every care to ensure the accuracy of our content, mistakes do happen. If you have found a mistake in this book, we would be grateful if you would report this to us. Please visit www.packtpub.com/support/errata and fill in the form.

Piracy: If you come across any illegal copies of our works in any form on the internet, we would be grateful if you would provide us with the location address or website name. Please contact us at copyright@packt.com with a link to the material.

If you are interested in becoming an author: If there is a topic that you have expertise in and you are interested in either writing or contributing to a book, please visit authors.packtpub.com.

Share Your Thoughts

Once you've read *Salesforce DevOps for Architects*, we'd love to hear your thoughts! Scan the QR code below to go straight to the Amazon review page for this book and share your feedback.

https://packt.link/r/1837636052

Your review is important to us and the tech community and will help us make sure we're delivering excellent quality content.

Download a free PDF copy of this book

Thanks for purchasing this book!

Do you like to read on the go but are unable to carry your print books everywhere?

Is your eBook purchase not compatible with the device of your choice?

Don't worry, now with every Packt book you get a DRM-free PDF version of that book at no cost.

Read anywhere, any place, on any device. Search, copy, and paste code from your favorite technical books directly into your application.

The perks don't stop there, you can get exclusive access to discounts, newsletters, and great free content in your inbox daily

Follow these simple steps to get the benefits:

1. Scan the QR code or visit the link below

https://packt.link/free-ebook/9781837636051

2. Submit your proof of purchase
3. That's it! We'll send your free PDF and other benefits to your email directly

1

A Brief History of Deploying Salesforce Changes

With Salesforce's own delivery model coming in the form of three major releases per year, the platform has evolved substantially since it was first made available back in 2000. From its early days as a predominantly sales tool, Salesforce has evolved to become a development platform in its own right. With this change came the need to bring true development best practices to your customizations and the need to deliver them effectively.

In this chapter, we'll be looking at the history of making and delivering changes on the Salesforce platform, to understand the current shortcomings of the built-in tools. This will help set the context for the necessity of a DevOps process and where the current state of the art sits today. We'll be covering the following main topics:

- The beginnings of customizing Salesforce

- Apex and Visualforce

- Sandboxes and change sets

- SFDX and scratch orgs

- DevOps Center

Unlike the rest of this book, this chapter does not necessarily provide actionable steps or best practice guidance that you can apply to your Salesforce implementations. However, one of the fundamental principles of being a good Salesforce architect is to understand the *why* of our decisions. By looking at the history of Salesforce as a development platform, and how it has continued to steer toward contemporary software development approaches and tooling, we can better understand the need for DevOps in the Salesforce ecosystem.

An introduction to the history of Salesforce as a development platform

For any sufficiently complex IT system, it is important to consider the full range of architectural considerations in both the implementation phase and the day-to-day running of the system. These considerations are not just technical aspects but those that sit at the business level as well – strong governance, accurate and up-to-date documentation, definable metrics, and a demonstrable return on investment to the business.

As Salesforce has grown, so has the need to apply these architectural factors to the work we do on the platform. Salesforce has become a *first-class citizen* in many organizations, acting as the digital hub to run a business. A proper change management process is therefore critical to avoid interruptions of service, and DevOps is the perfect approach to that requirement. DevOps promises faster, more accurate software releases, fewer errors, less downtime, and a faster path to recovery when problems occur.

We can reasonably pinpoint Salesforce first becoming a development platform in 2003. At the company's inaugural edition of Dreamforce, their flagship conference that continues annually to the present day, they announced a fundamental shift in how customers can customize the platform. Dubbed **sforce 2.0**, it was initially positioned as an *on-demand application server* and included some key capabilities, which we'll explore next.

Custom objects

The first major innovation introduced at this time was the ability to create additional custom objects, much like database tables, to complement the built-in objects provided by Salesforce for their core CRM capabilities. These custom objects could themselves contain custom fields and together provided the early framework for developing custom business applications on the platform.

Suddenly, Salesforce had moved from being just a sales CRM system and started moving toward becoming a platform to develop custom business applications. Salesforce teams were now able to start tailoring processes and applications to the core needs of their business, regardless of which industry they worked in. For example, some Salesforce customers would leverage this capability to start building out the ability to handle support cases for their business – something that didn't become a core platform capability until the announcement of Service Cloud in 2009.

S-Controls

S-Controls (initially called *sforce controls*) were one of the two programmatic elements of the new customization capabilities. Combining both functionality and user interface elements in one container, S-Controls could contain any items that could be displayed in a browser, such as Java applets, ActiveX controls, and web forms.

While they've been long since deprecated, S-Controls were the first method made available for developers to customize the platform in a programmatic way, and they allowed them to bring skillsets and programming languages from other non-Salesforce development into the platform. They enabled Salesforce developers to harness HTML and JavaScript for the creation of custom pages and user interface components. In this sense, they could be potentially viewed as an early forerunner of Lightning Web Components but without much of the best practice we use today.

SOQL

Sforce 2.0 also introduced **Sforce Object Query Language (SOQL)**, which provided a means of querying data from both standard and custom objects, with a syntax like the industry standard, SQL. This provided developers with a powerful mechanism with which to query the data in their Salesforce organization programmatically and act upon the results of these queries.

If we were to look at SOQL from an architect's perspective, we can see how this aligns with the need to ensure that your data quality is of as high a standard as your metadata. Clean, actionable data to drive business decisions should always be one of the key deliverables for an architect. SOQL provided an additional means of working with this data, whether operationally for the day-to-day business or as the beginning of a means to extract data from the platform for archival purposes. This latter use case is something that we'll explore later as we look at the importance of backups in a well-architected Salesforce DevOps strategy.

Sforce web services

One of the other fundamental new capabilities of sforce 2.0 was the ability to integrate Salesforce with other platforms, thanks to the exposing of the object model and business logic via web service APIs. Using the standards at the time, SOAP and WSDL, it was now possible to interact with your Salesforce organization from more traditional development environments and systems, over a network.

Workflows

The last major element introduced with sforce 2.0 was a business process automation engine called workflows. By defining workflow rules that responded to changes in your data, business logic could be triggered for things such as escalations, notifications, and automatic updates to data in response to events. Workflows were still very much a config, not code, means of delivering functionality, but as we'll see later, being a low-code solution does not mean that it should be ignored when it comes to DevOps.

Apex and Visualforce

At the 2006 edition of Dreamforce, Salesforce's flagship conference, co-founder Parker Harris revealed the most significant change to the Salesforce platform to date. Customers were now able to develop custom solutions using Salesforce's own programming language, called **Apex**, right within Salesforce itself.

A variant of the popular Java programming language, Apex enabled automation through code for the first time. Originally limited to triggers only, developers could now take a programmatic approach to responding to data changes.

Later in the evolution of the platform, Apex would adopt more of the object-oriented paradigm with the arrival of Apex classes, allowing developers to build a more structured, decoupled implementation than triggers alone could deliver.

Alongside Apex, the other major innovation to the Salesforce platform was Visualforce, introduced in 2008. Taking cues from other contemporary UI languages such as ASP or PHP, Visualforce blended HTML with programmatic elements and markup that connected back to your logic written in Apex. Visualforce went on to quickly supersede the S-Controls that were previously introduced, becoming the standard way to write custom user interfaces and pages in your Salesforce implementation.

With all these advances in the platform for development and customization, Salesforce then turned its attention to how to deliver them. Let's look at how this was initially introduced in the next section.

Sandboxes and change sets

As Salesforce continued to mature, the need to be able to safely make changes outside of production and move them across when ready became obvious. However, the pace of DevOps innovation did not seem to keep up with the rise of Salesforce as a development platform.

Sandboxes were introduced in the winter 2006 release, allowing customers to try out changes and enhancements in a safe environment away from production – but with a catch. The original implementation of sandboxes did not allow you to move those changes *back* to production, meaning that you had to recreate those changes again in your production environment manually. This would be both time-consuming and error-prone.

In recognition of this shortcoming, change sets were initially introduced in beta for the winter 2010 release, some four years after sandboxes, and finally, they became generally available in the Spring 2011 release. Change sets finally allowed the code and configuration work done in sandbox environments to be packaged up and moved between environments, whether from sandbox to sandbox, sandbox to production, or even production to sandbox. This opened up new possibilities to plan Salesforce environments as part of a mature application development life cycle – you could now have dev, QA, UAT, and staging environments ahead of production go-live. This was the first significant step toward achieving a DevOps process that matched those on other development platforms.

Metadata and Tooling APIs

To open the platform to better tooling for development and deployment, Salesforce introduced two important APIs – Metadata API in the Spring 2008 release and Tooling API in the Spring 2013 release. While they both fulfilled similar functions, there were some important differences in their aims and functionality.

Metadata API

At the simplest level, metadata is data that describes the *structure* of your data, but for the Salesforce platform, that is a bit of an oversimplification. The term *metadata* covers many of the configuration and customization elements of Salesforce as well – at the time of writing, Salesforce's own Metadata Coverage Report, available at `https://developer.salesforce.com/docs/metadata-coverage`, indicates 601 metadata types in the platform, the vast majority of which are covered in Metadata API.

Metadata API can be used to move this metadata between environments. You can retrieve the metadata as XML files from one Salesforce organization and deploy it into another. Much like change sets, the source and target for these operations can be sandboxes, production, or, as we'll learn about shortly, scratch orgs.

Additionally, Metadata API allows you to create, update, and delete metadata within a Salesforce org, and this unlocks a fundamental capability for both Salesforce development and to adopt a DevOps approach on the platform.

The Metadata API underpins most DevOps tools on the platform, whether that's Salesforce's own SFDX, the new DevOps Center, or the various third-party Salesforce DevOps solutions available. They all leverage Metadata API to coordinate the movement of your code and config between environments.

Tooling API

While Metadata API did much of the heavy work of managing metadata, Salesforce introduced Tooling API to provide further capabilities that better aligned to DevOps practices, such as smaller and more focused metadata retrieval and deployment, the ability to run unit tests and view both the test results and the associated code coverage, and support for some additional code debugging capabilities.

Being able to manage unit test cycles makes Tooling API another strong candidate for use in DevOps processes and tools. As architects, we need to ensure that we not only deliver code *quickly* but also that it is of the right quality – it doesn't break in isolation, it doesn't break existing code, it fulfills the requirements for which it was created, and it deploys between Salesforce organizations seamlessly. These are all factors of the Change Failure Rate, one of the fundamental DevOps metrics that we'll explore in the next chapter as we look at what the key considerations to develop a DevOps culture as architects are.

Tooling API is primarily targeted at those wishing to create additional development tools or apps for the platform, and its arrival heralded Salesforce development support in some of the popular IDEs of the day, which we will look at next.

The Force.com IDE and Mavensmate

With new tools that leveraged Metadata and Tooling APIs, it was no longer necessary to develop for the Salesforce platform from within the platform. To assist developers with this approach, Salesforce started looking at how best to deliver a standardized developer experience that matched the standards of the time. Let's run through the tools available at that time.

The Force.com IDE

One of the early IDEs that took advantage of this was Salesforce's own Force.com IDE.

Built on top of the modular plugin architecture of the popular Eclipse development environment that was predominantly used for Java, the Force.com IDE took advantage of the new APIs to allow developers to not only code with a proper editor but also to save their changes back in their development organizations, directly from the IDE, without having to switch back to the Salesforce user interface.

The Force.com IDE became very popular very quickly, as it was the first attempt to provide a modern environment for Salesforce developers, with some of the niceties that developers on other platforms such as Java or .NET had come to expect. However, it developed a reputation for being slow and unstable equally as quickly.

Mavensmate

As an antidote to the heavyweight installation of Eclipse and the plugin, and as a potential means to improve speed and stability, 2013 saw the arrival of another development tool for Salesforce – Mavensmate.

Mavensmate took the same plugin approach as the Force.com IDE, in that it effectively extended another editor called **Sublime Text** (and later, support was added for the rival Atom editor), but both the underlying editor and the Mavensmate plugin on the top were considerably more lightweight. This made working with Salesforce development easier, faster, and more stable than ever before, and Mavensmate became the choice of Salesforce developers everywhere on the basis of its speed and ease of use – not just for development but also to deploy changes, thanks to the use of the Metadata and Tooling APIs.

Introducing SFDX

The state of Salesforce change management had largely remained stable for several years. For the majority of Salesforce developers and admins, change sets remained the definitive means of delivering change from sandbox to production.

All this changed again when Salesforce released its SFDX toolchain in 2018. SFDX offered the promise of modern development and deployment practices, seen on other platforms, delivered through a command-line tool. Suddenly, the potential existed for advanced, scriptable deployments, more robust

IDE integration, and a new way to manage changes. Most importantly, it represented the move toward a source-driven development model for Salesforce, rather than the traditional organization-based model.

The SFDX **command-line interface (CLI)** was coupled with the introduction of scratch orgs. These are ephemeral development environments that can be spun up and torn down easily from SFDX, created using different configurations (or *org shapes*), and populated with test data. The ability to create them from a command lent itself to a new era of automated testing, as we shall see later, but it also reinforced the principle that organizations are now secondary to source code. If a scratch org expires, it's not a major issue because another one can be easily recreated from the source code.

Finally, Salesforce had recognized the need for tight integration with development tools and provided extensions for the popular **Visual Studio (VS)** Code environment, easing both development and deployment on the Salesforce platform, right from the IDE. Additionally, by building on open standards such as the **Open Command Line Interface Framework (OCLIF)**, it opened the tool up to extension via plugins, which were contributed from both inside and outside Salesforce, extending the capabilities of the SFDX CLI and filling some of the gaps that the tool didn't cover natively.

SFDX continues to be the Salesforce-recommended approach for developers working with the platform, especially around integrating it into CI/CD pipelines and other automation. As of December 2022, Salesforce is continuing a drive toward a unified CLI that combines the SFDX command line and the newer SF command line, which introduced a newer structure and a cleaner approach. This consolidation will hopefully result in an even more efficient command-line toolset that will increase the ease of building a robust DevOps pipeline.

DevOps Center

Salesforce has long acknowledged that the platform has outgrown change sets, but SFDX was (and still is) perceived by its customers as a tool solely for developers and those comfortable with the command line, despite the VS Code extensions that made it easier to work with. A considerable ecosystem of third-party providers such as Gearset, Copado, AutoRABIT, and Flosum had sprung up to provide platforms for robust DevOps that better matched the wider IT industry's best practices. These tools gave Salesforce developers and admins capabilities such as organization-to-organization comparisons, version control capabilities, static code analysis, and deployment pipelines.

Salesforce entered this space with the release of DevOps Center, which became generally available in December 2022. While not as feature-rich as the incumbent solutions from the third-party ecosystem, it represented a change of messaging from Salesforce to all users – a move away from change set deployments to something that was easy enough to work with, whether you were a low-code or pro-code admin or developer.

We'll be exploring the specifics of DevOps Center (and indeed, the leading solutions in the third-party Salesforce DevOps space) in a later chapter, but it's important to see how much of a fundamental shift in thinking this new product is, particularly when viewed in the context of the history of creating and delivering changes to the platform described earlier.

DevOps Center introduces much of the best practice in Salesforce DevOps that's slowly been established, incrementally, over the years and packages it up in an easy-to-understand native interface, right within the platform:

- It guides Salesforce practitioners toward a model in which source control is the version of truth for changes, rather than sandbox organizations

- It encourages the concept of isolated, incremental change through work items, or user stories – a concept popularized by the agile movement and popular in the DevOps strategy of many other platforms and organizations

- Most importantly, it gives better visibility and accountability for change delivery

These are factors of the overall architecture of a DevOps process, which we shall delve into later in this book. It doesn't cover every aspect thoroughly in the initial release, and it should very much be considered a DevOps *tool* rather than a DevOps *solution*, but as a means of educating Salesforce users on the basics of DevOps and weaning them off change sets, it's a very solid start.

Summary

In this chapter, we looked at the history of Salesforce as a development platform and saw how features were added over the years. We also explored the approach to delivering those changes on Salesforce, from change sets, through the various APIs and tools that utilized them, to the arrival of DevOps Center.

Armed with this knowledge, we can not only better appreciate how far the platform has come but also understand the reasoning behind some of the design choices we have today, gaining a little knowledge of older implementations, which can often prove useful when faced with having to work on older Salesforce organizations.

As architects, it's important to not take DevOps tooling for granted, and having the ability to work with a variety of different approaches and solutions, no matter how old, will help us to work with and improve the state of Salesforce DevOps for the implementations we deliver. In subsequent chapters, we'll look at some of the most recent tooling and, more importantly, the techniques and processes that shape modern Salesforce DevOps.

2
Developing a DevOps Culture

The core of a successful DevOps implementation does not lie with the technology and tooling used. Instead, getting the surrounding team culture in place and aligned with a new way of working is the most essential element that underpins DevOps.

In this chapter, we will cover the importance of the offline aspects of DevOps, and how a culture of collaboration and communication is fundamental to DevOps success. We'll see ways in which to drive adoption and alignment with best practices in your organization. Along the way, we'll explore the following:

- Why culture is key to a DevOps transformation and how we can start building it
- The need to strive for strong communication that drives collaboration
- Ways to drive adoption of and alignment to a DevOps approach

The need for a DevOps culture

The history of software development and its delivery has been long and ever-changing. As the landscape of technology has changed, so has the need for businesses to get that technology into the hands of customers. DevOps represents a drive to deliver according to that need, replacing monolithic software releases, lengthy project cycles, and opaque waterfall methodologies.

When we look at DevOps as a way of delivering change, it's very easy to get pulled into looking at the software tools first, but this should not be where your DevOps journey begins. It's equally important to keep in mind that any DevOps transformation should not be prescriptive; instead, it should align with you and your organization's way of working. This approach is equally important for those that have had prior DevOps experience with other teams or systems – there is no "one size fits all" approach to DevOps, and while experience can be brought to bear on building a DevOps culture with a new team, you should be mindful of tailoring it to fit the team.

However, there are some common elements that work consistently for high-performing DevOps teams, so you should contemplate making these a part of your plan to bring DevOps culture to life. Let's begin by looking at some of the characteristics of successful DevOps teams and the elements of DevOps culture they have adopted, before diving deeper into how to deliver them.

Strongly defined teams

As the name suggests, DevOps teams are a hybrid of IT Development and IT Operations teams, but the reality is not as straightforward. Successful DevOps teams comprise teams from the full end-to-end spectrum of software delivery, from business analysts gathering the requirements and architects designing solutions to those requirements through to developers implementing those solutions and operations delivering those requirements in your Salesforce environments.

It is within this cross-functional team structure that you need to establish strong buy-in for DevOps. A team that does not understand or appreciate the value of a process is unlikely to adopt DevOps – and it only takes a few shortcuts or out-of-process releases to damage the good work the rest of your DevOps team has done. It is vital that the entire team aligns and engages with DevOps as a way of working, to make the initiative successful.

A team that aligns with DevOps practices has shared responsibility for the entire application life cycle, from planning to deployment and maintenance, thus reducing standoffs and finger-pointing over who is responsible for fixing bugs or test failures. Additionally, DevOps encourages product teams to be more involved in the development process, ensuring that their input and expertise are considered throughout the application life cycle.

As architects, we need to convey the value that DevOps brings since for most teams – whether technical or on the business side – this tends to be the key factor that gets people on board. By showing how DevOps benefits everyone along the development journey we have outlined, we stand a better chance of getting teams on board with DevOps, compared to a hard enforcement of processes.

Companies that have yet to adopt a DevOps culture for software delivery may have lost trust in their delivery teams, bringing in heavyweight processes in an attempt to prevent the risk of future failures. Part of adopting a DevOps culture is restoring that trust by providing tools and processes that empower teams to succeed and allow any failures to be small, rather than bogging everything down by trying to avoid failure entirely.

In general, one of the benefits of DevOps and Agile is to be able to take small steps safely. DevOps and Agile methodologies advocate for small, incremental releases rather than large, monolithic deployments. This approach allows teams to identify and fix issues more quickly, reducing the risk of catastrophic failures. It also enables them to respond to changing requirements or market conditions more effectively. As a result, trust in the team's ability to deliver accurate results and adapt to change grows.

Closely working together

Hand in hand with strong teams is the need to collaborate and communicate with each other. This may seem an obvious need in all working teams, not just DevOps, but the principles of clarity, visibility, and cooperation really come to the fore with DevOps and are essential for its smooth running.

To break down the siloed approach to software delivery and work toward a common goal, the entire team needs to be aware of how projects are being delivered. Techniques such as Agile and tools such as Jira or Asana will certainly help with this, but that's only part of the picture of collaboration, as we'll explore shortly.

Constant evolution

No matter how mature a DevOps team may be, the highest-performing teams are always open to change and improvement. Through a continuous cycle of measurement, enhancement, and re-measuring, these teams are able to pinpoint areas where performance and accuracy gains can be made and then address them. The most common metrics they tend to focus on are based on the DORA metrics, as follows:

- **Deployment frequency**: How often a team releases to production
- **Change lead time**: How long it takes for a specific feature to reach production
- **Change failure rate**: The proportion of deployments that either fail to deploy or cause errors in production
- **Mean time to recovery**: How long it takes to recover from a production error or another issue

In the context of Salesforce, measuring against these metrics can be a bit different since it's a cloud-based platform with specific features and limitations. Metrics such as deployment frequency, change lead time, and mean time to recovery can be determined easily enough, especially if you have a ticketing system such as Jira or Asana for managing new work.

The change failure rate can be a little trickier, though, since it involves tracking unsuccessful deployments and the number of incidents or defects related to those deployments. There are a few ways you could approach this – we'll cover Salesforce-specific DevOps solutions and platforms in later chapters, but as an example using on-platform features, you could try the following:

- Use Salesforce's deployment history, available on the **Deployment Status** page, to track the success and failure rates of deployments. Identify failed deployments and the specific components that caused the failure.
- Keep a record of all production incidents, including those caused by recent deployments. You can use the Salesforce Case object to log and track incidents.
- For each failed deployment or production incident, analyze the root cause and determine whether it was due to a recent change. You can use the Salesforce Developer Console, debug logs, and test results to pinpoint the root cause of the issues.
- Divide the number of failed changes (deployments causing incidents or defects) by the total number of changes made during a specific period. Multiply the result by 100 to get the change failure rate as a percentage.

The origin of the DORA metrics

The DORA metrics came from a group called **DevOps Research and Assessment**, which was founded in 2015 by Nicole Forsgren, Gene Kim, and Jez Humble (and later acquired by Google in 2018), to better understand what factors led to high-performing DevOps teams. Since that initial research, these four metrics have become an industry-standard set of measurements of DevOps success.

Now that we've determined the need for, and elements of, a strong DevOps culture, let us look in more detail at some techniques for creating this culture.

Collaboration and communication

In an ideal DevOps team, the whole team works in the same way and toward the same goal – there should be a shared responsibility for the successful delivery of changes. Fundamental to this collaborative approach is strong communication, and this can take many forms, from the more formal approach needed for governance of the overall change management process down to the daily interactions that form part of your usual workflow.

Communication should be clear, informative, and present at every step of the delivery life cycle. For example, when using version control, teams should endeavor to always provide *meaningful* commit messages and comments on peer reviews. These aid teams to carry out the next steps of any change delivery process with *context*, not just the specifics of the change itself. There is often a balance needed between providing sufficiently detailed information and *relevant* information, and you should iterate on this level of detail to find the sweet spot that works for you and your team.

While this book is not an exploration of Agile principles, there does seem to be a strong correlation between successful DevOps teams and Agile practitioners since both disciplines foster these same principles of regular, clear, and concise communication to drive projects forward. Such techniques encompass all team members involved in delivering change so that everyone is informed and aware of the process and progress of work.

Equally, tools will help bring visibility and clarity to daily work. Software for managing features as they go through your DevOps process, such as Jira, Asana, Azure DevOps, and so on, can bring this overview to your processes when used properly and they integrate in some way into most DevOps tools to complete the picture. Many teams have started to eschew email as an internal communication medium, instead favoring the immediacy of messaging platforms such as Slack or Teams as a further means of breaking down silos and removing barriers between cross-functional teams.

The necessity of adapting to remote work has led to an increased reliance on digital communication tools and has changed the dynamics of team interaction in a number of ways. With teams distributed across various locations and time zones, it is essential to have tools that enable real-time collaboration and offer instant communication, file-sharing, and integration with other tools. In remote work, it is not always possible to gather everyone at the same time for discussions. Asynchronous communication tools, such as project management platforms, shared documents, and threaded discussions on messaging apps, allow team members to contribute at their convenience and keep everyone informed of progress.

With every adaptation that needs to be made with the shift to remote working, balance is key. With the shift to digital communication, remote workers may face an influx of messages and notifications. Messaging platforms have adapted by offering features such as channels, threads, and snooze options, allowing team members to prioritize and manage their communications effectively. However, it is equally important to maintain a sense of connection and engagement between team members. Messaging platforms facilitate informal interactions, such as virtual water-cooler conversations, quick check-ins, and social activities, helping teams stay connected and fostering a positive team culture.

Remote work has made it necessary for teams to communicate effectively without the context provided by face-to-face interactions. Modern methods of communication for distributed teams encourage team members to be more concise and clear in their communications, as well as more intentional with their responses.

Finally, as remote work relies on digital communication tools, ensuring data security and compliance with industry regulations becomes critical. Technological solutions have responded by offering end-to-end encryption, data storage options, and compliance features tailored to different industries.

Adoption and alignment

As we've seen, the adoption of a DevOps culture should come before the adoption of DevOps technology. Within each, however, the optimal approach is always to start slowly – it's often said that DevOps is a journey, not a destination, and to that end, we should begin with some planning.

Questions to start with

The best place to start any kind of journey is to look at where we would like to go, with a few questions:

- *What does the intended process look like?*

  Knowing your target scenario helps focus your efforts and prevents unnecessary disruption to your business. For example, is the ultimate goal to be able to deliver business requirements faster and incrementally, or do you want to work to a more scheduled, sprint-based approach, but have better visibility and control over the elements contained within that sprint? Having the aims well defined up front helps focus teams on delivering them.

- *What is the intended audience for the new process?*

  A new DevOps process will impact more than just development and operations teams. If you truly want to adopt an end-to-end Salesforce DevOps approach, you will need to align not just the technical teams but also those involved in the gathering and assigning of work tasks, those responsible for project management, release management, overall architecture, business approval, and more. We'll look at some of these governance aspects shortly.

- *What do we need to change in our current approach?*

  While it's not unheard of, it's rare that an existing process needs to be completely replaced. Take stock of your current delivery model and make note of what works and what doesn't work. Where are the bottlenecks that are slowing you down? How many attempts does it take to get something delivered to production? If we look again at the DORA metrics discussed earlier, where are we starting from? Getting a baseline set of metrics before you start a DevOps transformation is a solid way of measuring progress and improvement – and ultimately, your return on investment – as you begin to adopt Salesforce DevOps. Furthermore, having the ability to demonstrate the problem (and later, the improvements made) to executive stakeholders is invaluable in getting their buy-in for a DevOps transformation project.

With these questions front of mind, it becomes easier to start identifying the potential gains from adopting Salesforce DevOps, which, in turn, can help drive team alignment with the change. This step is essential – everybody involved needs to become a stakeholder in the move to DevOps and the best way to achieve this is to look at things from two viewpoints:

- *What are the benefits that DevOps will bring?*

  After identifying the teams that will be directly impacted by the adoption of DevOps as a means of delivery, work on conveying the benefits to them. Visibility of changes, more manageable and smaller units of work, faster delivery, robust testing, reasonably predictable release cycles – all of these things matter to Salesforce teams and the overriding principle of making their life easier is a strong driver for getting people on board with the change.

- *What are the risks of not adopting DevOps?*

  Equally, it's valuable to assess the risks of standing still and changing nothing. If you don't adopt a faster and more flexible delivery model, you risk being outmaneuvered by more agile competitors. If you don't implement a robust backup and recovery strategy, you risk losing your valuable business data or that of your customers. If you stick to more traditional delivery models, which can be lengthy and arduous, you risk dissatisfaction and burnout in your teams, which can lead to them moving elsewhere.

Making life easy for your teams

If your Salesforce team is new to DevOps concepts, techniques, or even terminology, then it can seem a daunting prospect for them to move to a new delivery model. However, like all large projects, the optimum approach is often to start slowly with small aspects of the process, then expand and iterate upon it.

For example, because the concept of source control has historically been a code-based domain for developers, many Salesforce Admins will be unfamiliar with this approach. This area alone is a good place to start – even if you don't necessarily dive straight into applying source control, the mere act of aligning Admins and Developers with a common way of working contributes to the communication and collaboration components of building a DevOps culture.

Having Admins and Developers work more closely together in this way also lends itself to another great set of techniques for fostering your DevOps culture. High-performing Salesforce DevOps teams make frequent use of mentoring and coaching to not only improve the overall skill set and confidence of the team but also as an aid to collaborative working and breaking down siloes to form a multi-discipline DevOps team.

Of course, it's not all about the process, and you should also ensure that your teams have the necessary tools to aid a smoother DevOps journey. As an architect, you should be ever-mindful of the Salesforce DevOps landscape and assess the components, such as version control providers, new tools or updates to existing ones, or even complete Salesforce DevOps platforms – some of which we'll look at in later chapters.

Governance and risk management

A DevOps culture should be ever-mindful of the need to manage and mitigate business risks, and a strong governance framework should be in place to provide this. It's important to appreciate that while DevOps unlocks the potential for rapid delivery of change, it is not a free-for-all without controls.

The governance of our DevOps process should be aligned with the governance in which your business, or that of your customers, operates. Without the correct processes in place, you risk losing the value of the alignment and adoption you fostered in starting your DevOps journey. You risk falling back to the use of lengthy, monolithic releases with dissatisfied customers waiting on changes that are buried deep in the backlog. You also potentially risk low-quality changes being delivered, which, in a worst-case scenario, can damage your systems, your data, and your reputation.

Regulated industries such as financial services and healthcare face unique challenges when it comes to software development and deployment. These industries are subject to a wide range of regulations, standards, and compliance requirements that govern how software must be developed, tested, and deployed. These regulations are in place to protect sensitive data, ensure data privacy, and prevent fraud and other criminal activities.

In financial services, regulations such as the **Sarbanes-Oxley Act**, **Payment Card Industry Data Security Standards** (**PCI DSS**), and **Anti-Money Laundering** (**AML**) regulations require financial institutions to implement strong controls around software development, testing, and deployment. Similarly, in healthcare, regulations such as the **Health Insurance Portability and Accountability Act** (**HIPAA**) and the **General Data Protection Regulation** (**GDPR**) require healthcare organizations to protect patient data and ensure data privacy. DevOps can help organizations in these types of industries comply with these regulations by providing a structured process for software development, which includes automated testing, security scanning, and continuous monitoring. This can help ensure that software is developed with security and privacy in mind and that any potential security vulnerabilities are identified and addressed before the software is deployed.

A good governance framework addresses these issues by implementing the necessary checks and balances throughout the entire life cycle. From prioritizing work and deciding which initiatives are driven forward through to the technical design and implantation considerations, governance allows stakeholders on all sides to input into success.

At the heart of this approach lies the Center of Excellence, which oversees this journey. It informs and guides the business goals as they apply to Salesforce, the approach used for delivery, and the technologies used. It is also responsible for communication with both stakeholders and end users across the organization, for identifying and managing business risk of projects, and for ensuring initiatives deliver value.

As such, a CoE often contains, or works alongside, distinct groups with specific responsibilities. A Change Management group, for example, will be the approving body for changes going into Salesforce and will make sure that the change is of suitable quality and has been thoroughly tested before it is allowed to be released to production. This would typically be through the definition of the required processes and behaviors it expects to see carried out to ensure quality deliverables, rather than it carrying out the testing itself, which would continue to be the responsibility of the technical teams.

A note of caution should be taken with Change Management groups, however. In the book *Accelerate: The Science of Lean Software and DevOps: Building and Scaling High Performing Technology Organizations* by Nicole Forsgren, Jez Humble, and Gene Kim, the authors emphasize the importance of fast feedback loops, continuous experimentation, and a culture of learning and improvement – factors that may suggest that traditional change management practices may not always align with the needs of high-performing DevOps teams.

A Steering Committee, on the other hand, is a business-led group that ensures that changes continue to align with business strategy, vision, and values. Across all these areas, there should be an executive sponsor that is empowered and available to make decisions and unlock business bottlenecks.

Making a case for a CoE to leadership

Architects looking to present a case for establishing a CoE to the leadership of their organization or customers should largely draw upon the same techniques for presenting any proposal to stakeholders. However, some specific elements should be considered a fundamental part of that proposal. Here are some typical areas to focus on:

Topic	Detail
Define purpose and goals	Articulate the objectives of the CoE, such as driving continuous improvement, sharing best practices, fostering collaboration, and accelerating DevOps adoption across the organization.
Build a business case	Create a compelling business case that demonstrates the benefits of a CoE, including potential cost savings, improved operational efficiency, faster time to market, and enhanced customer satisfaction. Showcase industry examples and relevant success stories.

Topic	Detail
Identify key stakeholders	Identify and engage key stakeholders, such as senior management, development, and operations teams. Involve them in the decision-making process and the subsequent establishment of the CoE.
Propose the CoE structure	Propose a structure for the CoE, including roles, responsibilities, and reporting lines. Estimate the budget and resources required to set up and maintain the CoE. Positions may include DevOps coaches, product owners, and continuous improvement specialists.
Develop a roadmap	Outline a roadmap for implementing the CoE, including milestones, timelines, and **key performance indicators** (**KPIs**). Provide a clear plan for leadership to follow and monitor progress.
Plan for change management	Recognize that implementing a CoE may involve significant cultural and organizational changes. Present a change management strategy that addresses potential resistance, communication, and training needs.
Foster collaboration	Emphasize the importance of cross-functional collaboration and knowledge sharing between teams. Propose tools and platforms that facilitate communication and collaboration, such as chat platforms, wikis, or video conferencing systems.
Pilot and iterate	Propose starting with a pilot program involving one or more teams to test and refine the CoE approach. Enable the organization to learn from the pilot, adjust, and gradually scale up the CoE as part of the wider DevOps adoption.
Regularly report progress	Ensure that the progress of the CoE is regularly reported to leadership, including successes, challenges, and learnings. Maintain support and commitment from senior management through transparency.
Demonstrate ongoing value	Continually highlight the positive impact of the CoE on the organization, including quantifiable improvements in efficiency, quality, and innovation. Maintain and grow support for the CoE and its role in the broader DevOps adoption.

Table 2.1 – Elements to consider in a proposal

Overcoming resistance and hesitation

There are several common reasons why people might initially resist the idea of implementing DevOps in their organization, believing that "it's nice, but it can't be done here." Let's address some of these reasons and provide counterarguments to help dispel these concerns:

Area	Resistance	Counterargument
Organizational structure and culture	The existing organizational structure and culture promote siloed teams and discourage collaboration	DevOps is an opportunity to break down silos and foster collaboration. Start with small changes, such as creating cross-functional teams, and gradually scale up DevOps initiatives as the organization adapts to the new approach.
Lack of skills and expertise	Team members lack the skills and knowledge to implement DevOps practices and tools	Invest in training and upskilling team members and consider hiring or partnering with experts to help guide your DevOps transformation. Continuous learning is a core principle of DevOps, so developing these skills should be viewed as an ongoing process.
Limited resources and budget	There is no budget or resources to invest in new tools, technologies, and training for a DevOps transformation	DevOps can help increase efficiency and reduce costs in the long run. Start small by leveraging existing tools and resources, and gradually expand your DevOps capabilities as you demonstrate ROI and gain organizational buy-in.
Fear of failure and disruption	Changing existing processes could lead to disruptions and negatively impact current projects	DevOps is about continuous improvement and learning from failure. Begin with small, low-risk projects to minimize potential disruptions and use the lessons learned to refine your approach before tackling larger initiatives.
Legacy systems and technical debt	Existing infrastructure and legacy systems make it difficult to adopt modern DevOps practices and tools	DevOps can help address technical debt and modernize legacy systems by promoting incremental improvements and fostering a culture of innovation. Prioritize the most critical aspects of your infrastructure and develop a roadmap for introducing DevOps practices.

Area	Resistance	Counterargument
Lack of management support	Management does not see the value in DevOps or is unwilling to invest in the necessary changes	Build a strong business case for DevOps by highlighting its potential benefits. Share success stories and best practices from other organizations and consider running a pilot project to demonstrate the value of DevOps firsthand.
Regulatory and compliance concerns	Adopting DevOps practices may conflict with compliance requirements in heavily regulated industries	DevOps can improve compliance by automating processes, ensuring consistency, and providing better visibility. Collaborate with your compliance and security teams to ensure that your DevOps practices align with industry regulations and organizational policies.

Table 2.2 – Reasons and counterarguments to dispel concerns

By addressing these common concerns and demonstrating the potential benefits of adopting DevOps, you can help overcome resistance and encourage stakeholders to embrace this transformative approach.

Summary

There is an often (mis)quoted saying, *"Culture eats strategy for breakfast,"* and seldom has this been more pertinent than in the world of DevOps. No matter how well crafted your strategy for adopting DevOps may be, it will not succeed if your team is not on board with the culture and mindset required. By promoting the advantages of a DevOps process and ensuring that the entire team works together to this model, with strong communication along the way, you have laid the foundation for a successful Salesforce DevOps transformation and can now build upon it with the tools and techniques we'll explore in the next part of this book. In the next two chapters, we'll first look at the essential role that testing plays across your DevOps life cycle, before looking at an example workflow that takes these elements into account with a typical SFDX and Git workflow.

> **Culture eats strategy for breakfast – or does it?**
>
> The quote is attributed to renowned management expert, Peter Drucker. While this version remains in popular use and demonstrates our point here, Drucker's original quote was *"Culture – no matter how defined – is singularly persistent."*

3
The Value of Source Control

As we move toward the technical aspects of Salesforce DevOps, we should start by exploring **source control**. In this chapter, we're going to cover the following main topics:

- Why source control is vital for the implementation of a DevOps process
- Fundamental Git operations for managing your changes
- Effective Git branching strategies for successful delivery with source control

Source control, also referred to as **version control**, is the technical backbone of modern DevOps, and all other tools and techniques are built upon that solid foundation. By tackling this topic first and looking at some of the common tasks it entails, you will have a solid foundation for the topics discussed later in this book, such as CI/CD automation.

Technical requirements

The examples in this chapter all pertain to the **Git** source control system and it is recommended that you have it installed if you want to follow along. Equally, a Git hosting provider is recommended. Many are available, such as GitHub, GitLab, and BitBucket. However, in our examples, we'll be using GitHub.

The importance of source control

While establishing a DevOps culture is the most important aspect of DevOps from a process perspective, as we saw in the previous chapter, it's fair to say that source control is the most important technical aspect. It underpins all the other tools and techniques of a mature DevOps process and enables deployments, peer review, rollbacks, and automation as part of a CI/CD process. Let's explore some of the advantages afforded by source control and the processes that build upon it.

Collaboration

DevOps is fundamentally a collaborative approach to software development, so effective collaboration is vital. Source control enables multiple developers to work on the same code base simultaneously while indicating when they could be overlapping or overwriting each other's changes during the development phase. Changes are merged later, and when coupled with appropriate reviews, they allow for rapid development and fewer defects, since changes are tested and reviewed far earlier in the development cycle. Only when manual and automated checks have passed does code make it higher up the environments toward production. It's worth noting that production issues are harder to track down and more expensive to deal with compared to development environments.

Traceability

As the importance of good governance grows across all processes and businesses, including software development, so does the need to have accountability and audit trails of software change. Source control facilitates this with a complete history of all changes to your code and configurations, detailing what was changed, by whom, and (with diligence around commit messages, comments, and references to change management tools such as Jira) why the change occurred. In addition to these audit trail benefits, a complete history also helps you find the origin of bugs and issues.

Automation

DevOps relies heavily on automation, and source control provides the foundation for automating many of the processes involved in software development, such as building, testing, and deploying code. For example, with source control, it's possible to automatically build, test, and deploy code to different environments every time a change is committed.

Continuous integration

Continuous integration (**CI**) allows developers to integrate their code changes from their development or feature branches into a shared integration branch, and then run automated tests to ensure that the changes do not break the existing system. This process is made possible by source control as it allows developers to easily merge their changes and track conflicts. By adopting this technique and regularly integrating changes into the main code, developers can detect issues earlier, which makes it easier to fix them.

Continuous deployment

Continuous deployment (**CD**) is a practice where code changes are automatically deployed to production after they pass through the CI process. This process is also made possible by source control as it allows the deployment process to be automated. This can be accomplished by using general-purpose CI/CD tools such as Jenkins, Travis CI, and CircleCI, or with Salesforce-specific tools such as DevOps Center, Gearset, or Copado. Regardless of the tool you choose, they can be configured to automatically deploy code changes to production when they pass through the CI process. This is the reason why CI and CD are usually grouped into the CI/CD process.

Continuous delivery (also CD)

The other CD you may hear concerning DevOps is **continuous delivery**. Its shared initials with continuous deployment often create a lot of confusion. The aim of CI/CD is continuous delivery: promptly and dependably delivering enhanced value to users. Distinct from continuous integration and continuous deployment, which are workflows or specific processes, continuous delivery delineates a working culture or methodology. Grounded in a practice of progressive enhancements, continuous delivery focuses on diminishing lead times and curtailing the development cycle, which includes swift feedback from all parties involved.

This approach enables Salesforce teams to aid their businesses in responding swiftly and more flexibly to evolving priorities and market prospects. Both CI and CD are processes that help teams accomplish continuous delivery.

Rollbacks

Source control allows for easy rollbacks, which lets you revert to a previous version of the code base if there are issues with the incoming changes. It is important to be able to roll back changes quickly and easily in case of bugs or other issues that may arise in the production environment. This is made possible by source control as it keeps a history of all the changes that have been made to the code base, making it easier to revert to a previous version if needed. However, keep in mind that not everything can be reverted in Salesforce. For example, if you are trying to revert a commit that contained a record type or a new flow and that change was deployed to an org, then you may have issues reverting that change. Record types cannot be removed via the Metadata API, and flows require you to specify the version number to be removed.

Incremental development

Another significant advantage of a source-control-driven approach to development and deployment is that it encourages developers to think incrementally – one commit at a time. This further supports many of the points covered previously – committing changes in smaller incremental chunks has the potential to make it easier to manage and merge work done by other team members, reducing the chance of code conflicts. It also makes debugging and tracking issues easier since you can compare the current version with the previous commit to see the net difference. Finally, it encourages better coding standards, in which smaller commits tend to promote more modular, decoupled code architecture.

Now that we've looked at the many advantages of using source control, and why it is so important to a mature DevOps process, let's look at some of the core Git tasks and commands that bring source control to life.

Fundamental Git operations

Before we dive into the sea of Git commands and how they come into play, it's essential to get a firm grasp of the basics of source control.

Commits

A commit is a snapshot of your project's files and directories at a specific point in time. Every commit is assigned a unique identifier (known as a SHA hash) and includes metadata such as the author, timestamp, and a descriptive message explaining the changes.

Commits aren't just frozen moments in time, though. They're also part of a larger narrative that reflects your project's evolution. In Git, commits are linked in a chain, with each commit referencing its predecessor. This allows you to traverse your project's history, compare versions, or even revert changes when necessary.

Staging

Before you can commit changes in Git, you need to **stage** them. The staging area, also known as the index, is like a preparation zone where you gather and organize your changes before making a commit. Staging changes allows you to create meaningful, well-organized commits that communicate what you've done and why.

When you stage a file, you are telling Git that you want to include updates to that file in the next commit. However, it is important to note that Git stages a file exactly as it is when you stage it. If you continue to make changes to a file after staging it, you will need to stage it again to include the latest changes in your next commit.

Repositories

A repository, often abbreviated to **repo**, is a container where your project lives. It's not just a storage space, though. A repository also includes a complete history of your project, tracking changes, branching paths, and the intricate web of collaboration. In Git, creating a new repository is as simple as using the `git init` command in the directory that contains your source code.

Putting source control into practice

While this book is not intended to give an *exhaustive* overview of Git's myriad of commands and options, there are a few key operations that make up Git's typical usage.

Firstly, it's important to note the difference between a local repository and a remote repository since many Git commands are specifically for moving changes between the two.

As the name suggests, a local repository exists on your local development machine and can be either a newly initialized repository or one that you have cloned from another (usually remote) repository. Operations carried out on this repository will remain on your local machine until you push those changes to a remote repository.

A remote repository is hosted on a remote server – either with a Git hosting provider or a physical server, perhaps within your own company's data center. This remote repository serves as the centralized source of truth from which other developers can get your changes and vice versa. With this distinction between local and remote repositories in mind, let's start looking at some common Git operations and the commands to carry them out.

Initializing a new repository

The initial step in any source control workflow is to create a repository in which to store your work, and while it is likely you will be working with a repository that already exists, creating a new repository can be achieved by running the following command in the directory that contains your source code. This will create a brand-new empty repository locally, into which you can then start adding files:

```
git init
```

Adding new files to the staging area

By default, Git will consider all files to be untracked and not part of your source control. Adding the files (also referred to as "staging" them) indicates that they should be included as part of your source control. Staging these files is the first part of a two-step process – first, we add files that we intend to commit; then, once we are sure everything that should be grouped as a single commit has been added, we can proceed to the second step.

You can add a single file to your local Git repository, like so:

```
git add <file>
```

Alternatively, you can add all files in the current directory, like so:

```
git add .
```

At this stage, they are not part of your local repository until you commit the changes, as shown in the next section. This is where it's important to note that the current directory is not the same as your local repository. Although there may be many files in the local directory, they don't form part of your local repository until you add and commit them.

Checking everything has been added before the commit

While not strictly required, it is recommended to get into the habit of checking that everything you wish to commit has been added. This can easily be achieved using the `git status` command. In the following example output, we can easily see changes that have been added, changes that have been made but not added, and files that are not currently being tracked for changes. This last category may be because the files have been added to the `.gitignore` file, which, as its name suggests, is a list of files and paths that Git should ignore, or they could be empty directories:

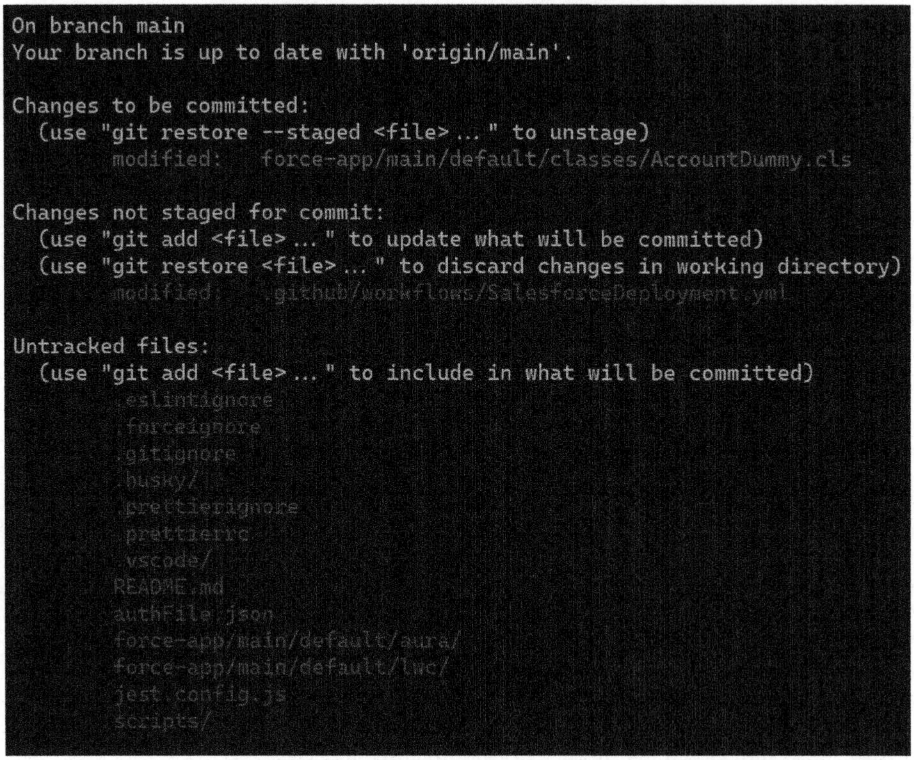

```
On branch main
Your branch is up to date with 'origin/main'.

Changes to be committed:
  (use "git restore --staged <file>..." to unstage)
        modified:   force-app/main/default/classes/AccountDummy.cls

Changes not staged for commit:
  (use "git add <file>..." to update what will be committed)
  (use "git restore <file>..." to discard changes in working directory)
        modified:   .github/workflows/SalesforceDeployment.yml

Untracked files:
  (use "git add <file>..." to include in what will be committed)
        .eslintignore
        .forceignore
        .gitignore
        .husky/
        .prettierignore
        .prettierrc
        .vscode/
        README.md
        authFile.json
        force-app/main/default/aura/
        force-app/main/default/lwc/
        jest.config.js
        scripts/
```

Figure 3.1 – Example output of the git status command

Committing changes to the local repository

Once you have staged your changes with the `git add` command, you can create a snapshot of these modifications in your local repository with the `git commit` command. When you commit your changes, it is important to include a descriptive message that explains the purpose of the commit. This makes it easier for you and your collaborators to understand the version control history.

Many tools that work with Git, including GitHub, make use of certain formats and tags in commit messages. These not only help provide additional context to developers but can also drive workflow integrations, such as in bug-tracking tools. Writing commit messages in this way involves following certain guidelines to maintain readability and effectiveness. A commit message typically includes a header or title, the type of commit (such as feat, fix, docs, and so on), an optional scope to specify the area of change, and a subject that concisely describes the change. It can also contain a detailed explanatory body and a footer referencing related issue IDs. The subject and header are often limited to 50 characters and the body wraps at 72 characters. The commit message should be clear and concise, explaining what the commit does and why. To commit your staged changes with a commit message, use the following command:

```
git commit -m "Commit message"
```

You can use the git log command to view commits made to your repository. By default, it will display an SHA-1 checksum, along with the author, date, and commit message of each commit. However, there are many options for filtering and searching the log, all of which you can find in Git's built-in documentation.

Connecting your remote repository

With our changes committed to our local repository, we need to ensure that our remote repository has been connected correctly and is ready to push our changes. If it is not already connected, we can use the git remote command to connect it and provide it with a working alias. Conventionally, this alias is often referred to as origin, but you can use any name you like. An example of this command is shown here:

```
git remote add origin https://github.com/myuser/myrepo.git
```

This command connects our remote repository at the URL specified, via the origin alias.

Pushing changes to a remote repository

Once you're confident that your local changes are stable and well tested, you can use the git push command to transfer these updates to the remote repository. This ensures that your changes are shared with other collaborators and makes the updated code accessible to anyone with access to the repository.

To perform a git push operation, simply run the following command in your terminal or Command Prompt:

```
git push
```

By default, this command pushes your changes to the branch of the remote repository that is currently checked out in your local repository. However, you can also specify the remote repository and branch you want to push to, if necessary:

```
git push <remote> <branch>
```

Merging changes from one branch to another

If you're working with an already existing Git repository, you may be working in a separate branch from the main branch – we'll be looking at a few example branching strategies in this chapter.

If this is the case, you will eventually need to merge your changes into the main branch, which can be achieved with the `git merge` command. This ensures that the main branch incorporates the changes in your branch, without conflicts. Git will automatically try to merge the changes, but if conflicts arise, you'll have to resolve them manually.

This manual resolution of conflicts involves going through the files that contain conflicts, such as lines of code that have been changed in both branches, and deciding which version should be kept as the final output. Git will automatically add sections marked with <<<<<<<, =======, and >>>>>>> to indicate where these conflicts exist within the file. The following code snippet demonstrates a typical example:

```
public class ExampleClass {
    public void doSomething() {
<<<<<<<
        System.debug('This is the current branch code.');
=======
        System.debug('This is the code from the branch being
merged.');
>>>>>>> branch-to-merge
    }
}
```

The first marker shows the start of the conflicting lines. The second marker acts as a separator between the conflicting versions – everything before the marker is in the current branch and everything after it is in the branch to be merged.

To resolve the conflict, delete the conflict markers and edit the code so that it reflects the intended version you wish to keep. It is important to consider the context and intention of the changes. For this reason, it is recommended to liaise with the author of the conflicting change wherever possible.

Merge strategies

When it comes to merging changes between branches, it's worth taking a brief look at merge strategies. These are the different approaches used by Git to determine how it handles the conflicting changes and merges them, as well as how it manages different situations during the merge process. Here are a few examples, although there are many more:

- **Recursive**: The recursive strategy is Git's default strategy and works for most common scenarios. It analyzes the commit history of both branches to determine a common starting point before the branches diverged and then applies changes from both branches. If it hits a conflict along the way, it will prompt for manual intervention.

- **Octopus**: The octopus strategy is used to merge multiple branches into a single branch. For example, you may want to merge multiple feature branches into a single release branch.

- **Resolve**: The resolve strategy is similar to the recursive strategy, in that it will attempt to automatically merge changes and pause for manual intervention if conflicts are detected. The difference in this strategy, however, is that it doesn't recursively analyze the commit history.

- **Ours**: The ours strategy is designed to give preference to the branch being merged into. Like the other strategies, it will automatically merge where no conflicts exist, but in the event of a conflict, it will discard changes from the incoming branch and keep the current version. As you might have guessed at this point, the opposing strategy, in which the incoming changes are favored, is called the **theirs** strategy.

- **Subtree**: The subtree merge strategy is used to merge changes from a remote repository into a subfolder of your current repository. This can be useful for very modular projects, or libraries of code that you wish to incorporate into larger projects.

These strategies are just a glimpse of the available options for merging in Git. You have the flexibility to choose the desired merge strategy by utilizing command-line options or configuration settings. Which merge strategy you choose depends on the specific needs and complexities of your project.

Creating a new branch

As we'll see in the next section on branching strategies, when you are about to start working on a new feature, bug fix, or any other change, it's a common practice to create a new branch, often referred to as a **feature branch**. This ensures that your work is isolated from the main branch, which is usually more stable and production-ready.

To create a new branch, you can use the `git branch` command, followed by the desired branch name:

```
git branch <branch_name>
```

Switching to a different branch

To switch to another branch from the current one in use, simply check out that branch, like so:

```
git checkout <branch_name>
```

Alternatively, you can create a new branch and switch to it with a single command using the `-b` flag:

```
git checkout -b <branch_name>
```

Now that you've created and switched to your new branch, you can start making changes to the code base without them affecting the main branch. Once your work is complete and has been tested, you can merge your feature branch back into the main branch, ensuring a clean and organized version control history.

Viewing commit history

The `git log` command allows you to see the history of all commits that make up your current branch – this could consist of commits directly to the branch, commits merged from other branches, or commits made from the original branch that your branch was created from. You can view this history, including any commit messages, like so:

```
git log
```

Reverting to a previous version of a file

It is possible to revert a specific file to a previous version, as opposed to reverting an entire commit that may contain multiple file changes. Using the commit hash from the log shown in the commit history and the name of the file you wish to restore from that point in time, you can check out the file, like so:

```
git checkout <commit_hash> <file>
```

Git rebasing

git rebase is a way to integrate changes from one branch into another. It involves replaying the commits from the feature branch on top of the base branch, which replaces the feature branch with an updated version that includes all the changes from the base branch.

The main principle behind `git rebase` is to maintain a linear history, which makes it easier to understand and follow the changes made to the code over time. A linear history means that there are no merge commits (a special type of commit when merges are made, to maintain the history of both branches going forward), only a straight line of commits.

`git rebase` also helps in resolving conflicts that may arise while merging. Instead of creating a merge commit, it replays commits one by one on top of the base branch, which can make conflicts easier to resolve. It's important to note that `git rebase` modifies the existing commits, and it can cause issues if other people have already pulled the feature branch. *Therefore, it's recommended to only use git rebase on branches that haven't been shared with others.*

In summary, `git rebase` is a powerful command that can help keep your Git history clean and easy to understand, but it *should be used with caution*. Now that we've looked at the foundational Git commands and why they are used in our workflow, let's discuss branching strategies.

Effective Salesforce branching strategies

When developing features in version control, a branching strategy establishes guidelines for how branches are utilized and managed. However, there is no single strategy that is ideal for every team. The best strategy for your team will depend on several factors, such as team size, team structure/complexity, the desired release schedule, and the current workflow.

For example, larger teams may require a more complex strategy to accommodate different roles, while a simpler strategy may be more suitable for smaller teams. Additionally, business requirements may dictate a specific release cycle, and the branching strategy should be able to accommodate those needs. Furthermore, it is important to consider how your current workflow and environment setup (for example, the number of sandboxes) may align with the chosen branching strategy.

Git as a backup

The first strategy we can look at is using Git as a lightweight backup of your Salesforce metadata. This approach is frequently the initial step teams take when they start version-controlling their metadata. They establish one branch per environment and begin transferring metadata from their orgs to the branches.

While this is a good initial approach to getting metadata into Git, the development life cycle is not truly source-driven in this way. Version control does not serve as the primary source of truth here, but rather as a retrospective record of the changes that have already occurred. It is still useful, but to fully reap the benefits of Git, it is important to ensure that once changes have been developed, they are placed into version control to facilitate a smooth flow between environments. Additionally, this model often results in isolated environment branches, where changes aren't exchanged between them in source control. Consequently, transitioning from this model to establish source control as the definitive source of truth can be challenging. This is primarily because the same file in each organizational branch lacks a shared commit history, which can make it difficult for Git to handle them.

For instance, with this workflow, it can be difficult to accommodate parallel development streams for multiple features. There are no pull requests in this model, which allows you to easily integrate peer review into the workflow.

Additionally, because changes are not regularly deployed from version control into the environments, there may be less confidence in the ability to roll back a release by deploying an older revision from version control.

It is important to remember that version control is primarily designed to assist teams in creating, tracking, and deploying new features. It should not be viewed as a comprehensive backup of Salesforce environments for disaster recovery purposes, as that is the role of backup solutions in a comprehensive DevOps strategy.

You can see an example of using Git as a backup, and how the branches mirror your Salesforce environments, in the following diagram:

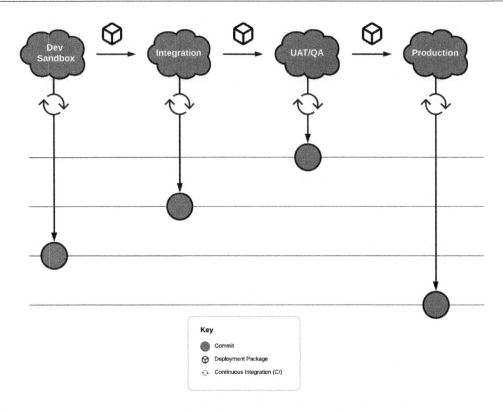

Figure 3.2 – Git as a backup

Trunk-based development

With **trunk-based development** (**TBD**), all developers work on a single branch, called the **trunk** or **main**. Feature toggles are used to hide incomplete work. Branches are short-lived and are merged back into the main branch as soon as possible. While the thought of merging your work into the main branch daily (or even multiple times a day) might seem daunting, many teams find that the benefits of TBD far outweigh the initial discomfort. Embracing TBD can lead to increased collaboration, higher-quality code, and a more streamlined development process.

In TBD, developers create branches for new features or bug fixes, but these branches are short-lived. They are merged back into the main branch as soon as possible, often within a day. To avoid unfinished features being pushed into production, TBD employs feature toggles (also known as feature flags). This allows teams to hide features until they are ready for production use. With everyone merging their changes into the main branch frequently, CI is necessary. Automated testing ensures that the main branch is always in a releasable state. You'll notice that the diagram for this approach (see *Figure 3.2*) and the feature branch one (see *Figure 3.3*), are extremely similar. The fundamental difference between the two strategies is that the branches for TBD are much more granular in their scope and short-lived:

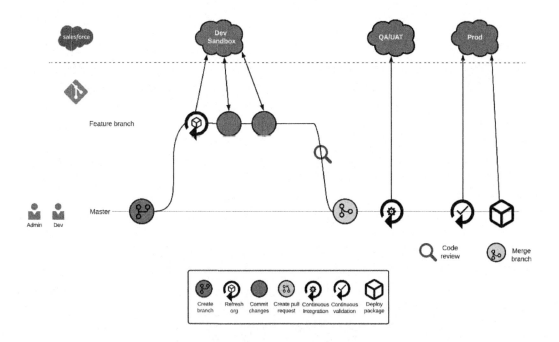

Figure 3.3 – TBD

The feature branch model

The feature branch model is a basic approach that integrates Git into the development process, rather than just being used for backup. While some teams may choose more complex branching methods, the feature branch model is a good starting point due to its simplicity. The master branch is the only long-term, permanent branch. When you work on new features or fixes, a separate branch is created from the main branch, and once completed, it is merged back into the main branch.

In this model, it is best to keep feature branches as short-lived as possible and delete them after use for cleanliness. Large features should be divided into smaller chunks and implemented one at a time to shorten the feedback cycle and decrease the likelihood of merge conflicts. It should be noted that any failure in the master branch is a blocker to the whole release process since it relies on all the prod-ready testing to happen on each feature branch, which is not always realistic.

The master branch is typically deployed automatically to a staging environment using a CI process, making the latest version readily available for testing. Once the version in the staging environment is satisfactory, a deployment from the master branch to the production environment releases the changes to the end users. As an option, before deploying to production, the changes can be deployed to a **User Acceptance Testing (UAT)** or **quality assurance (QA)** environment for further testing.

The following diagram shows a typical feature branch model and how changes in that branch are re-integrated into the master branch so that they can be deployed in your Salesforce environments.

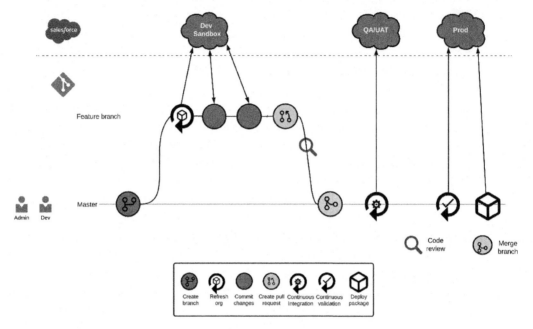

Figure 3.4 – The feature branch model

The protected master branch model

The protected master branch model is similar to the feature branch model, but it includes an additional long-lived branch for integration before merging into the master branch. In this model, the master branch is not updated until everything has been fully tested and is ready for release. The master branch is a more secure source of truth since only work that has been thoroughly tested in UAT is included in the branch.

However, one downside of this model is that it is not possible to propagate only a subset of changes if some are not ready yet. If some work has been tested and approved in UAT, but other work is not ready, it is difficult to selectively promote changes to the master branch. Instead, it is necessary to revert features that are not yet ready from the release branch. This inflexibility is a major concern for many teams, which is why this model is not as popular. If you find that you need to selectively promote changes regularly, then you have not selected the right branching strategy for your way of working.

The following diagram illustrates the protected master branch approach, with its separate integration branch for testing changes before they reach production:

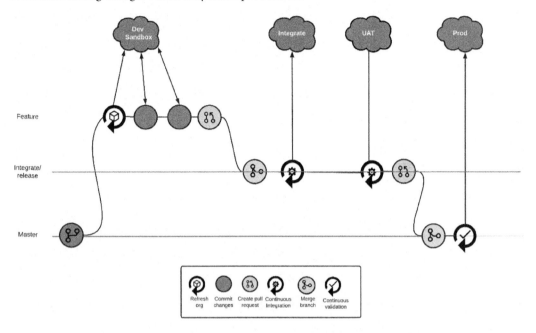

Figure 3.5 – The protected master branch model

The expanded branching model

Taking the process of isolating branches a step further, the expanded branching model includes several additional long-lived branches that correspond to the integration and UAT/QA environments. Instead of merging feature branches directly into the master branch, they are first merged into the integration branch. To move changes that are ready for release to the next environment in sequence, they are merged into the UAT/QA branch, and then into the master branch.

This approach allows for more precise control over which changes are deployed to each environment and allows for isolated evaluations of changes on a per-request basis. The expanded branching model is well suited to teams that prioritize gating and quality control over frequent releases. However, like every other branching strategy we've looked at, there are still some important caveats, particularly if merge conflicts are encountered. For example, if merge conflicts are found during the merge to UAT, then the entirety of the UAT branch will need to be merged in to resolve them, which would mean that a subsequent merge to master would bring in the whole of the UAT branch too, whether it is ready to be promoted or not.

You can see the correlation between branches and Salesforce environments in the following diagram:

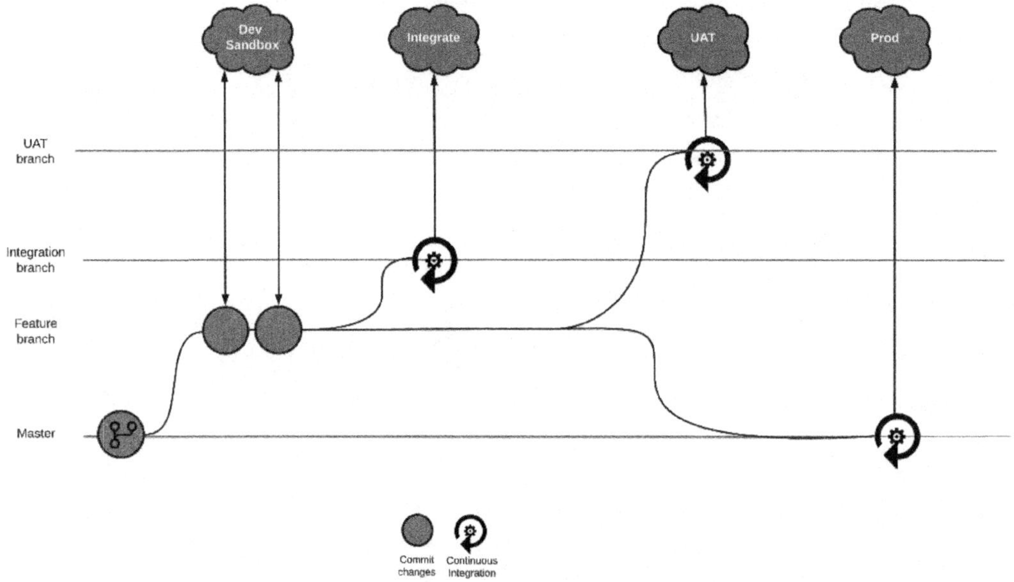

Figure 3.6 – The expanded branching model

Comparing the branching strategies

So, let's recap and summarize these four approaches:

- Using Git as a backup is pretty self-explanatory: we use it as a mechanism to save our metadata off-platform, which allows us to revert changes – although this is not easy if the change is several Git commits back and there are deep chains of dependencies. It also doesn't deliver any of the main benefits of a source-driven development approach.

- The TBD approach offers an array of advantages that streamline and accelerate software development. By promoting frequent integration of short-lived branches, it drastically reduces the occurrence of "merge hell," the oft-dreaded scenario of conflicting changes. The visibility of changes is also greatly enhanced as most work is carried out on the main branch, facilitating a clearer understanding of how alterations impact the project. TBD simplifies the development process by eliminating the need to maintain multiple long-lived branches and keeps the main branch in a perpetually releasable state, enabling any-time deployment and thus, quicker delivery of features.

- The feature branch model is great for teams that rapidly iterate – we use it ourselves internally and it allows us to deliver changes daily, or often more frequently than that. If your process requires more stage gates and checks along the way, this may not work for your longer dev cycles.

- The protected master branch model has multiple testing environments and an integration branch to support them, which means that your primary master or main branch is the source of truth. However, this model still acts as a queue, where items that require longer test cycles can hold up other changes until they're promoted.

- The expanded branch model allows for a more asynchronous approach to changes, with individual pieces of work that can be moved through the environments. This allows for questions in the style of "Bob, where are we with Jira 34533?" to be answered accurately in the style of "It's in UAT awaiting sign-off for release to production, Sarah."

Summary

In this chapter, we looked at the reasons why source control is fundamental to the adoption of DevOps:

- **Collaboration**: DevOps emphasizes collaboration in software development. Source control allows multiple developers to work concurrently on a code base without them having to interfere with each other's changes. By merging and reviewing changes later, teams can achieve faster development and reduce defects.

- **Traceability**: The growing need for governance in software development demands accountability and audit trails. Source control provides a comprehensive history of code and configuration changes, including details about the who, what, and why. This not only aids in auditing but also assists in identifying the origin of bugs and issues.

- **Automation**: DevOps emphasizes automation, and source control serves as a foundation for automating software development processes such as building, testing, and deploying code. This allows for the automatic execution of these tasks upon committing changes to the code base.

- **Continuous integration**: CI enables developers to frequently merge code changes into a shared repository and run automated tests, facilitated by source control. This practice helps detect and resolve issues early, streamlining the development process.

- **Continuous deployment**: CD automatically deploys code changes to production after passing CI tests, with source control enabling automation. This integration of CI and CD forms the CI/CD pipeline.

- **Rollbacks**: Source control enables easy rollbacks by maintaining a code base history, allowing you to quickly revert to previous versions in case there are bugs or issues in the production environment. This ensures you can efficiently and reliably handle unexpected problems.

We then explored some typical Git operations that you're likely to use regularly as you work on creating changes to your Salesforce orgs. Finally, we looked at some of the common Git branching strategies for Salesforce development, and the advantages and disadvantages of each.

In the next chapter, we will look at the next fundamental part of a mature Salesforce DevOps process – testing your changes effectively to ensure quality deliverables.

4

Testing Your Changes

One of the core tenets of DevOps is the ability to deliver robust changes that stand up to scrutiny, have fewer defects, and ultimately reduce the **Change Failure Rate** (**CFR**) metric. This can be largely achieved through testing our development changes.

In this chapter, we'll explore the importance of robustly testing Salesforce changes, the different types of testing that apply to your components, and how to ensure proper testing as part of your DevOps process.

We will be covering the following main topics:

- The importance of testing
- Apex testing
- Testing your **Lightning Web Components** (**LWCs**)
- Testing your flows

By the end of this chapter, you should be well equipped to create and run tests within Salesforce that exercise much of the functionality you implement, whether programmatically or declaratively. This will in turn help you deliver better quality deployments as your DevOps process matures.

Technical requirements

If you want to follow along with the examples in this chapter, as a minimum you will need to have the following installed:

- The Salesforce CLI
- Visual Studio Code
- Salesforce extensions for Visual Studio Code

Additionally, for the *Testing your LWCs* section, you will need to install Node.js (which will include **Node Package Manager** (**npm**)).

The importance of testing

Conventional wisdom states that the earlier a software bug is found, the easier it is to fix and the less impact and cost it is likely to have. Often referred to as a **shift-left** approach—in that given a process diagram moving from left to right in sequence, the further left you deal with an issue, the better—the idea is that by including robust and thorough testing in your DevOps workflow, you stand a much better chance of catching potential issues early. This approach applies not only to functional testing of your Salesforce changes but also to the security aspects of your design and development too—part of what has been dubbed *DevSecOps* in the wider IT industry.

If we look at the impact of testing in the context of our DORA metrics discussed in *Chapter 2*, we can easily see that testing directly impacts the CFR metric. Put simply, the more well tested your changes are, the less likely that errors are to be deployed into your later environments. *Test early, test often* is a phrase I've used across my years in software development to nicely summarize my approach.

When we look at testing in the wider aspect of DevOps, it's important to consider it in the context of not just the development or delivery phases of the application life cycle, but across every step from design to delivery. As architects, we should be mentally testing the requirements and design long before we get to implement any changes—picking holes and finding flaws is one of the greatest skills of a Salesforce architect. By making sure that a request is valid and its design stands up to scrutiny, with questions satisfactorily answered, you've tested the approach well ahead of time. This is considered to be the cheapest time to uncover flaws before developer hours (and thus cost) are spent on a project. It can be thought of as the software development equivalent to the phrase *measure twice, cut once* often quoted in the construction world.

There is an array of different aspects to testing that should be considered as part of your overall application delivery model. We'll cover some of the ones that are specific to the Salesforce platform's technology stack here, but to get a holistic view of testing as an architect, you should consider the following types of testing.

Integration testing

Thorough integration testing is critical for validating that different components and systems work together as expected. For Salesforce projects, key integrations to test include connections between Salesforce and external databases, third-party web services, interactions between Salesforce products such as Sales Cloud and Service Cloud, and custom Lightning components or other customizations.

Use a combination of automated API and UI testing, **end-to-end** (**E2E**) process validation, and manual spot checks to confirm all integration points consistently function as designed from end to end. Import and export data between systems to check for accuracy and completeness. Where possible, send test requests to web services to validate response handling, or as a fallback, provide mock responses for these requests.

Regression testing

Regression testing helps verify that existing functionality and integrations continue to work as expected after changes are made. Prioritize regression testing after deploying major updates, new features, or structural changes such as altering permissions or record-sharing rules. By building automated regression test suites that run quickly and frequently, focusing on critical business processes and key integration points most likely to be impacted by changes, you can quickly check and resolve any breaking changes.

Use a combination of automated UI testing, Apex tests to validate logic and handlers, cross-browser testing, and Salesforce API checks for data validation, and integrate regression testing into the deployment pipeline to run automatically.

Regression testing gives confidence that the system remains stable through ongoing enhancements and changes.

User acceptance testing

User acceptance testing (**UAT**) usually requires a dedicated Salesforce sandbox with test data, roles, and processes modeled on real usage patterns. Involve real users in UAT, to validate that new features meet business needs before full release. Identify power users across **business units** (**BUs**) to serve as UAT testers who deeply understand needs and workflows.

Be sure to structure formal test plans and reporting to ensure thorough real-world validation. Ahead of the start of your UAT process, you should provide testers with account access, sample data, and clear test scenarios mapped to business use cases.

Track and triage all issues uncovered during UAT, clarifying requirements with users and addressing issues before proceeding to production. It should be noted that in many larger organizations, much of this process is done by either a business analyst or dedicated testing resources, rather than the architect (whose role is more that of overseeing the process and ensuring it is carried out).

Large volume testing

Special testing is required to confirm the Salesforce platform can handle large data volumes and heavy user load. Use realistically large datasets in a test org to validate performance and stability at scale. Load the database with maximum expected data sizes, and import representative sample data. Use performance testing tools to simulate peak numbers of concurrent users, identifying governor limits or bottlenecks. Optimize configuration to support caching, indexing, and scalability best practices. Check for degradation over time as data volumes grow, tuning and adding resources as needed. Modeling production-level usage through large volume testing helps validate that the system can support business growth.

In the world of Salesforce DevOps, the two most common types of testing are unit testing and E2E testing, but as we'll see shortly, other important tests such as integration tests and regression tests should be considered as well.

Unit testing concentrates on verifying individual and separate functions within an application—these often relate to a specific individual change that you're developing. It's important to note that Salesforce enforces a minimum of 75% of Apex test coverage across your entire org for production deployments, and even more important to note is that this is not a guarantee that functionality is correct. A poorly written test can hide or distort actual issues, so unit testing should only be considered a part of your overall testing strategy. Additionally, if you specify a subset of specific test classes to run as part of a production deployment, then every Apex class being deployed needs 75%+ coverage individually rather than the org-wide or even deployment-package-wide average. All the more reason to aim for as high a percentage of coverage as possible.

Unit testing works best when you construct your application from small, testable units instead of monolithic Apex classes, flows, or even objects. Creating brief, quick unit tests that can be effortlessly executed motivates developers to include them in their development, regression testing, and **continuous integration** (**CI**) procedures. As a result, bugs are detected and resolved earlier.

Apex testing

Writing Apex code without proper testing can lead to issues, such as bugs and errors, which can negatively impact the user experience and ultimately harm the overall success of the project. This is where Apex unit testing comes in as a critical part of the development process that helps ensure that the code is functioning as intended, meets requirements, and can handle different scenarios. In this regard, Apex unit testing is essential for creating high-quality, robust, and maintainable code in Salesforce.

These tests should be designed to simulate both positive and negative scenarios. This means the code should not only be tested to ensure that it does what it is supposed to, but also tested to check that it *doesn't* do things it's not supposed to. Additionally, Apex unit tests should be written to test operations in a single context or a bulkified context, meaning they can test either a single record or multiple records at once. To improve test efficiency and isolate code under test, mocks and stubs can be used to simulate external dependencies, such as web services or database operations. By writing comprehensive unit tests that cover all possible scenarios and using best practices such as mock testing, Salesforce developers can build reliable, maintainable, and scalable applications.

As mentioned earlier, Salesforce enforces a minimum of 75% of unit test coverage of your code, but as good architects, we should always strive to get as close to 100% coverage as possible. The reality is that there will be some corner cases that are not reachable via unit tests—by targeting 100% coverage, these fall into a buffer between this high standard and the required 75%, so we should never have insufficient coverage in a well-written set of unit tests.

To illustrate a simple example of an Apex unit test, first, consider the following Apex class. It contains a static method that calculates the total price of products in a shopping cart. These products use a `Product__c` custom object that contains a `Price__c` custom field—the custom object is far simpler than the standard `Product2` object and associated objects for example purposes:

```
public class ShoppingCart {
    public static Decimal calculateTotal(List<Product__c> products) {
        Decimal total = 0;
        if (products != null) {
            for (Product__c p : products) {
                if (p.Price__c != null) {
                    total += p.Price__c;
                }
            }
        }
        return total;
    }
}
```

An initial attempt at a corresponding unit test class that includes both single and bulkified tests and covers positive and negative scenarios could look like this:

```
@isTest
private class ShoppingCartTest {
    @isTest
    static void SingleProduct() {
        // Create a single product
        Product__c p = new Product__c(Description__c='Product A',
        Price__c=100);
        insert p;

        // Calculate the total price
        Decimal total = ShoppingCart.calculateTotal(new
        List<Product__c>{p});

        // Verify that the total is correct
        Assert.areEqual(100, total, 'Total should be 100');
    }

    @isTest
    static void testMultipleProducts() {
        // Create multiple products
        List<Product__c> products = new List<Product__c>{
            new Product__c(Description__c='Product A', Price__c=100),
```

```
                new Product__c(Description__c='Product B', Price__c=50)
        };
        insert products;

        // Calculate the total price
        Decimal total = ShoppingCart.calculateTotal(products);

        // Verify that the total is correct
        Assert.areEqual(150, total, 'Total should be 150');
    }

    @isTest
    static void testNullProducts() {
        // Calculate the total price with null products
        Decimal total = ShoppingCart.calculateTotal(null);

        // Verify that the total is zero
        Assert.areEqual(0, total, 'Total should be 0');
    }

    @isTest
    static void testProductsWithoutPrice() {
        // Create a product without a price
        Product__c p = new Product__c(Description__c='Product A');
        insert p;

        // Calculate the total price
        Decimal total = ShoppingCart.calculateTotal(new
        List<Product__c>{p});

        // Verify that the total is zero
        Assert.areEqual(0, total, 'Total should be 0');
    }
}
```

In this example, the unit test class includes four test methods: `testSingleProduct`, `testMultipleProducts`, `testNullProducts`, and `testProductsWithoutPrice`. The first two methods test the `calculateTotal` method with different numbers of products, while the third and fourth methods test it with null and incomplete product data, respectively. The use of both single and bulkified tests ensures that the code can handle different scenarios and scales well. Additionally, the use of both positive and negative flows helps ensure that the code can handle both expected and unexpected input data.

Although this test class would work, many code scenarios would benefit from a @testSetup method, which creates the data used by the test. This data is rolled back at the end of the test.

If we consider the following trigger and corresponding handler class—which is illustrative, not a useful real-world example—we can create a test class for it that makes use of the @testSetup annotation. The trigger, handler class, and its test are shown here:

```
trigger ProductTrigger on Product__c (before insert, before update,
after insert, after update)
{
  if (trigger.isBefore)
  {
    if (trigger.isInsert)
    {
      //before insert logic
    }
    else if (trigger.isUpdate)
    {
      //before update logic
    }
  }
  else if (trigger.isAfter)
  {
    if(trigger.isInsert)
    {
      //after insert logic
    }
    else if (trigger.isUpdate)
    {
      //after update logic
    }
  }
}
public with sharing class ProductTriggerHandler
  {
    public static void beforeInsert(List<Product__c> products)
  {
    Decimal total = 0.0;
    for(Product__c prod : products)
    {
      total += prod.Price__c;
    }
    System.debug(total);
  }
```

```
}

@isTest
public with sharing class ProductTriggerHandlerTest
{
    @TestSetup
    static void setup()
    {
        // Create multiple products
        List<Product__c> products = new List<Product__c>{
            new Product__c(Description__c='Product A', Price__c=100),
            new Product__c(Description__c='Product B', Price__c=50)
        };
        insert products;
    }

    @isTest
    static void testTotal()
    {
        List<Product__c> products = [SELECT Id, Description__c,
        Price__c from Product__c];
        Decimal total = 0.0;
        test.startTest();
        for(Product__c prod : products)
        {
            total += prod.Price__c;
        }
        Assert.areEqual(150, total, 'Total should be 150');
    }
}
```

With this method, the @testSetup annotation is used to create multiple products that are used in the subsequent test methods. This eliminates the need to create duplicate product records in each test method, making the test code more efficient and easier to read. The first two test methods from our original test class now rely on the @testSetup method to create products and calculate the total price, while the remaining methods test different scenarios. The use of @testSetup helps ensure that the test data is consistent and the tests are more reliable.

We can further improve this test class by making use of the test.startTest() and test.stopTest() methods. These are used to separate the setup and execution phases of each test method and should be called immediately before and after the line(s) of code that specifically execute the code we wish to test. This ensures that the performance metrics captured by Limits.get*() methods and asynchronous operations started by the test method are isolated and not mixed with other operations performed before or after the test as part of preparing the test for execution. The use of `test.startTest()` and `test.stopTest()` also helps to avoid hitting governor limits during test execution, especially when testing bulk data operations.

It's important to be thorough and diligent in your Apex unit tests, but as we'll see in the next section, this should not be the only place that you apply a commitment to quality. We'll start by looking at how we can test LWCs.

Testing your LWCs

While Salesforce still has more than one approach for developing Lightning components, we're going to focus on testing LWCs, rather than the older Aura components. Salesforce introduced LWCs in December 2018, with the release of Salesforce's Spring '19 version. This was announced in a blog post by Salesforce on December 13, 2018, titled *Introducing Lightning Web Components*, available at `https://developer.salesforce.com/blogs/2018/12/introducing-lightning-web-components`.

When it comes to testing LWCs, we can take advantage of the fact that the architecture of this type of component is based on more common JavaScript standards and an open framework. This allows us to write our unit tests using the popular Jest testing framework (`https://jestjs.io/`), which is already used in the wider JavaScript community outside of Salesforce too. Jest is itself written in JavaScript and uses the Node.js engine to execute, and npm for installation and to manage its dependencies.

In the Salesforce world, there is a plugin for the SFDX command line called `sfdx-lwc-jest` that makes it easy to add Jest and its dependencies to your Salesforce projects.

If you run the following command in your project directory, it will install the necessary npm tools and the `@salesforce/sfdx-lwc-jest` package:

```
sf force lightning lwc test setup
```

With the capability to run Jest tests set up in your project, you next need to configure some tests for your LWCs. These tests are run locally on your development machine, independently of Salesforce, which makes it a lot easier to both run them at the development stage of your project and to include them as part of any test automation you add in your DevOps pipeline.

If you create an SFDX project using the standard template, it already has all these ready-to-write Jest tests. The `project.json` file is configured, as is `.forceignore`. This also creates a `__tests__` directory and a skeleton test file. However, if you have not created your project from the template, the steps for creating the appropriate structure are detailed next—in most cases, the template will take care of this for you.

Your first task should be to create a `__tests__` folder under the top-level folder of each component. For example, consider this example LWC folder structure:

▼ teamComponent

- teamComponent.html

- teamComponent.js

- teamComponent.js-meta.xml

Figure 4.1 – Example LWC folder structure without tests

In this example, adding the required `__tests__` folder would result in a structure like this:

▼ teamComponent

▼ __tests__

- teamComponent.tests.js

- teamComponent.html

- teamComponent.js

- teamComponent.js-meta.xml

Figure 4.2 – The same LWC folder structure, with the test folder and file in place

You should also add a wildcarded path to the `__tests__` folder to your `.forceignore` file in your project since you shouldn't deploy Jest tests to your Salesforce org—in fact, it will throw an error if you try to do this. Adding the following line to the `.forceignore` file should address this issue:

```
**/__tests__/**
```

Next, you will need to add the following line to the `scripts` section in your project's `package.json` file:

```
"test:unit": "sfdx-lwc-jest"
```

Your project is now configured for running Jest tests, and we'll now look at how to construct those tests for your components.

An example Jest test

Now that we have set up the prerequisites for running the Jest tests, we can look at a lightweight example test for our `teamComponent` component shown previously:

```
import { createElement } from 'lwc';
import teamComponent from 'c/teamComponent';

describe('c-team-component', () => {
```

```
    afterEach(() => {
        // The jsdom instance is shared across test cases in a single
        // file so reset the DOM
        while (document.body.firstChild) {
            document.body.removeChild(document.body.firstChild);
        }
    });

    it('renders the correct message', () => {
        const element = createElement('c-team-component', {
            is: teamComponent
        });
        document.body.appendChild(element);

        const pElement = element.shadowRoot.querySelector('p');
        expect(pElement.textContent).toBe('Welcome to the team!');
    });
});
```

In this test class, we import the createElement function from LWC to create an instance of the teamComponent component, and then we use Jest's describe and it functions to define a test case that checks that the component renders the correct message.

The afterEach function is used to reset the DOM between test cases, to ensure that each test case starts with a clean slate.

In the it function, we create an instance of the teamComponent component using createElement, add it to the DOM using document.body.appendChild, and then use querySelector to find the element that contains the message. Finally, we use Jest's expect function to check that the text content of the p element is equal to *Welcome to the team!*.

This is just an example and your test class will likely need to be more complex and cover additional use cases, but this should give you an idea of how to get started with writing unit tests for LWCs using Jest. Salesforce Trailhead has more detailed examples of testing your LWCs, including those that make use of @wire services. Now that we have our Jest tests written, let's look at how we run the tests against our code.

Running your Jest tests

To test an LWC in a Salesforce project using Jest, you can follow these steps:

1. Navigate to the root directory of your LWC component in your terminal.

2. Run the npm run test command. This will execute the Jest test runner and run any tests in the __tests__ directory or in the same directory as the LWCs being tested.

3. The Jest test runner will display the results of the tests in your terminal. If any tests fail, the Jest runner will output detailed information about the test failure.

4. You can also run individual tests by specifying the name of the test file or test suite that you want to run. For example, you can run a test named `teamComponent.test.js` by running the `npm run test teamComponent.test.js` command.

5. You can use additional options to customize the behavior of Jest, such as running tests in `watch` mode or generating code coverage reports. You can find more information on Jest options in the Jest documentation.

At this point, we now have a means of testing our LWCs, but that's only part of the puzzle. In the next section, we'll start exploring how to test the main declarative tool that Salesforce offers—flows.

Testing your flows

Flows are another extremely common means of developing complex functionality in Salesforce, and while they fall into the *clicks not code* category of Salesforce development, it is just as important to provide them with rigorous testing as it is for code-based solutions.

In Flow Builder, you can test your flow without leaving the interface. The UI contains two buttons for testing your flow: Run and Debug. Let's look at what they do:

*   The Run button executes the most recently saved version of the flow that is currently open in the editor.

*   The Debug button provides additional features beyond Run. In addition to running the flow, Debug allows you to input values for the flow's input variables and view debug details during the flow's execution. This allows you to verify how the flow processes data and identify any issues or errors.

Every time a flow runs in Salesforce, it initiates a flow interview. A flow interview is a unique instance of a flow that follows a specific path based on the parameters provided. These parameters can include input variables or components on a screen, which can lead the interview down different paths through the flow and trigger different actions.

By creating flow interviews that cover both positive and negative scenarios, you can test your flow's criteria, much like you would with Apex testing. However, breaking a flow into smaller tests may be challenging, as a flow interview tests the entire flow rather than just one decision at a time. You may need to create multiple flow interviews to cover all possible paths through the flow.

To simplify testing and ensure comprehensive coverage, it may be beneficial to break up the flow into subflows where possible. This architectural approach can help create more manageable and efficient tests for your flow.

As of the Summer '22 Salesforce release, it is possible to convert these flow interviews into flow tests. After successfully executing a flow interview in the flow debugger in Salesforce, you will see a **Convert to Test** action appear in the top-right corner of the page, next to **Edit Flow**. To convert the debug run to a flow test, click on **Convert to Test**, and a new test screen will appear in a modal window. You can create up to 200 tests per flow, so it should be possible to create a test for every path your flow can take:

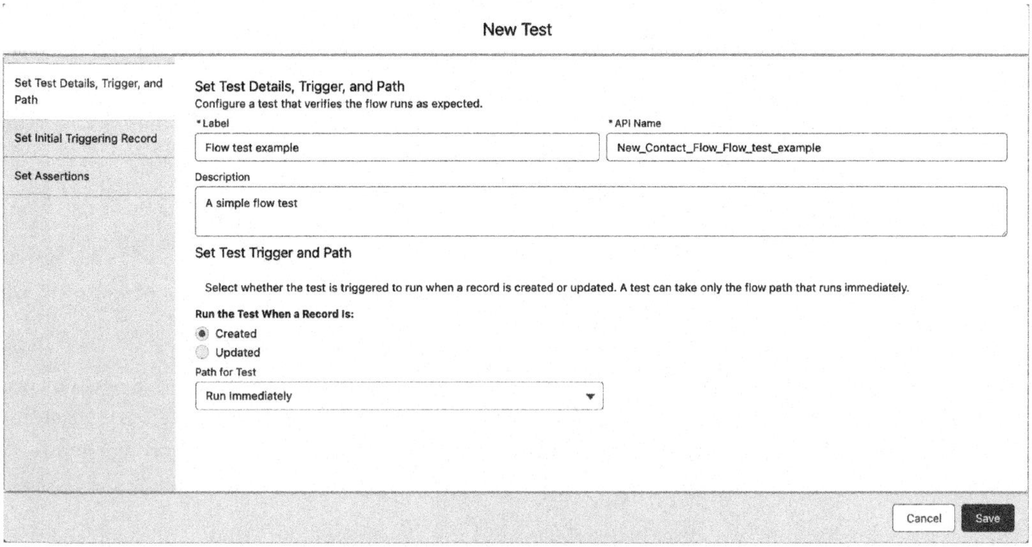

Figure 4.3 – Creating a new flow test

During testing of a flow in Salesforce, each assertion is evaluated to confirm that the flow behaves as intended, as illustrated in the following screenshot. However, it's important to note that a test can only verify whether a flow element was executed and whether the flow resource values were correctly set:

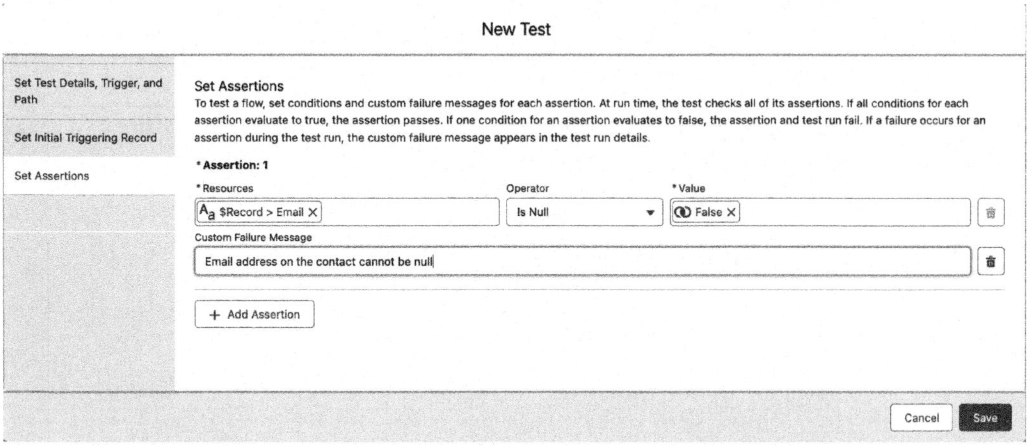

Figure 4.4 – Providing assertions for our new test, to validate our flow

At the time of writing, there are some important considerations around flow tests that an architect should consider when assessing them as part of an overall DevOps design:

- Flow tests are available only for record-triggered flows

- Flow tests don't support flows that run when a record is deleted

- Flow tests don't support flow paths that run asynchronously

- Flow tests cannot be automatically triggered as part of a deployment

- Flow tests can be based upon specific record IDs, but this can make the tests fragile since record IDs are not guaranteed to exist in other environments

- Flow tests don't count toward flow test coverage requirements

- This last point is of particular note because if you want to be able to deploy flows as **Active**, they need to have test coverage in just the same way that Apex code requires coverage (and at the same minimum level of 75%)

The process for this is less mature than that for code, but as a guide, for active processes and autolaunched flows, there is a requirement that at least one Apex test must achieve the required test coverage percentage of the flow tests. However, it's important to note that flow test coverage requirements do not apply to flows that include screens.

The lack of maturity in flow testing is largely around the absence of consistency between the flow tests that you can generate in the Flow Builder UI versus the tests required for coverage. Not only do these tests need to be written in code as Apex unit tests, but to see the current state of code coverage for the flows in your org, you need to query the `FlowTestCoverage` object—for example, from the Developer Console.

To determine the test coverage of your flows in Salesforce, you need to consider all active versions, regardless of whether they have test coverage or not, and all inactive versions that are the latest versions and have test coverage. Here are example queries for this purpose—to run them, you will need to ensure the **Use Tooling API** box is checked in the Developer Console.

First, you need to determine the number of flows (the latest versions of each) that have test coverage, like so:

```
SELECT count_distinct(FlowVersionId)
FROM FlowTestCoverage
```

Then, get the number of all active versions of flows—with or without test coverage—plus the inactive versions that are the latest versions that have test coverage:

```
SELECT count_distinct(Id)
FROM Flow
WHERE Status = 'Active' AND Id NOT IN (
    SELECT FlowVersionId
    FROM FlowTestCoverage )
```

To determine the test coverage percentage for your Salesforce flows, divide the count of the most recent flow versions with test coverage (second script) by the overall sum of active and inactive versions that possess test coverage, incorporating those lacking test coverage as well (initial script). If all this sounds unnecessarily complicated, you'd be right, and we can only hope that this area improves with subsequent Salesforce releases.

Summary

In this chapter, we looked at the reasons why testing your changes is a core principle of Salesforce DevOps. We also dove into some example tests, showing the differences in how they are constructed, depending on the approach you used to implement your Salesforce functionality—Apex code, LWC, or flows.

Now that we've looked at some of the building blocks of architecting a Salesforce DevOps process—culture, version control, and robust testing—in the next chapter, we'll start to look at how we bring these elements together by looking at some example workflows and scenarios of day-to-day delivery using the SFDX tool and Git. While these tools are one of many approaches to Salesforce DevOps, you'll benefit from seeing some of the principles we've discussed as real-world examples, which will bring a typical workflow to life.

5

Day-to-Day Delivery with SFDX

In this chapter, we'll see how we can apply what we've learned so far, using the SFDX suite of tools together with Visual Studio Code and Git, to manage our change delivery. It will by no means be the definitive way to do Salesforce DevOps and assumes starting a brand-new project from scratch, but it will show some common tasks and principles.

We will be covering the following main topics:

- Setting up the tools and your project
- The change lifecycle with Git and SFDX
- Sandboxes versus scratch orgs

By the end of the chapter, you should be able to replicate a simple workflow in your own Salesforce orgs for picking up an item of work from a ticketing system such as Jira or Asana, creating a new feature branch for it, using SFDX and VS Code to make your changes, and checking the code back in again. This is the most straightforward approach to DevOps and will give you the solid practical foundations you need.

Technical requirements

If you want to follow along with the examples in this chapter, as a minimum, you will need to have the following installed:

- The Salesforce CLI
- VS Code
- The Salesforce extensions for VS Code

You will also need a GitHub account (`https://github.com/`) in which to create a new Git repository and Git installed on your local machine (`https://git-scm.com/`).

Setting up the tools and your project

While in most real-world scenarios, it's highly likely that both your tools and your project would already be set up and ready for development on an existing implementation, we're going to cover setting up everything from scratch so that if you want to follow along with the example workflow, you could potentially do so from a fresh Developer Edition Salesforce org.

The Salesforce CLI

The Salesforce CLI is the primary tool for interacting with your Salesforce org from your development tools and is fundamental to automating processes for CI/CD as well.

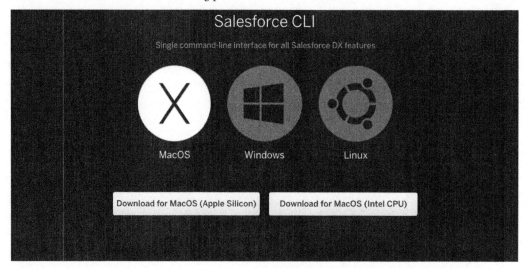

Figure 5.1 – Overview of the Salesforce CLI download page

To install the Salesforce CLI on Windows, macOS, or Linux, follow the instructions for the required operating system.

Windows

1. Go to the Salesforce CLI download page: `https://developer.salesforce.com/tools/sfdxcli`.
2. Click on the **Windows Installer** link to download the installer for Windows.
3. Run the downloaded executable file (`.exe`) to start the installation process.
4. Follow the installation wizard, accept the license agreement, and choose the desired settings. The default settings are usually sufficient for most users.
5. Complete the installation process by clicking **Install** and then **Finish**.
6. Open Command Prompt or PowerShell and type `sfdx --version` to verify the installation. If the installation was successful, you should see the installed Salesforce CLI version.

```
C:\Users\robjc>sfdx --version
sfdx-cli/7.196.5 win32-x64 node-v18.15.0
```

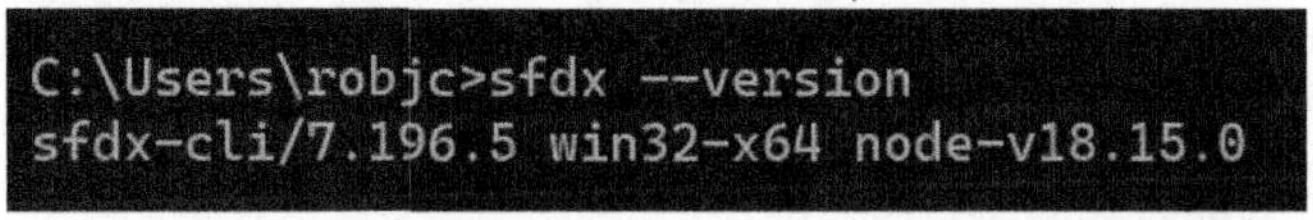

Figure 5.2 – Checking the installation of the Salesforce CLI on Windows

macOS

1. Go to the Salesforce CLI download page: `https://developer.salesforce.com/tools/sfdxcli`.
2. Click on the **MacOS Installer** link to download the installer for macOS that's appropriate for the type of Mac you have.
3. Open the downloaded `.pkg` file to start the installation process.
4. Follow the installation wizard, accept the license agreement, and choose the desired settings. The default settings are usually sufficient for most users.
5. Complete the installation process by clicking **Install** and then **Close**.
6. Open Terminal and type `sfdx --version` to verify the installation. If the installation was successful, you should see the installed Salesforce CLI version.

```
robcowell@Rob-Cowell's-MBP          sfdx --version
@salesforce/cli/2.23.20 darwin-arm64 node-v20.10.0
```

Figure 5.3 – Checking the successful installation of the Salesforce CLI on macOS

Linux

The Salesforce CLI for Linux is available as a tarball. You can find the download URL for the tarball that matches your system architecture here.

Architecture	Manifest file
x64	https://developer.salesforce.com/media/salesforce-cli/sfdx/channels/stable/sfdx-linux-x64.tar.xz
Arm	https://developer.salesforce.com/media/salesforce-cli/sfdx/channels/stable/sfdx-linux-arm.tar.xz

Table 5.1 – Manifest files for the Linux installation packages

1. To download one of these tarballs, use the wget command. For example, for the x64 platform, use this:

    ```
    wget https://developer.salesforce.com/media/salesforce-cli/sfdx/
    channels/stable/sfdx-linux-x64.tar.xz
    ```

2. Create a directory named sfdx:

    ```
    mkdir ~/sfdx
    ```

3. Extract the contents of the tarball version you downloaded:

    ```
    tar xJf sfdx-linux-x64.tar.xz -C ~/sfdx --strip-components 1
    ```

    The -C flag extracts the contents into the sfdx directory, while --strip-components 1 removes the root path component.

4. Modify your PATH environment variable to incorporate the Salesforce CLI bin directory. For instance, to configure it for your ongoing Terminal session, use the following command:

    ```
    export PATH=~/sfdx/bin:$PATH
    ```

5. To permanently update your PATH, add the relevant entry to your shell's configuration file. For example, if you are using the Bash shell, include this line in either your ~/.bashrc or ~/.bash_profile file:

    ```
    PATH=~/sfdx/bin:$PATH
    ```

6. Open Terminal and type sfdx --version to verify the installation. If the installation was successful, you should see the installed Salesforce CLI version.

Figure 5.4 – Verifying the installation of the CLI

Git

To install Git on Windows, macOS, or Ubuntu Linux, follow the instructions here for the appropriate operating system. For other Linux distributions, you may need to search for the appropriate documentation for your package management system.

Figure 5.5 – The Git client download page

Windows

1. Download the Git for Windows installer from the official website:

    `https://git-scm.com/download/win`

2. Run the downloaded executable file (`.exe`) to start the installation process.

3. Follow the installation wizard, choosing the desired settings. The default settings are usually sufficient for most users.

4. Complete the installation process by clicking **Install** and then **Finish**.

5. To verify the installation, open the Git Bash terminal by searching for it in the **Start** menu or using the context menu in a folder by right-clicking and selecting **Git Bash Here**.

6. In the Git Bash terminal, type `git --version` and press *Enter*. If the installation was successful, you should see the installed Git version.

```
C:\Users\robjc>git --version
git version 2.27.0.windows.1
```

Figure 5.6 – Confirming the successful installation of Git for Windows

macOS

1. Check whether Git is already installed by opening the Terminal app and typing `git --version`. If Git is installed, you'll see the version number. If not, proceed to the next step.

2. Install **Homebrew**, a package manager for macOS, by following the instructions on the official website: `https://brew.sh/`.

3. Once Homebrew is installed, open Terminal and type `brew install git`.

4. Wait for the installation process to complete.

5. Verify the installation by typing `git --version` in Terminal. If the installation was successful, you should see the installed Git version.

```
robcowell — robcowell@Robs-MacBook-P
robcowell@Robs-MacBook-Pro          git --version
git version 2.40.0
```

Figure 5.7 – Confirming the successful installation of Git on macOS

Ubuntu Linux

1. Open Terminal (*Ctrl* + *Alt* + *T*).

2. Update the package list by typing `sudo apt update` and pressing *Enter*.

3. Install Git by typing `sudo apt install git` and pressing *Enter*.

4. Confirm the installation by typing `Y` when prompted and pressing *Enter*.

5. Wait for the installation process to complete.

6. Verify the installation by typing `git --version` in the Terminal. If the installation was successful, you should see the installed Git version.

```
robcowell@alphatron          git --version
git version 2.34.1
```

Figure 5.8 – Confirming the successful installation of Git on Linux

VS Code and extensions

Microsoft VS Code is available for Windows, macOS, and Linux systems. The installer can be obtained from https://code.visualstudio.com/download – simply follow the instructions for your operating system.

More important to Salesforce development using VS Code are the extensions that allow integration with both Git and SFDX right from within the IDE:

1. Open VS Code.

2. Click the extensions view icon on the sidebar or press *Ctrl + Shift + X* (Windows/Linux) or *Cmd + Shift + X* (Mac) to open the **Extensions** panel.

3. Search for Salesforce Extension Pack in the search bar.

4. Click the **Install** button on **Salesforce Extension Pack** by Salesforce. This will install a collection of extensions, including Salesforce CLI Integration, Apex, Aura Components, Lightning Web Components, and more.

Creating a new SFDX project and connecting it to your Salesforce org

Now that we have all the required tools installed, we can start getting a project together on which to work. We will create a new SFDX project from within VS Code and connect it to our Salesforce environment. We'll also connect it to our Git source control so that we can truly work in a source-driven way. Let's look at the steps needed to connect everything together:

1. Set up an SFDX project using the Command Palette:

    A. Open the Command Palette with *Ctrl + Shift + P* (Windows/Linux) or *Cmd + Shift + P* (Mac).

    B. Type SFDX: Create Project and press *Enter*.

    C. Choose **Standard** as the project template and press *Enter*.

    D. Enter a desired name for your project and press *Enter*.

    E. Choose a folder to store your SFDX project and press *Enter*. This will generate a new SFDX project structure in the specified folder.

2.   Set the default org for your project using the Command Palette:

   A.   Open the Command Palette with *Ctrl + Shift + P* (Windows/Linux) or *Cmd + Shift + P* (Mac).

   B.   Type SFDX, then set a default org and press *Enter*.

   C.   Choose an alias to use when authenticating with your Salesforce org.

Now you have installed and set up the VS Code extensions for Salesforce using the Command Palette and are ready to start developing Salesforce applications.

The change lifecycle with Git and SFDX

In many organizations, teams make use of workflow management systems such as Jira or Asana to capture, refine, and assign work items for development teams. In this example, we're going to assume that Jira is in use, but this is purely for illustrative purposes to replicate a reasonably typical real-world scenario. It is definitely not essential to use Jira, or any equivalent system, to follow these examples. We will be looking at ticketing systems in more detail in *Chapter 8*.

Getting a Git repository to work with

In *Chapter 3*, we looked at some of the most common Git operations and their corresponding commands. In most real-world scenarios, you are likely to have a pre-existing repository to work with. However, there may be scenarios where you are starting a project with Git for the first time, so let's look at the main ways to prepare Git for work:

1.   git init will create a brand-new local repository on your machine to work with. At this point, there is no equivalent remote repository. You can refer back to *Chapter 3* if you need a reminder of how to connect one, for example, on GitHub.

2.   git clone will create a copy of a remote repository on your local machine – including the version history and all the branches and commits it contains. It will create the correct directory structure for you, ready to work with.

3.   git checkout is used to switch branches within an existing repository. When you use this command, your local working folder will be updated to reflect the contents of that branch.

Getting the latest changes from the main branch

Obtaining the latest main branch changes before development ensures a current code base, minimizes merge conflicts, and streamlines the integration of new features or fixes:

1.   In VS Code, click the **Source Control** icon in the left sidebar.

2.   Click the **...** (ellipsis) button at the top and choose **Pull** to fetch and merge the latest changes from the main branch.

Creating a new feature branch

The feature branch model is a simple Git-based development approach, ideal for beginners. It maintains up-to-date metadata on the main branch, which should always be release-ready. Definitions of what constitutes "release-ready" or "production-ready" can vary wildly and largely depend on the level of testing applied, both of individual changes and the overall holistic view of your production system and any integrations it may have. For the purposes of demonstrating a workflow here, we shall significantly simplify our definition to mean that changes have had functional testing in your development org, any code reviews (both automated and manual) have been carried out, and a pull request has been approved.

Developers create new branches from the main for features or fixes, merging them back upon completion. Short-lived feature branches minimize merge conflicts and promote tidiness. Smaller deliverables reduce feedback cycle length. To create the feature branch from within VS Code, complete the following steps:

1. In the **Source Control** panel, click the branch icon at the bottom-left corner of the window.

2. Type in the name of the new feature branch (e.g., `feature/JIRA-1234`) and press *Enter* to create and switch to the new branch.

Working on your changes

You should now be able to start your development work against your feature branch. This can be a combination of configuration work in the connected Salesforce org or code-based development in the Salesforce IDE.

The Salesforce extensions for VS Code simplify moving your metadata changes back and forth between your local machine and your development org. Many of the underlying Salesforce CLI commands are available in either the Org Browser, the Command Palette, or as context-sensitive menu options when right-clicking on files.

Retrieving metadata

1. Open the Org Browser in the side panel in VS Code (you can find it with an icon that resembles a cloud).

2. If it's your first time using the Org Browser, or if the metadata for your org has changed, click the refresh icon to retrieve the metadata from your org.

3. The Org Browser displays a list of metadata types. You can click the arrow next to a metadata type to expand it and see the individual components of that type.

4. To retrieve a metadata component, click the cloud download icon next to the component's name. This retrieves the component and adds it to your local project.

Deploying metadata

1. Navigate to the files or folders you want to deploy in your local project structure.

2. Right-click on the selected items.

3. From the context menu, choose the **SFDX: Deploy Source to Org** command. This deploys the metadata to your org.

4. Note that the Org Browser does not directly facilitate deployment, but the standard deployment commands in the Salesforce extensions for VS Code are used instead.

Once your development is complete, test your changes in Salesforce using scratch orgs or sandboxes, as appropriate. We will be looking at the differences between the two types of Salesforce development environments later in this chapter.

Committing your changes

The two-step process of committing changes involves first staging the alterations and then executing the commit. Staging selects modifications for a commit while committing records the staged changes as a new snapshot in the local repository, maintaining development history. You can complete the staging and committing of your changes like so:

1. In the **Source Control** panel, review the changes you have made.

2. Stage the changes by clicking the + icon next to each changed file or by clicking the + icon next to **CHANGES** to stage all changes.

3. Enter a meaningful commit message describing the changes related to the Jira ticket (e.g., "`JIRA-1234: Implemented new feature`").

4. Click the checkmark icon at the top to commit the changes to your feature branch.

Pushing your feature branch to the remote repository

Once our changes are added to Git locally, we can then move those changes up to the remote repository as follows:

1. In the **Source Control** panel, click the **...** (ellipsis) button at the top and choose **Push**.

2. If prompted, select your feature branch (e.g., "`feature/JIRA-1234`") to push it to the remote repository.

Creating a pull request

Creating a pull request in Git is a collaborative process where a developer proposes merging their changes from one branch into another, often from a feature branch into the main branch. This allows for code review, discussion, and potential modifications before integrating the changes. This is also the stage in which automated checks are carried out, such as running tests and static analysis, and this makes pull requests a useful tool for solo developers, not just multi-person teams.

To create the pull request via GitHub, follow these steps:

1. Open your browser and navigate to your repository on GitHub.
2. Click the **Compare & pull request** button next to your recently pushed branch.
3. Review the changes, and add any additional information or context related to the Jira ticket.
4. Assign the appropriate reviewers and click **Create pull request**.

Alternatively, if you have the `GitHub Pull Requests and Issues` extension installed in VS Code, you can create your new pull request from within the VS Code IDE as follows:

1. Open the VS Code Command Palette by pressing *Ctrl + Shift + P* (Windows or Linux) or *Cmd + Shift + P* (macOS).
2. Type `Github: Create Pull Request` and select the option from the list that appears.
3. Select the base and compare branches for your pull request.
4. Enter a title and description for your pull request.
5. Review your changes and make any necessary adjustments.
6. Click the **Create Pull Request** button to submit your pull request.

Addressing feedback and updating the pull request

Quite often, there can be feedback and changes required to your pull request during the review process. This is a normal part of the review process and helps to deliver quality releases to production by capturing changes early. Thankfully, addressing these changes is as easy as your original commits to Git were – let's look at the steps required:

1. If changes are requested during the review process, make the necessary updates in VS Code.
2. Commit and push the changes to the feature branch in the same way as you did for the original commit of your changes.
3. The pull request will automatically update with your new changes.

Merging the pull request

Once we reach the stage where our pull request has been approved and any required changes are complete, we can safely merge it into our upstream branch, like so:

1. Once the pull request has been approved, click the **Merge pull request** button in GitHub.
2. Delete the feature branch if it is no longer needed, either on GitHub or in VS Code.

Updating your local main branch

All that remains for us to do now is to refresh our local copy of the main branch to ensure we have all the latest changes and everything is correctly in sync. The following steps will achieve this:

1. In VS Code, switch back to the main branch by clicking the branch icon at the bottom-left corner and selecting **main**.

2. Pull the latest changes exactly as you did at the start of the process.

We have now completed a typical lifecycle of developing a Salesforce feature using SFDX and Git. This represents the most basic DevOps workflow – and in many teams, it can remain as simple as that.

In the next section, we're going to look at some subtle differences between the most common Salesforce development environments – sandboxes and scratch orgs – and see the use cases for each.

Sandboxes versus scratch orgs

Scratch orgs and Salesforce developer sandboxes serve similar purposes in providing environments for development and testing; however, they differ in several key aspects, which we will discuss here.

Sandboxes

Salesforce sandboxes are a copy of your Salesforce environment, including metadata and customizations. Sandboxes are typically used for testing and development purposes such as creating and testing new features, integrating with other systems, or replicating production issues. Developers can use sandboxes to test new features or customizations without affecting the production environment. Sandboxes can also be used for training and **user acceptance testing** (**UAT**) to ensure that changes are thoroughly tested before deployment. Additionally, sandboxes can be used for integration testing, disaster recovery, and as a backup in case of data loss or system failure.

Salesforce sandboxes are used for development and testing, and four different types are available, each with different features, purposes, refresh cycles, and storage limits:

- The Full Copy sandbox is a complete copy of your production environment, including all metadata and data. It is typically used for testing and development purposes that require a full replica of the production environment, such as performance testing, **UAT**, and training. However, you should be aware that these sandboxes can only be refreshed from production every 29 days. Full Copy sandboxes also don't support source tracking, so they are not suited for being your primary development environment for SFDX.

- The Partial Copy sandbox includes a subset of your production environment data, as well as all metadata. It is typically used for testing and development purposes that require a smaller dataset than a Full Copy, such as feature development or regression testing. This type of sandbox is not provided as standard and is an additional license cost from Salesforce. Unlike the Full Copy sandbox, Partial Copy sandboxes can be refreshed every five days, but like the Full Copy sandboxes, they don't support source tracking.

- The Developer sandbox is a dedicated environment for individual developers or small teams. It includes all metadata but no data. It is typically used for individual feature development or testing. Most orgs will have far more Developer sandboxes available than the Full Copy or Partial Copy ones (usually limited to one of each unless you purchase additional ones). They can be refreshed daily but don't bring across any data, and have a much smaller data capacity.

- The Developer Pro sandbox is similar to a Developer sandbox but has a larger storage capacity. It is typically used for more complex development and testing tasks, such as integrations or app development.

Scratch orgs

Scratch orgs are disposable, temporary environments that can be quickly created and deleted. They are primarily used for agile development, such as building and testing new features in a short amount of time.

The lifespan of a scratch org is inherently temporary, with a maximum duration of 30 days. This ephemeral nature encourages developers to follow a source-driven development approach, where the version control system serves as the single source of truth. In contrast, Developer sandboxes are more persistent environments that may exist for extended periods, making it easier for developers to unintentionally accumulate outdated or unused code and configurations.

Scratch orgs are designed to be lightweight and rapidly configurable. They can be created and customized with specific features, settings, and data needed for a particular project by adjusting the scratch org definition file. This makes it easy for developers to create multiple scratch orgs tailored to different projects or tasks. On the other hand, Developer sandboxes are created as a copy of the production environment, including all customizations and a subset of the data, which can make them less cumbersome and time-consuming to set up and configure.

By default, when a scratch org is created, it doesn't have any connection to the features or metadata enabled in your production org. It's created according to a generic template with a base set of features. This means that the newly created scratch org won't reflect your production org's specific characteristics or customization, which can be challenging if you're developing and testing features tied to those specific settings or metadata.

To overcome this, Salesforce introduced the concept of a definition file. A definition file is a JSON file that specifies the shape of the scratch org or the characteristics that you want the scratch org to have. It can define preferences for features, settings, and editions. For example, the definition file might include instructions to enable certain Salesforce features, such as Einstein Analytics or person accounts.

Creating a definition file manually allows you to tailor your scratch org to match your production environment. However, manually creating a definition file that exactly matches a complex production org can be time-consuming and potentially error-prone.

To help with this, Salesforce has introduced the concept of an org shape. An org shape is essentially a snapshot of your production org's features and settings, which you can use as a template when creating scratch orgs. By using an org shape, you can quickly and accurately recreate the environment of your production org in a scratch org without having to manually specify all the settings in a definition file.

The preceding combination of being short-lived, lightweight, and configurable means that scratch orgs are more conducive to supporting **continuous integration and continuous delivery (CI/CD)** processes. The disposable nature of scratch orgs allows developers to rapidly create, test, and destroy environments as needed, enabling seamless integration into CI/CD pipelines. Developer sandboxes, with their longer lifespan and more complex setup, may not be as well suited for such automated workflows.

Summary

In this chapter, we covered an end-to-end lifecycle of using the standard stack of Salesforce and source control tools. Let's recap what that process entailed.

We looked at how to initialize or clone a Git repository to the local machine, ensuring we had the latest version of the code base. Using VS Code, we were able to easily access and manage the source code, as well as run SFDX commands within the integrated terminal or from the built-in Command Palette within VS Code and the Salesforce extensions pack.

Before starting the development process, we created a new branch in the Git repository to represent the specific feature or task we were working on. This branch is typically named according to the associated Jira ticket to maintain traceability and organization. Once the feature branch was created, we switched to the new branch and started implementing the required changes.

As part of the development process, we made use of SFDX tools to create, retrieve, and deploy metadata components. Although we used a sandbox environment in our example, we could also have leveraged scratch orgs – temporary Salesforce environments – to test and iterate on our changes before finalizing the code. Throughout this process, we committed our changes to the feature branch, providing clear and concise commit messages to maintain a comprehensive history.

Once the development was complete and the changes were thoroughly tested, we pushed the feature branch to the remote Git repository. At this point, we were then ready to create a pull request to merge the feature branch into the main branch. The pull request serves as an opportunity for team members to review the changes, provide feedback, and suggest improvements. It also acts as a quality assurance measure to ensure that the code base remains stable and maintains the desired level of quality.

Upon receiving approval from the team, we could then merge the feature branch into the main branch using the pull request. The main branch was then ready to be deployed to a staging or production environment for further testing and validation.

Once the deployment was successful, the feature branch could be deleted, both locally and on the remote repository, to maintain a clean and organized code base.

The use of pull requests, Jira ticket-based feature branches, and the collaborative review process ensures a high-quality, traceable, and maintainable code base throughout the Salesforce development lifecycle.

This entire workflow was achieved with freely available tools and provided the simplest entry point to a Salesforce DevOps process. As your needs grow, it will become more important to look at the power of automation, especially in the context of CI/CD.

We will look at CI/CD in more detail in *Chapter 7*. Ahead of that, though, in the next chapter, we'll take another approach to Salesforce change management by looking at packaging.

6
Exploring Packaging

There are many ways to deliver Salesforce changes between environments and still adhere to DevOps principles. One of the popular mechanisms is the use of Salesforce packages, which can be either managed, unmanaged, or unlocked packages.

In this chapter, we'll look at these three types of Salesforce packages, their use cases, and considerations:

- **Unmanaged packages** – Used to share customizations or applications with other organizations or users without any built-in versioning or upgrade capabilities.

- **Unlocked packages** – Designed for efficient application life cycle management, modular development, and versioning within a single organization. They are also a popular means of distributing open source solutions on the Salesforce platform.

- **Managed packages** – Designed to distribute custom applications, extensions, or integrations built on the Salesforce platform to multiple organizations or customers, with protection of the code used to build them, versioning, and upgradability.

By the end of the chapter, you will have a clear idea of not only the differences between these different types of packages but also when to use them and how to build them in Salesforce.

Technical requirements

For unmanaged, unlocked, and 2GP-managed packages, there shouldn't be any additional requirements other than your Salesforce environment – ideally either a **Sandbox** or a **Developer** Edition.

For 1GP-managed packages, you will need a separate packaging org when developing a managed package for distribution. A packaging org is a separate Salesforce org used to develop, package, and distribute managed packages.

For Salesforce ISV partners, this would typically be a **Partner Developer Edition** org, which has additional features and higher limits compared to a regular Developer Edition org. These are for use by Salesforce registered partners and aren't for general everyday use by most Salesforce customers.

An example project for testing package commands is provided in the Chapter6 folder of the GitHub repository associated with this book.

Unmanaged packages

Unmanaged packages form a part of Salesforce's original implementation of packaging, and as such, form part of what is now known as **first-generation packaging (1GP)**. They are used to bundle and share customizations, applications, or templates between different organizations or users. Unmanaged packages provide a way to distribute components, allowing developers to modify or build upon them as needed after installation.

Since unmanaged packages are part of 1GP, they follow a development and packaging process that is seldom source-driven. This means that the components within the package are typically selected from an org rather than a branch in a version control system. The lack of source-driven development with unmanaged packages makes it difficult to establish a streamlined and efficient DevOps process that involves version control, continuous integration, and continuous deployment.

Another limitation of this approach is that unmanaged packages do not support versioning of the packages themselves or in-place upgrades. Any updates or changes to the components within an unmanaged package must be done manually in the target org after installation. This can lead to challenges in managing and maintaining customizations over time, especially in larger and more complex Salesforce implementations.

The absence of a package-specific namespace in unmanaged packages also means that their components merge into the target org's metadata without any separation. This can lead to naming conflicts and potential issues during deployment, making it more difficult to manage dependencies and maintain a clean metadata structure in the target org. If an unmanaged package is installed into a namespaced org, the components will inherit the org's namespace.

As you can see, there are several limitations to the original 1GP approach and this is why Salesforce replaced it with **second-generation packaging (2GP)**, which is what is now recommended.

As we've discussed, unmanaged packages are not ideally suited for use as part of your DevOps strategy, so let's look at unlocked packages, which were introduced with Salesforce's 2GP implementation.

Unlocked packages

Salesforce unlocked packages are a modern, flexible, and modular packaging solution that allows developers and administrators to bundle, deploy, and manage customizations and applications built on the Salesforce platform. They are part of Salesforce's source-driven development approach, which emphasizes version control systems and continuous integration pipelines for efficient development and deployment processes.

Unlocked packages address the challenges of managing and deploying customizations in large-scale and complex Salesforce implementations. By breaking down applications and customizations into modular units, they enable teams to manage and distribute these components more effectively. This modular approach promotes better collaboration, easier version control, and a streamlined development process. Unlocked packages are aimed at both developers and administrators who want to leverage best practices in application life cycle management, streamline their deployment processes, and reduce the complexity associated with metadata deployments.

Unlike managed packages, which are primarily used for distributing applications to multiple companies or customers, unlocked packages are designed for use within a single company. They are especially useful for enterprises with large Salesforce teams that require a structured and maintainable way to manage and deploy customizations across various environments, such as development, testing, and production. By providing a scalable and modular approach to Salesforce development, unlocked packages help organizations optimize their Salesforce implementations and drive better business outcomes.

Since unlocked packages are a source-driven approach to packaging, there is a greater reliance on the use of the command line to create them. You will need to be using the **Salesforce DX (SFDX)** approach to managing your metadata, and thus have a Dev Hub enabled. To do this, follow these steps:

1. Log in to your Salesforce org.
2. Click on the gear icon in the top-right corner and select **Setup**.
3. In the **Quick Find** box, type Dev Hub and select it.
4. Toggle the **Enable Dev Hub** switch to **On** and enable **Unlocked Packages** on the same screen.

Once this is enabled, you can then work with your Dev Hub org from the command line – whether that's a standalone one or the embedded terminal in VS Code. To create a new unlocked package, run the following command:

```
sf package create --name MyPackageName -t Unlocked --path force-app -v
MyDevHub
```

Replace MyPackageName with the name of your package and MyDevHub with the alias you used when authenticating with your Dev Hub org.

At this point, it is assumed that you have a local project and that you have committed your code to Git. While source control of your changes is not essential for creating the package, as part of a DevOps process, this would be a good time to ensure your Git repository is up to date before creating your new package. With your updated metadata components in your local project, you can create a new package with the following command:

```
sf package version create -p MyPackageName -d force-app -k MyPassword
--wait 10 -v MyDevHub
```

Replace `MyPackageName` with the name of your package, `MyPassword` with a password for the package (optional), and `MyDevHub` with the alias you used when authenticating with your Dev Hub org.

After creating a new package version, the added metadata components will be included in the unlocked package. You can install this package in your target Salesforce org with the following command:

```
sf package install --package MyPackageName@1.0.0 -o MyTargetOrg -w 10
```

Again, you will need to replace `MyPackageName@1.0.0` with the package name and version, and `MyTargetOrg` with the username or alias of your target org. It is worth noting that if a password was set in the preceding version creation, it will have to be supplied here with the `-k` flag for the installation to work.

Since unlocked packages have the foundation of a source-driven development approach rather than an org-driven approach, it is much better aligned to the use of DevOps throughout your entire process. By making use of source control and breaking down larger code bases into modular groups of functionality that could potentially be in their own separate Git repositories, you can be much more flexible in your approach to delivery using unlocked packages.

The one potential catch in this degree of modularization, however, is that there are sometimes situations in which there are pieces of metadata that overlap multiple packages. For example, if you have two distinct pieces of functionality that both make use of or depend upon the `Opportunity` object, you could potentially end up with a situation where there is a circular dependency on changes across packages.

A workaround to this could be to have a centralized `core` package that the other packages all reference. During the development of new functionality outside of this package, you would ensure you have installed the latest version of this core package in your development environment.

A better approach is to make good use of namespaces in your unlocked package development. Namespaces should be an integral part of creating Salesforce unlocked packages. They guarantee uniqueness – if someone already has an Apex class named `MyClass`, your `MyClass` won't conflict with it, which avoids tricky naming clashes.

Namespaces also enable effective versioning of packages. Salesforce uses the namespace to manage multiple versions of a package, knowing which are compatible and how to handle upgrades or rollbacks.

Additionally, namespaces provide another means to provide clear separation of package code. It becomes evident which components belong to a particular package, isolating its code from the rest of the org's metadata. This aids in debugging and maintenance.

At the code level, rather than at the point of packaging, there are some additional benefits to be found. Namespaces remove ambiguity when third-party systems integrate with your package's APIs and components. References are clear even with dynamic SOQL or REST calls, and namespaces allow control over which components are globally accessible versus private. Boundaries can be set on what's exposed for general use.

When creating a package, the first step is registering a unique namespace identifier. This ties all components to that namespace. Next, the namespace is included in the package metadata when building a new version – during installation, Salesforce leverages the namespace to separate incoming components, avoiding conflicts. In code and configuration, components can be referenced with their namespace prefix, such as `namespace__MyClass`.

However, namespaces also come with some downsides. They lock you into a permanent identifier that can't easily change later. Complexity gets introduced by referencing namespaced components. Migrating existing `un-namespaced` code can require cumbersome adjustments. The availability of intuitive namespaces may be limited. Debugging across multiple namespaced packages can become complicated.

Overall, the benefits outweigh the limitations, especially for manageability and version control. But it's important to be aware of the cons and plan your naming and development accordingly.

Thankfully, Salesforce also recognizes this challenge and provides another package type to cover this eventuality. Let's explore these org-dependent packages a little further.

Org-dependent packages

The other type of unlocked package that Salesforce provides, org-dependent packages, tackles the problem of dependencies by deferring compilation and validation of your changes until installation time. This means that these dependencies don't necessarily need to be in your development org or in your source control for you to build the package – you can depend on metadata that exists in the target org.

This type of unlocked package is ideal for Salesforce orgs that are large, complex, and have been in use for a long time and thus have accumulated a lot of changes. Unpicking these changes into separate modules is lengthy, challenging work, but by having a package type that is able to depend on unpackaged metadata in the target org, you can defer (or even avoid) the need to refactor your entire org.

Creating an org-dependent package is incredibly simple, too – the command is the same as that for creating an unlocked package, but with the `--orgdependent` flag specified, such as in the following example:

```
sf package create --name MyPackageName -t Unlocked --path force-app -v
MyDevHub --org-dependent
```

You might be tempted to make all your unlocked packages org-dependent to gain the advantage of just-in-time validation, but there are some key drawbacks to org-dependent packages that ultimately mean you should always assess the correct package type for your use case:

Feature	Unlocked packages	Org-dependent packages
Installation flexibility	You can install these packages in any org, regardless of the metadata they contain.	You can only install these packages in orgs that have the specific metadata that the package depends on.
Dependency validation time	The package dependencies are checked when you create the package version.	The package dependencies are checked when you install the package in an org.
Dependency on other packages	These packages can depend on other packages.	These packages cannot depend on other packages.
Dependency resolution	You need to resolve all the dependencies before you can create the package.	You do not need to resolve any dependencies before you can create the package.
Supported metadata types	Refer to the unlocked packaging channel of the Metadata Coverage report for the list of supported metadata types.	Refer to the unlocked packaging channel of the Metadata Coverage report for the list of supported metadata types.
Development and test environment	Use scratch orgs to develop and test your unlocked packages.	Use a sandbox that has the dependent metadata. You can also enable Source Tracking in sandboxes to develop your org-dependent unlocked package. Test the package in a sandbox org before installing it in your production org.
Code coverage requirement	You must have at least 75% code coverage for the Apex code in your package before you can promote and release it.	There is no code coverage calculation, but you should test your Apex code well.

Table 6.1 – A comparison of unlocked and org-dependent packages

In the next section, we're going to look at the final type of packaging in Salesforce, managed packages.

Managed packages

Salesforce managed packages are developed, packaged, and distributed by Salesforce partners – also known as **independent software vendors** (**ISVs**). These packages provide a way to extend the functionality of Salesforce by adding new features, processes, or applications without having to build them from scratch. Managed packages are distributed through the Salesforce AppExchange, which is an online marketplace for Salesforce applications, components, and services. AppExchange allows developers and partners to publish their managed packages for Salesforce customers to discover, evaluate, and install them directly into their Salesforce environments.

Managed packages often can be customized to meet specific business needs while maintaining the core functionality provided by the package, but the level of customization possible will vary depending on the metadata contained within the package. The Salesforce DX Developer Guide has a section on what can and can't be changed in managed packages and can be found at `https://developer.salesforce.com/docs/atlas.en-us.sfdx_dev.meta/sfdx_dev/packaging_packageable_components.htm`.

The package provider is responsible for maintaining and upgrading the package, ensuring it stays compatible with the latest Salesforce releases and industry standards. This reduces the burden on the organization using the package, especially if it is using the package as installed with no further customizations or changes to the metadata in the package.

Salesforce stands out from other development platforms such as Java or C# due to its strong emphasis on backward compatibility and API stability for developers. When you build applications on top of the Salesforce platform, you can have confidence that the core APIs you rely on will not suddenly be deprecated or altered unexpectedly.

With languages such as Java or C#, core libraries or methods can be deprecated with just a notification that they will be removed in an upcoming release. This forces you, as a developer, to continually refactor your code to stay current. But Salesforce takes a very different approach to managing upgrades and keeping customers happy.

Once an Apex API is released as part of a managed package on Salesforce, its method signature is locked in place. The API functionality may evolve over time, even to the point of throwing new exceptions, but the original method and signature will remain intact. This prevents the common problem developers face of having to hastily refactor their own customizations just to install an upgrade to a dependent package.

Additionally, managed packages undergo a thorough security review process by Salesforce to ensure they meet the necessary standards for performance, data protection, and privacy. This provides an additional layer of trust for organizations using these packages.

Typically, the life cycle of managed packages differs only in the approval and distribution stages. Managed packages are developed in scratch orgs and distributed through the Salesforce AppExchange. Participating in this marketplace requires you to enroll with Salesforce as an ISV partner with a valid business case for your package. Once approved, you can then move on to producing your package.

Here's how the distribution process typically works:

1. Development
2. Testing
3. Packaging
4. Security review
5. AppExchange listing
6. Installation and configuration
7. Ongoing support and upgrades

Development

The package creator develops the managed package using Salesforce tools such as Apex, Visualforce, Lightning Components, and more, ensuring compatibility with Salesforce.

Testing

Like any other piece of Salesforce development, the metadata and code for the package should be fully tested, not just to ensure that it is functionally complete but also to meet the stringent expectations for security that ISV partners should adhere to.

Salesforce provides several tools to help guide developers through this process, such as Salesforce Code Analyzer. This tool makes use of the Salesforce Graph Engine to do a deep walk through the code, following dependencies and looking for common security issues – particularly those around record access – using a technique called **data flow analysis (DFA)**. DFA is a method that helps you to understand complicated parts of computer code better. It looks at the whole code all at once to figure out what's going on in it. It does this by breaking down the code's steps, including things such as evaluating conditions, creating classes, and calling methods and static calls. It also tries to guess the value of the variables and fields at each step along the way. This all helps to give a better picture of how the code works.

The analyzer also makes use of other open source analysis engines, such as PMD and ESLint, to round out the coverage of these checks.

Packaging

Historically, managed packages followed a lengthy process along the lines of 1GP, as discussed earlier, which involved the following:

- Selecting the components to be included, such as Apex classes, Visualforce pages, Lightning Components, custom objects, and more

- Setting the package properties, such as the package name, namespace, version number, and description

- Defining dependencies on other packages or Salesforce features, if any

- Designating the package as managed to ensure versioning, upgradeability, and intellectual property protection

The package can then be uploaded to the Salesforce environment, generating an installation URL for distribution.

With the advent of 2GP, this process has become much more simplified. First, ensure that all components required for your package are in your project directory (typically in the `force-app` folder). This project should be linked to a corresponding scratch org and the required namespace should be specified in your `sfdx-project.json` file.

The process for creating the actual package is more straightforward than the old 1GP approach, differing from unlocked packages by one simple command-line parameter, `-t Managed`, as shown in the following:

```
sf force package create -n "My Managed Package" -t Managed -r force-
app
```

Security review

Before a managed package can be listed on the AppExchange, it must undergo a security review process. This process involves the following:

- A comprehensive assessment of the package's code and components to identify potential security vulnerabilities, such as injection attacks, insecure storage of sensitive data, and improper access controls

- Ensuring that the package adheres to Salesforce's security guidelines, best practices, and compliance requirements

- Submitting a security review request to Salesforce, along with relevant documentation and test cases

- Addressing any security issues identified by Salesforce during the review process and resubmitting the package for approval

Once the package passes the security review, it is granted the **Passed Security Review** status, signaling to customers that it meets Salesforce's security standards.

AppExchange listing

After passing the security review, the package can be listed on the Salesforce AppExchange. Listing the package involves the following:

- Creating an AppExchange listing with essential information about the package, such as its name, description, features, pricing, and support details
- Adding screenshots, videos, or other media that showcase the package's functionality and benefits
- Associating the listing with the managed package using the installation URL generated during the packaging process
- Submitting the listing for approval by Salesforce, which will review it for quality, branding, and content guidelines

Once the listing is approved, it becomes publicly available on the AppExchange, allowing customers to discover and evaluate the package.

Installation and configuration

Salesforce customers can find, evaluate, and install managed packages from the AppExchange by following these steps:

- Browsing the AppExchange to discover packages that address their specific needs using search, filters, and categories
- Evaluating the package by reviewing its description, features, pricing, customer reviews, and any available demos or trials
- Installing the package by clicking the **Get It Now** button on the AppExchange listing, which initiates the installation process in the customer's Salesforce environment
- Granting access and setting up security settings for the package during installation, ensuring it aligns with the organization's security policies
- Configuring the package post-installation by customizing settings, adjusting layouts, or setting up any required integrations

Once installed and configured, the managed package becomes an integral part of the customer's Salesforce environment, extending the platform's functionality to address their specific needs and requirements.

Ongoing support and upgrades

After the package is installed and configured, the package provider is responsible for offering ongoing support and updates. This ensures that the package remains compatible with the latest Salesforce releases, industry standards, and customer expectations. The ongoing support and upgrade process typically involves the following:

- Monitoring and addressing customer feedback, questions, and issues through support channels such as email, phone, or online forums.

- Regularly releasing updates to the package to fix bugs, enhance features, and add new functionality. These updates are created as new package versions that customers can choose to install at their convenience.

- Ensuring compatibility with the latest Salesforce releases, making any necessary adjustments to maintain seamless integration with the platform.

- Staying up to date with industry trends, customer needs, and technology advancements to ensure the package remains relevant and valuable to customers.

- Informing customers about important updates, new features, and best practices through communication channels such as newsletters, webinars, or in-app notifications.

The ongoing support and upgrades provided by the package provider contribute to the package's long-term success, customer satisfaction, and overall value.

Packaging models' pros and cons

Packaging serves as a distribution method for development updates in a broader DevOps process, aligning with source-driven software development principles. As various package types offer distinct use cases and strengths, selecting the most suitable delivery model is crucial to optimizing your workflow within the DevOps life cycle.

Let's remind ourselves of the differences:

Package type	Pros	Cons	Primary use cases
Unmanaged	Easy to customize	No version control	Sharing code and configurations for learning purposes
	Allows for code editing	No automatic upgrades	Sharing sample solutions
	No namespace requirements	Security concerns due to editable code	Collaborative development
		No support for managed package features	Can be used by Professional Services teams where there's a common customization that many customers require, but which itself may need the odd tweak for each customer
Unlocked	Easy to customize	No automatic upgrades	Deploying reusable components across multiple orgs
	Version control	Manual upgrade process	Sharing modular solutions
	Allows for code editing	Security concerns due to editable code	Facilitating internal collaboration and development
	Supports managed package features (e.g., namespaces)	Requires Salesforce DX and source-driven development	
Managed	Automatic upgrades	Limited customization	Commercial app distribution
	Version control	Code not editable	Distributing apps on the AppExchange
	Enhanced security due to uneditable code	Requires namespaces	Protecting intellectual property
	Supports managed package features (e.g., namespaces)	2GP requires Salesforce DX and source-driven development (although 1GP can still be done without DX patterns)	

Table 6.2 – The pros and cons of each package type

Breaking up an existing monolithic application

Migrating a mature, monolithic application to Salesforce's package development model can be a major undertaking filled with complexities and challenges.

On the complexity side, code refactoring is often needed to break tight couplings and fit components into modular packages. Dependency management becomes critical to untangle interconnected components. Introducing namespaces can add complexity in updating all references. Data models may need reworking to fit the new packaged schema. Permission sets and profiles will likely require redefinition. Automation and CI/CD pipelines need adaptation to handle packaging, versioning, and dependencies. Keeping various org environments in sync with the correct package versions is complex to orchestrate.

In terms of challenges, the transition will require extensive investment in resources and time. There will be a knowledge gap as teams learn the new model. Testing strategies need an overhaul, potentially including rewriting tests and scripts while setting up new test environments. Maintaining backward compatibility could limit changes, forcing the need for legacy system support. Once transitioned, version management across packages and customers multiplies the complexity. Stakeholders accustomed to quick deployments may resist the slower, more controlled package life cycle. Apart from staffing costs, expenses such as training, downtime, and tools will accumulate.

To smooth the transition, a phased, gradual approach can help. Extensive training and expert consulting will build the necessary skills. Detailed documentation provides a knowledge base. Feedback channels give early visibility of issues. Risk assessments and rollback plans mitigate pitfalls. Proper resource allocation, both human and computational, lays the groundwork.

While difficult, migrating a monolithic application to the package model can ultimately enable modular, scalable development and easier maintenance. With careful planning and execution, the long-term benefits may outweigh the complexities of getting there.

Summary

In this chapter, we've looked at packaging as a technique for deploying our code changes and compared the different types of packages available. For each type of package, we have seen the steps required to bundle our Salesforce changes into those packages for further distribution.

We've also seen that these changes can follow a source-driven DevOps process if we select the appropriate type of package. Packaging by no means replaces DevOps processes; rather, it is a technique that forms part of DevOps on the Salesforce platform. Equally, it is not the only means of delivering your changes for scenarios outside of the ISV Partner space.

In the next chapter, we'll start looking at bringing all the elements of our source-driven workflow together and adding some automation as we investigate the CI/CD automation of our processes. This represents an alternative delivery mechanism for our changes that doesn't require packaging.

7
CI/CD Automation

In this chapter, we'll learn how to automate our DevOps processes with **Continuous Integration and Continuous Delivery (CI/CD)**. We'll also look at some popular tools for achieving this.

By leveraging the power of CI/CD, we can create a more efficient, reliable, and streamlined workflow for our Salesforce development and operations. This approach allows us to quickly react to changes, reduces the risk of deployment failures, and ultimately, helps us deliver better-quality software.

We will cover the following main topics.

- **Introduction to CI/CD**: Firstly, we will define CI/CD, explain its benefits, and discuss how it fits into a DevOps strategy. We'll also highlight the key principles and best practices to follow when implementing CI/CD.

- **GitHub Actions**: This section will focus on GitHub Actions, a flexible and powerful CI/CD tool that integrates directly with your GitHub repositories. We'll explore how to set up workflows, automate tests, and handle deployments, all within the GitHub platform.

- **Jenkins**: A longstanding favorite in the CI/CD community, Jenkins is another tool we'll dive into. We'll show you how to configure Jenkins for Salesforce projects, create pipelines, and leverage its extensive plugin ecosystem.

- **Salesforce-specific tools**: Salesforce offers several tools that can aid in CI/CD, such as **Salesforce DX (SFDX)** and the Salesforce CLI. We'll discuss how to leverage these tools to streamline your CI/CD process and tackle Salesforce-specific challenges.

- **Practical use of the CI/CD pipeline**: We'll finish by looking at the advantages that our newly-built CI/CD pipeline affords us as part of a robust DevOps implementation.

By the end of this chapter, you should have a robust understanding of the role of CI/CD in Salesforce DevOps, the tools available for implementing it, and the steps you can take to begin automating your own processes.

Technical requirements

For Jenkins, you'll need a server that can host the Jenkins software. This could be a physical server, a virtual machine, or a cloud-based server. The specific requirements will depend on the scale of your projects, but as a minimum, you should plan for at least 1 GB of memory, 50 GB of disk space, and a modern CPU. It's worth noting that, for learning purposes, it is possible to run Jenkins on your local development machine if you want to follow the processes and steps in this book, but for real-world use, as part of your DevOps toolchain, a dedicated hosting solution is recommended.

SFDX and the Salesforce CLI are crucial tools for Salesforce DevOps. To use them, you'll need to install the Salesforce CLI on your system. If you've not already got them in place, you can revisit *Chapter 5*, which covers setting them up in detail.

To implement CI/CD in Salesforce, you'll need an active Salesforce developer account. If you're working with a team, you'll also need an SFDX "hub" organization, where you can create and manage scratch orgs.

A crucial part of CI/CD is version control. GitHub is the most widely used platform and is recommended for its excellent integration with CI/CD tools. You'll need a GitHub account and a repository for your Salesforce code.

The source code for this chapter is available at `https://github.com/PacktPublishing/Salesforce-DevOps-for-Architects/tree/main/Chapter7`.

Introducing CI/CD

The world of software development has evolved dramatically over the years, with an increasing focus on agility, efficiency, and quality. In this context, CI and CD have emerged as key practices that can drive significant improvements in development workflows. In this section, we will explore the core concepts of CI/CD, their benefits, and their role in a DevOps strategy.

Continuous Integration (CI)

CI is a process in which developers commit their code into a shared repository frequently. Each of these commits can then undergo an automated build and test cycle to identify problems in the early stages of the development life cycle. This CI process helps to reduce integration problems and allows the development team to receive immediate feedback on any issues.

Continuous Delivery (CD)

CD takes the ideas of CI one step further. It automates the software release process as far as being ready for production but falls just short of the actual production deployment. This practice ensures that the code and config contained in the repository (usually the main or master branch) are always in a production-ready state, reduces the risk and effort of deployments, and allows teams to deliver updates and improvements to customers more quickly and regularly. The software is deployment-ready after automated testing, but a human decision is required on when to deploy to production.

Together, CI and CD form the backbone of modern DevOps practices. They promote a culture of collaboration, fast feedback cycles, and a focus on high-quality output. Implementing CI/CD can lead to more efficient development processes, fewer bugs reaching production, and a better product for your users.

In the context of Salesforce, CI/CD can bring additional benefits. Salesforce projects often involve multiple developers working on several aspects of a complex system. With CI/CD, you can ensure that changes are integrated and tested frequently, reducing the risk of conflicts and errors. Also, automated deployments can simplify the process of pushing changes to testing, staging, and production environments.

However, it's important to note that implementing CI/CD is not just a matter of using certain tools or following specific steps. It's a cultural shift that requires buy-in from the entire team, a focus on automation and testing, and an ongoing commitment to improving your processes. This may involve improving existing testing practices or addressing technical debt and poor architecture – all of which can be prerequisites for properly implementing CI/CD. While these changes can seem daunting, the benefits of adopting CI/CD typically outweigh the effort required. In the following sections, we'll delve into the specific tools and practices that can help you bring the benefits of CI/CD to your Salesforce projects. Even though the initial effort may be substantial, the payoff from improved automation, testing, and delivery processes is well worth it. With team commitment and a focus on continuous improvement, CI/CD can transform how you build and deliver on Salesforce.

CI/CD pipeline

A crucial concept within the CI/CD landscape is that of a pipeline. A CI/CD pipeline is a series of steps that your changes, whether in the form of code, metadata, or even data, will go through to make their way from development to production. It automates the process of integrating code changes, validating them with tests, and delivering them to the end users. It is usually visualized as a series of stages, each with a specific purpose. When a change is introduced (for example, when a developer pushes code to the repository), it triggers the pipeline, and the change moves through the stages. Let's look at some of the typical pipeline stages:

- **Build stage**: This is where the code is compiled, dependencies are fetched, and the software is packaged for deployment. For a Salesforce project, this might involve creating a new SFDX scratch org, pushing the code to the org, and running any required scripts.

- **Test stage**: Automated tests are run against the build to ensure it behaves as expected. This could include unit tests, integration tests, and functional tests. In a Salesforce context, this must involve running Apex tests and possibly testing other components, such as Visualforce pages or Lightning components.

- **Deploy stage**: If the build passes all tests, it can be deployed to a staging environment for further testing, and if it passes there, it can be deployed to the production environment. Salesforce-specific tools such as SFDX and change sets can be used for these deployments. Ultimately, these tools are wrappers around the Metadata API, which remains the sole underlying way to deploy changes.

- **Monitor stage**: After deployment, the application is monitored to ensure it's functioning correctly in the production environment. Any issues that arise can be fed back into the development process.

Each of these stages is typically automated, meaning that the change can progress from one stage to the next without manual intervention, assuming that all checks pass. This automation is a key benefit of CI/CD pipelines, as it reduces the risk of human error, speeds up the delivery process, and provides quick feedback to the development team.

Each stage is designed to catch different types of issues. For instance, the build stage might catch syntax errors, while the test stage could catch functional bugs, and the monitoring stage could identify performance issues or errors in the live environment. Using tools such as PMD for static code analysis, or other code linters, such as ESLint for your Lightning Web Components, reinforces consistent code style and best practices across the entire development team. With rules encoded into the tools, developers get immediate feedback if they violate conventions. This promotes readable, maintainable code and, of course, can be added to your pipelines to run automatically.

In the context of Salesforce, a CI/CD pipeline can help manage the complexities of developing in a multi-tenant, metadata-driven environment. It allows teams to develop, test, and deploy changes in a controlled, repeatable way, reducing the risks associated with manual deployments and ensuring high-quality output. In the coming sections, we'll discuss how to implement such a pipeline using popular tools such as GitHub Actions and Jenkins.

GitHub Actions

In our journey into the realm of CI/CD, we encounter various tools that help facilitate these practices. One of these tools, which stands out for its simplicity and tight integration with the GitHub platform, is GitHub Actions. This powerful automation tool allows you to create custom **Software Development Life Cycle (SDLC)** workflows directly in your GitHub repository.

GitHub Actions enables you to automate, customize, and execute your software development workflows right in your repository. You can deploy workflows in the same place where you store code and collaborate on projects. This translates into faster, more streamlined development cycles as you can manage CI/CD from within your GitHub projects, without needing to rely on external tools.

In GitHub Actions, workflows, jobs, and actions have a hierarchical relationship, which allows you to organize and structure your CI/CD process. This hierarchy has the following levels:

- **Workflow**: A workflow is the highest level of organization. These automated processes are typically stored in your repository and can be configured for a number of DevOps tasks against your GitHub project, such as building, testing, packaging, or deploying your changes. Workflows consist of one or more job nodes and can be triggered automatically by various events, such as a push or pull request. The `.github/workflows` directory of your repository holds `.yml` or `.yaml` files where workflows are defined.

- **Job**: Jobs are the second level of organization within a workflow. Each job will execute in an environment defined by the `runs-on` directive. A single workflow can execute numerous jobs, which, by default, operate concurrently, although you can adjust them to run one after the other. Each job is composed of several steps, each performing specific tasks. These jobs can utilize either the same runner or different ones.

- **Step**: Steps represent the most granular level of work within a job. Each step is responsible for executing a single command or action. They can either carry out commands, which are any shell commands, or actions, which are reusable code chunks. These actions could be developed by you, developed by GitHub, or sourced from the community through a public repository.

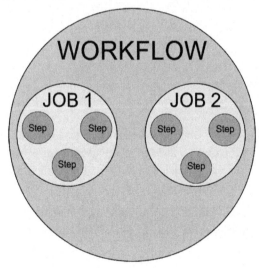

Figure 7.1 – The hierarchical relationship between workflows, jobs, and steps

A step in a job can be either a command that runs in a shell or an action. In the following example, each step in the job either runs a command in a shell (such as `npm install sfdx-cli --global`) or uses an action (such as `actions/checkout@v2`).

GitHub Actions provides more than just the ability to establish CI/CD pipelines. It also allows for the automation of a broad spectrum of tasks, such as issue triaging and package publishing. This makes it a multifaceted tool essential for any developer's toolkit.

For Salesforce developers and architects, tasks can be automated using GitHub Actions, such as running Apex tests, deploying code to scratch orgs, and promoting changes to staging and production environments. In the following sections, we'll delve deeper into how to set up and use GitHub Actions for Salesforce CI/CD.

GitHub workflows in action

Let's start by looking at a real-world example of a Git workflow and then walk through what it is doing. Consider the GitHub workflow shown here:

```
name: Salesforce CI
on:
  push:
    branches: [ main ]
  pull_request:
    branches: [ main ]
```

This GitHub workflow is initiated whenever push or pull request events occur on the main branch. We then need to define the job(s) within the workflow:

```
jobs:
  deploy:
    runs-on: ubuntu-latest
```

In this instance, we have defined a singular job named `deploy`, which executes in an `ubuntu-latest` environment. The `runs-on:` field in a GitHub Actions workflow configures the kind of machine that the job will be run on. This field can assume a variety of values, which, in turn, determine the type of runner used for the execution of the job.

A runner is a server equipped with the GitHub Actions runner application, tasked with executing jobs. The `ubuntu-latest` value indicates that the job should run on the latest stable Ubuntu virtual machine hosted by GitHub.

Next, we will define the steps that the job should execute. Firstly, we do some preparation by checking out the code in our repository and installing the Salesforce CLI to run additional steps with the code:

```
    steps:
        - name: Checkout
          uses: actions/checkout@v2

        - name: Install Salesforce CLI
```

```
        run: |
                wget https://developer.salesforce.com/media/salesforce-
cli/sfdx/channels/stable/sfdx-linux-x64.tar.xz
                mkdir ~/sfdx
                tar xJf sfdx-linux-x64.tar.xz -C ~/sfdx --strip-
components 1
                echo "$HOME/sfdx/bin" >> $GITHUB_PATH
                ~/sfdx/bin/sfdx version
```

The first step uses `actions/checkout@v2` to check out the source code of the current repository. With GitHub Actions, it's possible to utilize actions that are contained in your own repository, in a public repository, or within a Docker container image in GitHub's own collection of published images. The `uses:` keyword in your GitHub Actions workflow is used to specify these actions.

In this case, `actions/checkout@v2` refers to the checkout action from the `actions` repository, and `v2` is the tag of the version you want to use. This checkout action checks out your repository under `$GITHUB_WORKSPACE`, so your workflow can access it.

By specifying `v2`, you are instructing the workflow to use the second major version of the checkout action. This version could include new features, changes, or bug fixes compared to the previous version (`v1`). The maintainers of the action define these versions according to semantic versioning rules.

It's good practice to specify a version (instead of using the default branch, usually `main` or `master`) to protect your workflows from potential breaking changes introduced into those branches.

The second step is to install the Salesforce CLI globally. The Salesforce CLI is used to authenticate with your Salesforce org and run your Apex unit tests. However, the Salesforce CLI isn't pre-installed on GitHub's virtual environments, so you need to install it in your workflow.

The Salesforce CLI has two main distribution methods – as a binary executable file and as a Node. js package installed through npm. We chose to use the binary distribution in our script, as the npm installation can run into permissions issues when trying to add extra plugins. The npm package requires Node.js and needs to be installed globally, which typically requires sudo permissions. Using sudo can lead to filesystem permission problems down the line. The binary distribution avoids these problems, which is why we opted for that method. The Node.js npm package is also available, but we avoided it due to the potential permission issues when adding plugins. Now, we can move on to the next step in our job:

```
# The URL is stored in the Github Secret named DEVHUB_SFDX_URL
# so here we store the URL into a text file
        - name: 'Populate auth file with SFDX_URL secret of integration
org'
            shell: bash
            run: |
                    echo ${{ secrets.DEVHUB_SFDX_URL}} > ./DEVHUB_SFDX_
URL.txt
```

In the preceding step, we are making use of GitHub's per-repository secrets to retrieve a stored value and copying that value into a temporary file *only for the life cycle of this job*. The file contains an SFDX authorization URL, which allows the job to connect to our Salesforce Developer Hub org easily.

There are three choices available to create this authentication file. The simplest approach involves redirecting the output of the `sf org display --verbose --json` command to a file. As an illustration, consider the scenario of utilizing an org that you have already authorized:

```
sf org display -o <OrgUsername> --verbose --json > authFile.json
```

Inside the resulting JSON file, you can find the URL stored in the `sfdxAuthUrl` property within a results object. Please note that the `force:org:display --verbose` command only displays the refresh token for orgs authorized with the web server flow, not the JWT bearer flow.

Additionally, you have the option to generate a JSON file with a top-level property called `sfdxAuthUrl`, which contains the authentication URL. Alternatively, you can create a plain text file that solely includes the URL without any additional content.

The SFDX authorization URL follows this format:

`force://<clientId>:<clientSecret>:<refreshToken>@<instanceUrl>`

The URL uses `force://` instead of `http://` or `https://`, and `instanceUrl` does not include `https://`. It is just the domain name.

The next step authenticates with the Salesforce org using the newly created file, which contains the authorization URL, and gives it the alias `HubOrg`:

```
- name: Authenticate to Salesforce
    run: |
        sf auth sfdxurl store -f DEVHUB_SFDX_URL.txt -a HubOrg
```

Having authenticated our Dev Hub, we are now able to automatically generate a new scratch org for our testing needs and transfer our code into it:

```
- name: Create A New Scratch Org
    run: |
        sf org create scratch --target-dev-hub HubOrg --set-default
--definition-file config/project-scratch-def.json --alias ciorg
--wait=10

    - name: Push changes to new Scratch Org
    run: |
        sf project deploy start --target-org ciorg
```

With this new scratch org in place, with the `ciorg` alias, we can execute our Apex tests:

```
- name: Run all Apex tests
      run: |
          sf apex run test -o ciorg -l RunLocalTests -r tap -d test-
 results
```

Finally, we delete the scratch org when we've finished. This is an important step, since Salesforce enforces limits on how many active scratch orgs you can have in each Dev Hub:

```
- name: Delete scratch org
      run: |
          sf org delete scratch --target-org ciorg --no-prompt
```

Each step within a job operates in its own distinct context. However, using GitHub workflow syntax, these individual steps can be orchestrated to interact and cooperate with each other. The workflow configuration provides the ability to establish dependencies between steps, such as specifying that a step must wait for the successful completion of another before it starts. It also allows one step to utilize the output from another, among other interactions. This flexible configuration enables complex automated processes to be built from a collection of individual steps.

GitHub Actions provides a versatile platform for tailoring your CI/CD pipeline when working with SFDX. With its capability to run a wide array of tasks, from executing shell commands to running scripts or even third-party software, GitHub Actions can be uniquely customized to fit your specific needs.

This adaptability is also applicable to SFDX, where you can utilize GitHub Actions to automate numerous tasks. These can include executing unit tests, deploying code to various environments, and even overseeing data migration. By leveraging the power of GitHub Actions, you can create an efficient, reliable, and automated CI/CD pipeline that enhances the development and deployment process for your SFDX projects.

While the preceding steps will provide you with a basic automated workflow for using GitHub Actions for your Salesforce CI/CD needs, you can extend it with more automated testing, static code analysis, approval processes, and more. You find extensive documentation and tutorials in the official GitHub Actions documentation at `https://docs.github.com/en/actions/learn-github-actions`.

If you want an alternative approach to your CI/CD, you could instead look at Jenkins. It has a considerable number of plugins available, can be self-hosted to give you more control of your implementation, and has a more intuitive UI to set up and manage your pipeline. In the next section, we'll look at Jenkins in a little more detail.

Jenkins

Jenkins is an open source automation server that has solidified its place as an essential tool in the DevOps community. It has been a go-to choice for many organizations due to its extensive feature set, its plugin ecosystem, and the high degree of flexibility and control it offers.

Jenkins is engineered to manage a range of DevOps activities and processes, from a straightforward CI server to a comprehensive CD hub, accommodating any kind of project, regardless of the size or complexity. It allows you to automate the different stages of your delivery pipeline, providing continuous feedback to the project team about the health of their project.

One of the significant advantages of Jenkins is its extensibility through plugins. With over 1,000 plugins in the Update Center, Jenkins integrates with practically every tool in the CI/CD toolchain. You can use it to build, test, and deliver code in any language, to any platform. This extensibility makes Jenkins a versatile tool that can adapt to a wide range of project needs.

Jenkins uses a distributed architecture that can easily scale as your needs grow. You can set up Jenkins to distribute work across multiple machines, enabling projects to build, test, and deploy faster. This distributed nature of Jenkins is particularly beneficial for large and complex projects.

Much like GitHub Actions, Jenkins can be configured to handle tasks such as running Apex tests, creating and managing SFDX scratch orgs, and deploying metadata to various Salesforce environments. Jenkins can also be integrated with version control systems, such as Git, enhancing its capabilities within a Salesforce CI/CD pipeline.

The first part of setting up a Jenkins CI/CD pipeline for Salesforce is the installation of Jenkins itself. This varies slightly depending on your operating system. Jenkins is a Java-based application, so it runs on any platform that supports Java. It's advisable to always ensure that your system packages are up to date before starting any new installations.

If you're running Ubuntu Linux, the process begins with updating your system packages via the `apt update` and `apt upgrade` commands run in your terminal. You then need to install Java, as Jenkins requires it to run. The OpenJDK package is a good option and can be installed with `apt install openjdk-17-jdk`. At the time of writing, JDK 20 is the most recent version of the Java SE platform. However, JDK 17 LTS holds the status of being the most up-to-date **Long-Term Support (LTS)** release for the Java SE platform.

Next, you should add the Jenkins repository to your sources list, which is a prerequisite for the Jenkins installation. You can accomplish this by fetching the Jenkins repository key with the `wget` command and adding it to your system's software repository list. The key is required to authenticate and ensure that packages installed on your system are from a trusted source. You can download the Jenkins repository key directly from Jenkins' own servers with the following `wget` command in your terminal:

```
wget -q -O - https://pkg.jenkins.io/debian/jenkins.io.key | sudo
apt-key add -
```

The -q option tells wget to operate quietly, meaning it won't output progress information. The -O - option tells it to write the downloaded content to standard output, represented by -. This content is then piped, using the | symbol, into the sudo apt-key add - command, which adds the key to your system's list of trusted keys.

Next, you need to add the Jenkins repository to your system's software repository list. This is done by appending the Jenkins repository URL to the list of repositories stored in the /etc/apt/sources.list.d/ directory. You can do this with the following command:

```
echo deb http://pkg.jenkins.io/debian-stable binary/ | sudo tee /etc/
apt/sources.list.d/jenkins.list
```

The echo command prints its argument, in this case, the Jenkins repository URL and the type of packages to use (binary). This output is piped into the sudo tee command. The tee command is used to append the input it receives to a file, in this case, the jenkins.list file in the /etc/apt/sources.list.d/ directory.

Once these commands have been run, your system's package manager is set up to install Jenkins and keep it updated. The next step would be to update the package list with sudo apt update, and then you can proceed with installing Jenkins via sudo apt install jenkins.

For macOS users, you'll first need to install Homebrew, a package manager that simplifies the installation of software on macOS. Once Homebrew is installed, you can use it to install OpenJDK, and then Jenkins itself. Just like with Ubuntu, once Jenkins is installed, you should start the service and make sure it's set to start automatically when the system boots.

On Windows, the process is slightly different. You'll need to download the Jenkins WAR file directly from the Jenkins website and have the latest version of JDK installed from Oracle's website. After setting up the JAVA_HOME environment variable, you can run Jenkins by navigating to the directory where the Jenkins WAR file is stored and using the java -jar command.

In all three cases, once Jenkins is running, you can access the Jenkins dashboard by navigating to http://localhost:8080 in a web browser. You'll be guided through the rest of the setup process, which includes setting up an admin user and configuring security settings.

After Jenkins is installed and running, you'll need to prepare it for SFDX. SFDX comprises a suite of tools designed to enhance and simplify all stages of the development and deployment process. It requires the Salesforce CLI, so you'll need to install that on the same machine as Jenkins. We covered the installation of the Salesforce CLI earlier, in *Chapter 5*, if you need a reminder of the process.

Once the Salesforce CLI is installed, you'll need to ensure Jenkins can interact with it. This is done by adding the path to the Salesforce CLI in the Jenkins system configuration settings. You can navigate to these settings via the **Manage Jenkins | Configure System** menu on the Jenkins dashboard.

Jenkins operates by using plugins for specific tasks and integrations. For SFDX, the key plugins you need to install are the Pipeline plugin, the Git plugin, and, depending on your choice of version control solution, either the GitHub plugin, the Bitbucket plugin, or any plugins that may be specific to your Git provider. In this example, we're going to focus on the GitHub option. The Pipeline plugin enables the creation of CD pipelines in Jenkins, while the Git and GitHub plugins enable Jenkins to interact with Git repositories.

These plugins can be installed via the **Manage Plugins** menu in the Jenkins dashboard. After they're installed, Jenkins will be able to interact with SFDX and pull code from a GitHub repository, forming the basis of your CI/CD pipeline.

The addition of Git support via the plugin enables Jenkins to monitor a Git repository for changes, pull those changes when they occur, and then take certain actions based on those changes. Jenkins achieves this by using webhooks and polling. Webhooks are triggers that are sent from GitHub to Jenkins when a change occurs, while polling means Jenkins will periodically ask GitHub whether there has been a change.

To set up a webhook, you'll need to navigate to your repository on GitHub, go to the **Settings** tab, and then go to the **Webhooks** menu. From there, you can add a new webhook, with the payload URL pointing to your Jenkins instance followed by `/github-webhook/` (e.g., `http://your-jenkins-url/github-webhook/`). Make sure **Content Type** is set to `application/json` and the events you are interested in are selected (such as `Just the push event`).

If webhooks are not an option due to network restrictions, you can opt to have Jenkins periodically poll GitHub for changes. This is done through the **Poll SCM** option in the job configuration.

The actions that Jenkins takes in response to detected changes are defined in a **Jenkinsfile**, which contains all the stages of your Jenkins pipeline. It's checked into source control, providing an easy way to version it and allowing it to be shared across multiple jobs.

A basic Jenkinsfile for a CI/CD workflow – pulling changes, running unit tests, checking whether they pass, and then deploying to the next environment if they do – might look something like this:

```groovy
#!groovy

node
{
    def SF_CONSUMER_KEY = env.CONNECTED_APP_CONSUMER_KEY_DH
    def SERVER_KEY_CREDENTALS_ID = env.JWT_CRED_ID_DH
    def TEST_LEVEL = 'RunAllTestsInOrg'
    def SF_INSTANCE_URL = env.SFDC_HOST_DH
    def SF_USERNAME = env.HUB_ORG_DH
    def sfdxcli = tool 'sf'
```

In this first section, we set up some variables. As we're referencing credentials, it's recommended that you don't hardcode them into the Jenkinsfile but, instead, pull them from environment variables on the server that is running Jenkins. Once these are set up, we can start with the first stage of our pipeline, as follows:

```
stage('Pull changes')
{
        echo 'Pulling changes from the repository'
        checkout scm
}
```

This first stage of the pipeline simply pulls the latest changes from our source control, ready for Jenkins to work with. In the next section of the file, we can wrap everything else with the set of credentials we wish to use for interacting with Salesforce, so that all the stages contained inside the code block use the same details. These credentials are supplied in the form of a **JSON Web Token (JWT)** file and then added to the configuration with a reference to that file – instructions on creating this, as well as a connected app within Salesforce, can be found in the official documentation at https://developer.salesforce.com/docs/atlas.en-us.sfdx_dev.meta/sfdx_dev/sfdx_dev_ci_jenkins_config_env.htm:

```
    withCredentials([[file(credentialsId: SERVER_KEY_CREDENTALS_ID,
 variable: 'jwt_key_file')]])
```

With these credentials in place, we can do a similar thing with the working environment, so that all commands run in the context of the code we just retrieved from source control:

```
    {
        withEnv(["HOME=${env.WORKSPACE}"])
```

Now that we have our build environment in place, we can start moving the code to our Salesforce environment. In this first step, shown as follows, we use our credentials to authenticate to our SFDX Dev Hub:

```
    {
        stage('Auth to Salesforce')
        {
                echo 'Authenticating to Salesforce'
                rc = bat returnStatus: true, script:
"\"${toolbelt}\\sfdx\" force auth jwt grant -i ${SF_CONSUMER_KEY}
--username ${SF_USERNAME} -f \"${jwt_key_file}\" -d -r ${SF_INSTANCE_
URL} -a HubOrg"
                if (rc != 0) { error 'hub org authorization
failed' }

                println rc
        }
```

Once our Dev Hub is authenticated, we are able to create a new scratch org for our code testing, as shown:

```
stage('Create scratch org')
{
        echo 'Creating scratch org'
        script
        {
                rc = bat returnStatus: true, script:
"\"${toolbelt}\\sf\" org create scratch --target-dev-hub HubOrg --set-
default --definition-file config/project-scratch-def.json --alias
ciorg --wait=10"
                if (rc != 0)
                {
                        error 'Salesforce test scratch org
creation failed.'
                }
                println rc
        }
}
```

We can now push our changes to the newly created scratch org in the next stage, as follows:

```
stage('Push To Test Scratch Org')
{
    echo 'Pushing changes to test scratch org'
        script
        {
                rc = bat returnStatus: true, script:
"\"${toolbelt}\\sf\" project deploy start --target-org ciorg"
                if (rc != 0)
                {
                        error 'Salesforce push to test scratch org
failed.'
                }
                println rc
        }
}
```

At this point, we have a freshly created scratch org populated with our latest changes. We can use this to run the full suite of unit tests and ensure our tests pass, with another section in our CI/CD pipeline, as follows:

```
stage('Run tests in scratch org')
{
        echo 'Running tests in scratch org at test level
${TEST_LEVEL}'
```

```
                    script
                    {
                        rc = bat returnStatus: true, script:
"\"${sfdxcli}\\sf\" apex run test -o ciorg -l ${TEST_LEVEL} -r tap -d
test-results"
                        if (rc != 0)
                        {
                            error 'Salesforce test run failed.'
                        }
                        println rc
                    }

                }
```

Finally, we tidy up by deleting the scratch org – this helps preserve the number of active scratch orgs governor limit in our Salesforce dev hub:

```
            stage('Delete scratch org')
            {
                echo 'Deleting scratch org'
                    script
                    {
                        rc = bat returnStatus: true, script:
"\"${toolbelt}\\sf\" org delete scratch --target-org ciorg --no-
prompt"
                        if (rc != 0)
                        {
                            error 'Salesforce test scratch org
deletion failed.'
                        }
                        println rc
                    }
                }
            }
        }
}
```

This Jenkinsfile uses a declarative pipeline syntax, which has a more rigid structure than the scripted pipeline syntax. It begins with the node keyword, indicating the start of the pipeline.

Each stage contains one or more steps to be performed. As you can see, this structure is like that of GitHub Actions, which we covered in the previous section.

The checkout scm command is a built-in Jenkins command that fetches the source code from the repository defined in the Jenkins job.

The various other steps run commands in the Salesforce CLI. This is a very basic example; a real-world Jenkinsfile would be more complex. For example, you might want to add error handling, send notifications based on the job result, or add stages for things such as code analysis or integration testing. It's worth noting that Jenkins, while enormously powerful, is more complex than setting up GitHub Actions, and it's worth spending time getting familiar with the tool and how Jenkinsfiles work in more detail. The official Jenkins website at `https://jenkins.io` has a wealth of material to guide you, not least of which is the Jenkins Handbook – `https://www.jenkins.io/doc/book/`.

Salesforce-specific tools

In the world of Salesforce development, there is an essential need for tools specifically designed to accommodate Salesforce's unique architecture and development paradigm. Two of these tools that hold particular importance are SFDX and the Salesforce CLI, acting as central figures in the Salesforce development process and enhancing the efficiency of CI/CD pipelines.

SFDX, which is an approach to Salesforce development supported by a suite of development tools provided by Salesforce, not only fosters source-driven development but also facilitates team collaboration and orchestrates testing and deployment continuously. It's built with an ecosystem-centric approach, ensuring seamless integration with other tools within the DevOps landscape. The Salesforce CLI, a fundamental component of SFDX, serves as a command-line tool that allows the scripting of a multitude of tasks across Salesforce orgs, ranging from creating scratch orgs and managing data to executing Apex code.

The real potential of SFDX and the Salesforce CLI unfolds when integrated with external CI/CD tools such as Jenkins and GitHub Actions. These tools, although powerful, lack an innate understanding of Salesforce's metadata-driven and multi-tenant architecture. That's precisely where SFDX and the CLI step in, bridging the gap between these external tools and the Salesforce-specific tasks.

Imagine a scenario where a developer pushes code to a GitHub repository. GitHub Actions could initiate a workflow, leveraging the Salesforce CLI to create a new scratch org, push the updated code, and execute Apex tests. Similarly, Jenkins can incorporate Salesforce CLI commands within its build steps, enabling it to handle tasks such as creating and managing scratch orgs or deploying metadata.

Beyond triggering actions and facilitating workflows, SFDX and the Salesforce CLI also enforce best practices in Salesforce development. SFDX's source-driven approach encourages developers to rely on version control systems as the source of truth. The Salesforce CLI, with its broad command range, promotes automation, thereby reducing errors and enhancing the quality of your Salesforce code base.

Both SFDX and the Salesforce CLI are continuously updated by Salesforce. They remain tightly integrated with Salesforce's own development, always staying aligned with the latest Salesforce features and improvements. Therefore, by incorporating these tools into your CI/CD pipeline, you are not just addressing today's needs but are also poised to harness future advancements in Salesforce development.

SFDX and the Salesforce CLI serve as invaluable tools in constructing an efficient and effective CI/CD pipeline for Salesforce. They provide the critical link between the Salesforce platform and external CI/CD tools such as Jenkins and GitHub Actions, enabling them to handle Salesforce-specific tasks. By capitalizing on these tools, you can build a robust, automated, and future-proof CI/CD pipeline, revolutionizing your Salesforce development process, reducing manual effort, minimizing errors, and accelerating delivery.

Practical use of the CI/CD pipeline

Once an automated CI/CD pipeline is in place for Salesforce development, new disciplines and practices can emerge to take full advantage of its capabilities. The most immediate benefit is the real-time visibility that the pipeline dashboard provides into the health of the entire process. Build statuses, test results, deployment records, and other key indicators can be monitored to quickly identify pipeline failures and rapidly troubleshoot any issues before they become major problems.

Increased visibility facilitates practices such as incorporating quality gates into the process. Required standards such as code coverage thresholds can be enforced, ensuring quality before releases. With CI, developers gain the confidence to merge code frequently into a shared mainline repository, promoting effective trunk-based development.

Another major advantage is how the pipeline tightens and shortens feedback loops. Automated testing and rapid build/deploy cycles mean developers get near-instant feedback on any changes. Issues can be identified and fixed immediately, before more work piles up.

Automation also reduces risk when releasing frequently. Advanced teams can implement automated rollback procedures to instantly reverse bad deployments directly from the pipeline. Of course, data from pipeline metrics can be analyzed to find opportunities for tuning – key indicators such as lead time, deployment frequency, and change failure rate reveal areas for continuous improvement.

With the new visibility and automation the pipeline facilitates, developers are freed from tedious manual quality checks to focus their energy on writing great code. They can release faster with confidence, knowing automation is handling testing, quality enforcement, and promotion up the pipeline behind the scenes. This allows teams to fully leverage modern development practices that increase agility.

Summary

In this chapter, we've explored a couple of solutions to implement a Salesforce CI/CD pipeline, using freely available tools. In looking at the setup for both GitHub Actions and Jenkins, we saw that the fundamental steps of the pipeline are the same, but with differences in the specific implementation.

We've also seen that these tools depend heavily on the Salesforce CLI tool and the SFDX approach to managing your metadata, to carry out the steps that make up the CI/CD pipeline. Of course, the use of SFDX is not mandatory – anything that leverages the Metadata API could be used instead, but it's worth noting that building the necessary scripts to manage this entire process represents a significant development and maintenance effort by whoever is responsible for managing your DevOps toolchain. This can be mitigated by adopting DevOps solutions and platforms that are designed to work specifically with Salesforce only. We'll cover some of the options on the market in later chapters.

In the next chapter, we'll continue to round out our overall DevOps implementation by looking at ticketing systems, which allow for better management of work items and not only help bring a clearer picture of progress on your development changes but also contribute to breaking those changes up into smaller units of work, which lends itself to the DevOps principle of releasing early and often.

8
Ticketing Systems

In this chapter, we'll discuss the benefits of tracking your Salesforce changes in a ticketing system and how it contributes to a more efficient DevOps process. We'll then look at three of the most common tools for tracking the progress of changes in Salesforce:

- **JIRA** is an issue-tracking and project management software developed by Atlassian that allows teams to plan, track, and release software

- **Asana** is a work management platform that helps teams collaborate, communicate, and coordinate work across projects

- **Azure Work Items** are development tasks that are tracked in Azure DevOps to manage agile development processes and ship software more frequently

By the end of the chapter, you will have a clear idea of not only the differences between these different types of packages but also when to use them and how to build them in Salesforce.

Technical requirements

While this chapter isn't intended to be a direct step-by-step guide for the products covered, should you wish to explore them, each one provides a free trial with which to learn:

- JIRA – `https://www.atlassian.com/software/jira`

- Asana – `https://asana.com/`

- Azure DevOps – `https://azure.microsoft.com/en-gb/free`

The benefits of tracking your work

The foundation of any successful project relies on an organized approach toward task management and tracking. Utilizing a ticketing system in Salesforce DevOps offers multiple advantages.

Transparency

All tasks and their statuses are visible to team members, fostering open communication and promoting teamwork. When everyone has visibility into what needs to be done and who is working on what, it eliminates duplicative work and makes coordinating easier.

This visibility provides benefits at multiple levels – for individual team members, team managers, cross-functional stakeholders, and leadership. For team members, having all tasks and current statuses in a central ticketing system lets everyone see what needs to be worked on and who is working on what. Immediately, developers can check which tickets are **In progress** versus **In code review** or **Ready for testing**. Testers can view what items are queued up for validation.

This real-time visibility eliminates duplicating efforts since people can coordinate based on the latest information. Team members don't waste time working on the same task or miss blockers that are impeding progress. For managers, ticketing transparency helps gauge team workload, identify bottlenecks, and assess resource needs. A ticket backlog provides data to plan capacity. Tickets waiting for acceptance reveal where processes are slowing down.

Across teams such as product, UX, development, and QA, ticketing gives cross-functional transparency. Stakeholders can monitor progress on features or projects that require collaboration. Insight into each other's workstreams enables better coordination.

For leadership, ticket data rolls up into reports that reflect completion rates, cycle times, and throughput. This high-level transparency helps executives understand team productivity, prioritization, and progress toward strategic goals.

Accountability

Each ticket is assigned to a particular team member, which aids in individual performance tracking. With tickets tied to individuals, it is clear who is responsible for completing specific tasks that support monitoring productivity.

With a ticket assigned to a specific person, there is no ambiguity about who owns the work. Responsibilities are clear, which prevents tasks from slipping through the cracks if no one takes charge. Team members can be held accountable for meeting deadlines and delivering results.

Having tickets tied to owners enables monitoring productivity at an individual level. Both team members and managers can quickly check the status of a person's assigned tickets to assess workloads and completion rates. This supports tracking performance and progress.

If certain tickets are stalled, it's evident which team member needs to be approached to remove roadblocks. Similarly, when tickets exceed **service-level agreements** (**SLAs**), the accountable owner can be notified to take expedient action. From a project management perspective, being able to filter and view tickets by assignee makes it easy to gauge capacity and balance workloads across the team. Adding or removing team members from tickets helps scale resources appropriately.

Beyond just assignments, some ticketing systems allow setting due dates, time estimates, and reminders. These features provide further accountability guardrails to help team members manage their time and priorities.

Prioritization

Ticketing also facilitates prioritization. Tickets can be marked with priority levels or tagged, which allows the team to focus on the most business-critical items first.

One method is assigning priority levels such as P1, P2, and P3 to tickets. P1 tickets would be critical issues or high-priority features that need to be worked on first. P2 and P3 tickets have lower priority and can be queued up behind higher-priority work.

Teams can also categorize tickets based on the type of work such as bugs, improvements, new features, and so on. Critical bugs that are impairing production systems would get prioritized above feature enhancements.

In agile frameworks such as Scrum, prioritization is managed through product backlogs. Backlog items are ordered with the highest-value items at the top to be completed first in upcoming sprints. Some ticketing systems have built-in processes for validating and ranking requested work relative to business value before adding tickets. This gates entry into the backlog based on priority. Within a sprint backlog, assigning point values to tickets based on estimated effort also allows ordering by priority. Larger point tickets get worked on earlier.

At the team level, daily standups provide an opportunity to re-prioritize if any urgent or blocked tasks come up. Adjusting ticket priorities keeps the team focused. From a portfolio perspective, tagging tickets by strategic themes or objectives aids leadership in assessing priority across multiple projects and products.

Documentation

In addition, ticketing provides central documentation. Instead of valuable information being scattered across tools and conversations, details about tasks are documented within each ticket, creating a knowledge base that persists over time. This includes background details and context, requirements, acceptance criteria, design specifications, configurations, procedures, code snippets, testing steps, communications, and more.

Without ticketing, these important work details end up scattered across Slack conversations, emails, wikis, documents, Post-it notes, and individual notebooks. Critical information gets siloed and hard to find. However, with a unified ticketing system, everything related to a task is documented in one place in an organized manner. Team members can easily get up to speed on a ticket by reviewing its history and attachments.

Searching tickets allows quickly finding past solutions that can be applied to current issues or requirements. It prevents duplicating efforts when similar work has already been completed and documented. Well-documented tickets create organizational memory that persists even when team members leave or roles change. Historical tickets become valuable references and training resources.

From a process perspective, ticketing enables standardizing documentation practices across teams. Template ticket types can be defined to guide consistent information capture as tasks flow through workstreams.

Collaboration

In each of the chapters so far, collaboration is a recurring element of a successful Salesforce DevOps strategy. Having a unified ticketing system also aids collaboration across teams such as product, development, QA, support, and so on. It creates a shared source of truth for cross-functional transparency.

This transparency has a great deal of practical advantages. While individual items will still be controlled by the product owner in the early stages, a visible backlog presents a good opportunity for the development team to have input into stories that they feel might be too large or complex and need to break apart. It also allows the team to sketch out high-level implementation plans for stories and keep them together so that an individual developer isn't left having to create a solution on their own, and that there's a degree of consistency of approach regardless of who specifically picks up a ticket.

Ticketing systems create a common platform for these diverse teams to gain visibility into each other's workstreams. For example, the product team can monitor engineering tickets to track progress on new features. Support can check the status of pending bug fixes. This insight across departments enables the identification of dependencies and risks early. Seeing blockers ahead of time allows teams to proactively collaborate on solutions instead of reacting down the line.

Tickets provide a centralized communication channel beyond just status updates. Teams can use the `@mention` function for relevant members for input, clarifying requirements, request approvals, or escalating issues through comments. For complex projects, people from different teams can be assigned jointly to collaborative tickets. This ensures alignment through shared ownership.

Some ticketing systems have agile project management capabilities, such as Kanban boards. This provides a visual collaborative workspace to manage tickets flowing through various stages. The ability to convert issues into actionable tickets and vice versa streamlines hand-offs between teams. Seamless transitions reduce fall-throughs during cross-functional workflows. An additional benefit of Kanban boards is the ability to limit the amount of work in progress at any given point in the life cycle. Not only does this help not overload development teams, but it also provides great visibility of the efficiency of your process. The limit in a particular column might mean things aren't leaving quickly enough, are coming in too quickly, or both.

Reporting and analytics

Ticketing systems collect valuable data that can be used to generate insightful reports and metrics on development workflows. This supports data-driven decisions and process improvements. Common ticket reports include summarizing workload by assignee, ticket type, priority, project, and so on. These views help identify bottlenecks and resource gaps.

Trend reports track things such as tickets opened/closed over time. Analytics around cycle time – from ticket creation to completion – help monitor the efficiency of development processes. Cycle time by ticket type or project provides insights into what areas need streamlining. Dashboard views can visually track ticket backlogs and SLA adherence. Other key metrics are lead time, throughput, and WIP limits – all of which help optimize process flows.

Reporting on time logged against tickets aids the accuracy of release and sprint planning based on historical velocity. Comparing estimated versus actual time helps improve effort estimation. For productivity, reports can show ticket completion rates by individual team members. Analyzing patterns may indicate the need for training, tooling improvements, or reallocations.

Overall, data analytics helps correlate how process changes impact ticket throughput and cycle time. This guides where to focus optimization efforts for maximum gains.

Potential pitfalls

While ticketing systems in Salesforce DevOps offer considerable advantages, it's crucial to acknowledge their potential pitfalls. One major risk is mistaking a backlog of tickets for actual planning. A well-maintained backlog is undoubtedly beneficial, but it's no substitute for comprehensive plans, such as quarterly roadmaps, that provide a broader strategic view of the project's objectives and timelines.

Another challenge lies in the nature of the content within the tickets. Relying solely on tickets for documentation can lead to fragmented and scattered information. This fragmentation makes it difficult to form a coherent, up-to-date picture of the project, as opposed to when well-organized, centralized documentation is available. It's vital to complement ticketing systems with robust documentation practices to ensure clarity and continuity.

Lastly, the explicit handover of tickets between teams, if not managed thoughtfully, can lead to siloed operations. This runs counter to the ethos of DevOps, which emphasizes collaboration and integration across different teams. It's essential to foster a culture where ticketing enhances communication and cooperation rather than creating barriers between different parts of the organization.

JIRA

JIRA, developed by Atlassian, is one of the most popular ticketing and project management tools, widely used for bug tracking, issue tracking, and agile project management. One of its main strengths is its flexibility. Teams can customize their workflows, create custom fields, and use various plugins to suit their unique needs. It integrates seamlessly with Salesforce, providing a unified and efficient workspace.

In a Salesforce DevOps context, JIRA can streamline the work process by creating a ticket for every task, bug, or feature. These tickets can be assigned, prioritized, and tracked until completion. JIRA's reporting features give useful insights into the team's performance, while its robust search capabilities help quickly find issues or tickets.

JIRA plays an integral role in managing end-to-end Salesforce development processes and enhancing DevOps collaboration through its flexible workflows and customizability.

Let's look at a typical project workflow that uses JIRA to manage tasks. Our example assumes a reasonably large enterprise team made up of multiple roles, as this is the most typical use case seen with JIRA implementations.

The JIRA project life cycle

When starting the quarterly road mapping process, product managers rely on JIRA epics to define the major themes, features, and initiatives slated for the upcoming release. These high-level epics establish goals and direction for the team. As the product team delves further into details, those broad epics become populated with granular user stories, bugs, tasks, and subtasks. This hierarchy of issues captures both the big-picture vision and the incremental work needed to deliver on it.

By sprint planning, JIRA contains a trove of well-defined issues ready for execution. The Scrum team heavily utilizes JIRA's agile capabilities to estimate issues, apply story points, and negotiate scope for the sprint. Release plans take shape by mapping dependencies and structuring issues into coherent sprints. Owners are assigned, risks discussed, and assumptions challenged so the team is aligned.

Once the sprint is underway, developers take ownership of JIRA issues to build solutions to complex problems. JIRA is tightly integrated into the entire development workflow for traceability and automation. User stories are worked on in feature branches in Git that reference the JIRA issue number. All commits explain the work done and map to an issue in commit messages. Pull requests for peer code reviews also call out the issues they address.

This connectivity between Git and JIRA provides end-to-end traceability on code changes tied to issues. It also enables automation opportunities. Code builds can intake JIRA issue IDs to automatically link failures and test results as comments or child issues. Transitioning issues through workflow stages can trigger events in continuous integration such as build jobs, deployments, or notifications.

For example, when a developer completes coding for a user story, they merge the feature branch to the main branch. This triggers a continuous integration job that runs Apex tests and static analysis. If any failures arise, they are logged as child issues of the story in JIRA for the developer to address. Successful builds can automatically deploy the code changes to a Salesforce sandbox for QA testing. JIRA issues then progress to the QA testing and validation stages of the workflow.

QA engineers take an active role in Salesforce DevOps by automating validation to accelerate release cycles while improving quality. JIRA supports this through linked test cases, defects, and tight integration with CI/CD pipelines. QA logs detailed test steps, results, questions, media, and other issue comments as they verify user stories against acceptance criteria.

For efficient regression testing, they build automated test suites using frameworks such as Selenium and Jasmine for UI testing, and Apex unit tests for logic testing. These automated tests execute as part of continuous integration against feature branches and mainline code. QA sets up quality gates, so builds only progress if tests pass and code coverage thresholds are met.

Static code analysis is also baked into builds to check for vulnerabilities and enforce custom rulesets around code quality and best practices. Failures from any of these checks are logged as child issues or bugs, providing an audit trail on quality evolution.

When all automated validations pass and QA completes exploratory testing, the user story transitions through the JIRA workflow. This can often trigger a continuous delivery workflow to automatically deploy and validate the changes in a Salesforce sandbox. Downstream teams are notified of the deployment for user acceptance testing. However, there are some caveats to be aware of in this approach – if that deployment fails for some reason, you also need to handle that and revert the status to whatever it was before, which can certainly be more complex. It's also worth noting that some teams enforce a "swim lane limit" on their JIRA boards to prevent too much work sitting at any one status. So, even if you do manage to revert the status of a ticket that is associated with a failed deployment, there might not be room to move it back to a work-in-progress status. To address these types of issues, many teams take the opposite approach, in which a JIRA ticket status is only updated upon successful deployment.

This comprehensive automation of unit, integration, UI, performance, security, compliance, and deployment testing enables rapid feedback on quality. JIRA provides traceability on tests, validations, and code changes tied to issues being delivered, while automation frees up QA staff for higher-value testing while enforcing quality standards.

JIRA is invaluable in enabling the communication rhythms and transparency needed for Salesforce DevOps collaboration. Standups centered around JIRA issues provide quick status checks on blockers and progress. Retrospectives leverage JIRA data on cycle times and velocity to continuously improve processes.

JIRA helps embed DevOps practices even without explicit agile frameworks. Breaking work into small issues enables rapid delivery and feedback. Tracking issues through defined workflows mirrors pipeline orchestration. Automated hand-offs based on JIRA transitions increase collaboration across teams.

Powerful reporting and dashboards spotlight trends, risks, and dependencies. Activity streams and notifications keep everyone informed of issue changes in real time. This level of transparency supported by JIRA fosters shared ownership across silos.

Requirements and acceptance criteria logged in JIRA aid collaboration between developers, QA, security, and other teams. Smooth hand-offs happen by aligning early on issue details rather than last-minute surprises.

JIRA provides a digital backbone that enables Salesforce teams to inspect and adapt quickly based on real-time data. Tight integration with version control, test automation, and CI/CD pipelines accelerates feedback cycles.

Standups, retros, sprint planning, and work coordination all revolve around JIRA. It is an indispensable tool that empowers teams to deliver faster while improving quality and processes. JIRA can help cement an environment of continuous improvement, transparency, automation, and collaboration – the foundations of DevOps.

A high-level JIRA workflow

Your first step should be to create a JIRA project for your Salesforce release, with issue types for user stories, bugs, tasks, and so on. Within this project, you should then create epics to capture major features and initiatives for the release, and then break those epics down into user stories.

Developers pick up user stories from the backlog for sprint planning. Stories are estimated and prioritized before the user stories in the sprint are moved to **In Progress**.

Developers commit code to Git feature branches, referencing the JIRA issue number that relates to the user story. Once the work for an individual user story is complete, developers open pull requests when feature branches are ready for review. Pull requests link back to JIRA.

After some code review by peers, the pull requests are merged into the main branch, which may kick off automated builds. These builds execute Apex tests and static code analysis, with any failures tracked as issues in JIRA.

Successful builds can deploy code to a full copy sandbox for QA testing. QA tests user stories and logs any bugs as issues in JIRA for the developers to remediate. When user story acceptance criteria are met, QA moves the story to the **QA Approved** state.

A project manager should review the completed stories, with the product owner providing final approval. The project manager then batches approved stories for deployment to production via change sets.

A release manager typically coordinates the User Acceptance Testing (UAT) process and final deployment to production. After a successful release, the user stories are then marked as closed.

In the final review phase following a release, metrics can be gathered on team velocity, defect rates, and so on, and then the process repeats for subsequent sprints and releases.

This covers major steps such as sprint planning, CI/CD, code changes tied to issues, QA testing, approvals, and releases. The workflow is highly customizable in JIRA for each team's needs – this is just a reasonably typical example.

Asana

Asana provides a powerful work management platform designed to help teams effectively coordinate, track, and deliver work across the organization. At its core, Asana enables the creation of flexible workflows that map to team processes with customizable stages to track task status. Tasks can be organized in list views, kanban-style board views, or calendar views based on what works best for each team.

Adopting Asana as the project management platform of choice can significantly enhance a Salesforce development team's ability to plan, track, and collaborate on everything from new feature requests to production bug fixes. By mirroring their entire development life cycle across differentiated Asana projects, teams gain end-to-end visibility and control across the process.

For example, creating separate projects for **Backlog**, **In Development**, **Code Review**, **QA Testing**, and **Production Release** provides a logical way to segment work as it flows from idea to deployment. Teams can further organize by dividing each project into sections based on workstream, application, or initiative. This helps cluster-related tasks and ensures continuity of effort.

With this foundation in place, let's walk through how Asana can optimize productivity and coordination from initial intake through final release.

The Asana project life cycle

First, requirement gathering is streamlined by creating a task for each new feature or enhancement request. The task can include a high-level description, expected delivery timeline, assignment to the appropriate developer or team, links to related documentation or tickets, and any other supporting details.

Capturing requests in Asana provides traceability and easy reference later in the process. Custom fields can be defined to match the team's way of working – for example, indicating the priority, level of effort, dependencies, or associated releases for each task.

During sprint planning and backlog grooming, managers can survey the landscape of outstanding requests and schedule the highest-value ones into upcoming iterations. Setting milestones and dependencies between tasks ensures proper sequencing and delivery of functionality.

Once tasks are ready for active development, they can be moved into the **In Development** project. This provides developers with a clear view of their workload for the sprint. As work gets completed, developers can easily update the task status, log hours, attach screenshots or code snippets, and provide any other relevant commentary right within Asana.

For developers, Asana acts as a central workspace to track and execute their assigned tasks during the development phase. As soon as work is identified during sprint planning, corresponding tasks are created in an **In Development** Asana project and assigned to developers based on their roles and capabilities.

These tasks contain all necessary context such as descriptions, due dates, story points, links to tickets or specs, and tags indicating the applications or features being worked on. By consolidating all this information in Asana, developers have clarity on what needs to be done without having to dig through inboxes or chat histories.

As work begins, developers can break down larger tasks into granular subtasks to represent stages of completion. They can also log hours directly within Asana to capture the time spent on each task. Inline comments allow developers to provide updates on progress, ask clarifying questions, or request feedback.

Code samples, screenshots, and other relevant artifacts can be attached to tasks as they are generated. Mentioning colleagues brings them into the conversation as needed. This creates a running record of progress and knowledge sharing that lives with the task.

For blocked or delayed tasks, developers can quickly raise red flags by updating statuses and notifying managers. Upon completion, tasks are marked as **Ready for QA**, which automatically routes them to the next stage in the workflow. Integrations with source control tools such as Git and Jenkins mean code commits and builds can automatically advance tasks through the pipeline.

Upon feature completion, work moves into the **Code Review** project where QA engineers validate implementation according to specifications. If issues are identified, they can spawn new bug tasks linked to the parent for traceability. This tightens the feedback loop for developers. Once approved by QA, thoroughly tested code progresses to user acceptance testing and staging deployment.

Automated integrations can be configured to update the task status upon successful deployment to each environment. This saves teams time manually tracking release activity. As work nears production readiness, the change log within Asana gives managers full context into what is slated to be released. Immediately, they can review all completed tasks, affected components, dependencies, and expected impact.

This level of transparency keeps managers informed and surfaces any roadblocks early. Team members can also be `@mentioned` in comments to loop them into discussions or solicit feedback on work in progress. If additional needs come up, new subtasks can be defined while retaining ties back to the original parent task.

With the full narrative visible, any last-minute changes can be minimized. After sign-off, the **Go** button can be clicked on approved production tasks. Peer reviews and spot checks post-deployment provide validation that everything rolled out smoothly.

Now complete, tasks get marked as **closed** in Asana, creating a permanent audit trail from inception to completion. When sized correctly, tasks closed per sprint indicate team velocity, which can influence future planning and resourcing. Reviewing cycle time per task also uncovers any lags between environments.

Ongoing governance of Asana is required to shape role-based permissions, customize fields, set up automation, and monitor adoption. Project and task templates will help codify best practices and give teams a head start. Regular Asana training will ensure that team members are getting the best use of the full breadth of functionality.

In common with other ticket-based task management systems, Asana contributes significantly to communication and collaboration within mature DevOps teams. For standups, tasks assigned to each developer are front-and-center with the latest updates visible. Team members can easily reference blocked tasks, new impediments, and the help needed to unblock progress. Managers gain insight into velocity across working threads.

Retrospectives are enhanced by looking at historical Asana data on cycle times, workload distribution, and completion rates by developer. This spurs data-driven root cause analysis and process improvements.

Backlog grooming is facilitated by having all candidate stories and defects sequenced in Asana with priority, scoping, and effort details. This information guides decision-making on what gets pulled into upcoming sprints.

The common thread is Asana centralizing all tasks, statuses, and supporting context to inform conversations. Unlike chat or email, this knowledge persists attached to tasks for future reference. Asana's flexibility supports any preferred cadence of team rituals.

By providing transparency into who is doing what and by when, Asana fuels collaborative problem-solving, removal of blockers, and continuous improvement – core DevOps tenets. In this way, Asana contributes significantly to alignment, visibility, and velocity for Salesforce teams on the DevOps journey.

A high-level Asana workflow

Begin with creating Asana projects to represent each stage of your Salesforce development life cycle (e.g., **Backlog**, **In Development**, **Code Review**, **QA Testing**, and **Production Release**). Within each of these Asana projects, create sections for different workstreams such as new features, bugs, enhancements, and so on. When new tasks are created in Asana, link them to the corresponding Git repo for your project and branches that will contain the code changes for each task.

As developers work on tasks, they commit code changes frequently to Git branches named after the associated Asana task IDs. Upon completing development, developers push their feature branches to Git and move the Asana task into **Code Review**.

The QA team then pulls the feature branch to locally validate changes described in the Asana task, with any failures logged as new tasks. Once approved, the QA team merges validated code into a release candidate branch in Git. This triggers deployment to downstream environments.

Before the final production deployment, the Git diff is reviewed alongside the Asana change log as a final check. After the release branch is deployed to production, it is merged into the main branch.

All tasks related to the release are closed in Asana and, optionally, Git commit logs are linked to Asana tasks to maintain end-to-end traceability. As part of the release review process, code coverage and quality metrics are taken from Git to provide input on developer performance and areas needing improvement.

By integrating Git version control into this workflow, code changes are synchronized with project planning and testing processes in Asana. This provides comprehensive visibility and traceability.

Azure Work Items

Unlike the previous two solutions, Azure Work Items are a subset of the functionality of a much larger overall DevOps solution – one targeting multiple platforms, not just Salesforce. Azure DevOps provides a large set of collaborative development tools, including Azure Boards, and the Azure Work Items contained therein, for work tracking. When we look specifically at the parallels with JIRA or Asana, then Azure Boards, with its Work Items feature, helps teams plan, track, and discuss work across the entire development cycle.

Work Items in Azure DevOps are a way to track tasks, bugs, features, and more. They can be organized into a hierarchy, so you can break down a large feature into manageable tasks and track progress at each level. You can visualize your work with Kanban boards, backlogs, custom dashboards, and reporting tools.

Azure DevOps acts as the source of truth for development tasks while Salesforce provides customer insights directly from service, sales, and marketing teams. Viewing each of these data sources, with their different perspectives on the current state of your Salesforce system, creates a valuable view of priorities. For example, customer service agents can view Azure DevOps bugs and features within Salesforce cases to stay updated on issue resolution for customers. They can easily link bugs to support cases to showcase customer impact to developers.

Meanwhile, developers gain visibility into which bugs are linked to high-value accounts and opportunities nearing close. This helps technical teams prioritize the most critical defects over lesser items. Seeing the full context of each work item enables smarter triage and efficient use of development resources. Quicker resolution of high-priority defects improves customer retention and satisfaction.

On the flip side, when development teams complete items linked to Salesforce records, the changes instantly sync both ways. For instance, when a developer resolves a critical bug, the customer service agent sees the update in Salesforce immediately. This avoids unnecessary back-and-forth communication and keeps customers informed through centralized data.

With this bi-directional sync, work item updates in either system remain in real-time sync. Avoiding stale or duplicate data ensures accuracy and a single source of truth across departments. This increases process efficiency for collaborating on defect resolution.

Further enhancing collaboration, Salesforce users can easily track progress on Azure DevOps work from within familiar CRM views. For example, customer service managers can create custom Salesforce dashboards to monitor bug resolution timelines. Account managers can view features planned for a client right on the account record. There is no need to cross-reference disparate systems as all data lives natively in Salesforce. This simplifies how non-technical users interact with vital development tasks without needing to learn Azure DevOps.

Turning to the developer side, importing Azure DevOps Work Items into Salesforce grants new levels of customer insight to inform technical tasks. In traditional siloed models, developers have limited visibility into client needs and business objectives. By linking work items to accounts, opportunities, and support cases, the full context of each item becomes clear.

With this customer focus, developers can understand the experience and frustration behind certain bugs. Seeing linked support cases with exact user steps to reproduce an error brings clarity faster than traditional isolated tickets. Engineers gain empathy and appreciation for the customer journey, which inspires building features that truly solve pain points.

The Azure Work Items life cycle

Now, diving deeper into Azure DevOps' role specifically in the development phase of the DevOps life cycle, seamless Azure integration facilitates developer productivity and collaboration. Within a single Azure DevOps workspace, development teams can plan agile sprints, create work items, conduct repositories for source code, execute builds, manage testing, track defects, deploy to staging environments, and more.

For example, a developer working on a user story can easily view linked bugs, test cases, branches, and builds all in one place. This removes toggling between disjointed systems to piece together context. Azure Boards tie connected items together for efficient coding with reduced overhead. Within boards, developers can assign granular tasks to individuals and track the hours spent on each item. This level of visibility enables accurate tracking of capacity and sprint progress. Automated burndown charts plot completion over time to pinpoint scope creep or blockers needing resolution.

For task management, customizable workflows enabled by Azure Boards allow the creation of subtasks, priority designation, status changes, assignment to individuals, tracking of remaining work, and more. Developers can break down larger stories into executable checklists of actionable development items.

With tasks established, developers utilize Azure Repos for secure source code management across Git and GitHub. Advanced version control features such as branching and merging enable developers to isolate changes during new feature creation. Repos safeguard code integrity throughout the coding process.

Next, by integrating with Azure Pipelines, developers can automatically build, test, and deploy with every code change to provide rapid feedback. Full traceability from commit to deployment simplifies root cause analysis. Failures get flagged quickly to maintain velocity.

For testing, developers leverage Azure Test Plans to create test cases that automatically integrate with builds. Testers can easily track which test cases need execution, view the status of test runs, and log defects. Linking bugs to failing tests accelerates resolution.

Throughout development, teams utilize collaborative tools such as customizable team dashboards, built-in wikis, and discussion threads for improving visibility and alignment. With everything housed in Azure, developers reduce task switching and stay focused. By centralizing the dev life cycle into Azure DevOps, developers gain an agile, productive, and collaborative environment that is purpose-built for modern development. Integrating these capabilities with customer data from Salesforce completes the contextual picture that developers need to deliver innovative solutions.

A high-level Azure Work Items workflow

To use Azure Work Items for tracking changes in a system using Azure DevOps Repos as the Git provider, you begin by setting up a project in Azure DevOps. This project serves as the central hub for both your code in Azure Repos and your project management activities in Azure Boards, which include your work items.

Once your project is established, the next step is to configure Azure Repos within this project. This involves initializing a new repository or importing an existing one into Azure Repos. This repository will store your code and track changes made over time.

After setting up your repository, the focus shifts to Azure Boards, where you manage your work items. These work items can range from features and user stories to tasks, bugs, and more, representing the different aspects of your project. The key here is to link these work items directly to the changes in your Azure Repos. This linking provides traceability and a clear history of what code changes relate to which project tasks.

To establish this link, when committing changes to your repository in Azure Repos, you include references to these work items in your commit messages. Azure DevOps automatically links these commits to the mentioned work items. For example, including a phrase such as `Fixes AB#123` in your commit message would link that commit to work item 123 in Azure Boards.

Within Azure Boards, you can view the development status and associated commits for each work item. This visibility allows you to track the progress of your development directly from the work items, offering a comprehensive view of both coding and project management activities.

This high-level workflow is integral for teams using Azure DevOps for their software development. It ensures a seamless integration between code management and project tracking, enhancing the overall efficiency and transparency of the development process.

For more detailed instructions and best practices, you should consult the official Azure DevOps documentation provided by Microsoft, which offers comprehensive guides and step-by-step tutorials for setting up and managing these integrations.

Using an Azure Work Items workflow with GitHub

It is equally possible to use GitHub as your main Git provider and still take advantage of the tracking capabilities of Azure Work Items. We first install the Microsoft Azure Boards application from the GitHub Marketplace, which authorizes the integration between the two systems. Within GitHub, under **organization settings**, we can verify that the Azure Boards GitHub app has been authorized correctly.

Next, in the Azure DevOps portal, we connect the Azure Boards organization to the designated GitHub account through **GitHub Connections**. Here, we specify the Azure DevOps organization, project, and repositories to sync with GitHub. Critical mappings are then configured in Azure Boards under the *repository mapping* section, aligning GitHub repos to Azure DevOps teams and branches.

With the integration setup, developers can now create pull requests and commit code changes within GitHub, referencing related Azure DevOps work items directly in the commit messages using the work item ID format prefixed with AB (for Azure Boards). For example, adding `AB#206` to your commit message would link to work item ID 206.

In the other direction, you can click the **Add Link** button on a work item and select **Existing Item** to add the URL link to a GitHub commit, pull request, or issue. This bidirectional linking between the two systems gives full traceability between coding activity and project tasks, user stories, bugs, and other work items managed in Azure Boards. The integration provides an efficient development workflow to maintain progress visibility as code evolves.

Summary

In this chapter, we've discussed the enormous value and benefits that having a task tracking or ticketing system can bring when integrated into your DevOps workflow – both at a technical level through Git integration and in terms of giving visibility and organization of your work.

We looked at some of the common choices of tools that provide the capabilities needed to manage your tasks in a DevOps pipeline, as well as a high-level workflow for getting started with each system. Hopefully, this will give you both insight and inspiration to bring order to your development life cycle with these solutions. To aid your decision-making process, here's a brief overview of each tool's strengths and weaknesses:

Feature	JIRA	Asana	Azure Work Items
Strengths			
Project Management	Advanced agile management, strong bug tracking	User-friendly, great for task and project management	Comprehensive agile planning, integrated with Azure DevOps
Customization	Highly customizable, adaptable to complex workflows	Simple, easy to use, with basic customization	Highly customizable, supports complex workflows
Integration	Deep integration with other Atlassian products	Good integration with various apps, including Salesforce	Strong integration with Microsoft products and services
Reporting	Robust reporting and analytics	Basic but user-friendly reporting	Detailed reporting, analytics, and dashboards
Collaboration	Good for technical teams, detailed tracking	Excellent for cross-functional team collaboration	Effective for teams deeply integrated with the Microsoft ecosystem

Feature	JIRA	Asana	Azure Work Items
Scalability	Scales well for large and complex projects	Suitable for teams of all sizes	Ideal for large teams, especially in enterprise environments
Weaknesses			
User Interface	Complex interface, steeper learning curve	Limited features for complex project management	Can be overwhelming for non-technical users
Pricing	Can be expensive, especially for large teams	Premium features require paid plans	Can be costly, especially with additional Azure services
Flexibility	May be overly complex for simple projects	Less flexible for complex, technical projects	Tied closely to other Azure services, less standalone capability
Initial Setup and Learning Curve	Requires time to set up and learn, especially for non-technical users	Easy to start with but has limitations for scaling	Requires familiarity with the Microsoft ecosystem
Collaboration Outside Technical Teams	Less intuitive for non-technical team members	Excellent for all team types	Best suited for teams already using Microsoft tools

Table 8.1 – A comparison of ticketing systems' strengths and weaknesses

In the next chapter, we'll move on to another of the core pillars of Salesforce DevOps – backing up your data and your metadata. We'll cover why it's important to consider both as part of a robust backup strategy and discuss how the effectiveness of any backup lies in your ability to restore it quickly and easily.

9

Backing Up Data and Metadata

In this chapter, we'll explore the critical importance of backing up both data and metadata as part of a comprehensive Salesforce DevOps strategy. We'll discuss the substantial costs that organizations face from data loss and system outages in terms of lost productivity, revenue, and reputation. Viable backups can drastically reduce disruption by enabling rapid restoration after incidents. Key capabilities such as external storage, automation, integration, security, and smart restoration functionality will be explored to help you architect backups for Salesforce.

This chapter stresses capturing both metadata and data within backups to fully protect business continuity. Metadata's indispensable role in securing data, providing context, enabling automation, and preserving configurations will be highlighted. Similarly, effective techniques for backing up Salesforce's flexible data model at scale will be covered. You will learn how to integrate backup tools into development workflows to amplify their value beyond just protection, and architect streamlined recovery processes.

We will cover the following main topics:

- *Why backups should be part of your DevOps process*: We'll start by looking at the fundamental role that regular and accurate backups play as part of an overall DevOps strategy.

- *Metadata backups*: In this section, we'll look at how it's important to have a plan for backing up your metadata schema, not just the data contained within it.

- *Data backups*: Next, we'll discuss the considerations you need to factor into your data backups.

- *The recovery process*: Backups are only half the challenge – in this section, we'll tackle the steps and processes to consider when restoring from backups.

- *Incident and disaster recovery planning*: Efficient data recovery is driven by effective planning for when things go wrong. This section covers factors to take into account when you're planning your approach.

- *Securing backup data*: Your backups need to be as secure as your Salesforce implementation. So, in this section, we look at how to enforce security around your backups.

- *Navigating GDPR and CCPA regulations for data backups*: The data you back up is subject to the same rules and regulations as your working data. In this section, we'll touch upon the two most common regulations that may apply to your data backups – the **General Data Protection Regulation (GDPR)** and the **California Consumer Privacy Act (CCPA)**.

- *Data retention considerations*: In this section, we'll review some of the areas that may affect your data retention policy for how long you keep your backed-up data.

- *Options for Salesforce backup*: Finally, with the aforementioned topics covered, we'll look at the current options available for effective Salesforce backups.

By the end of this chapter, you will understand the pivotal role effective data and metadata backups play in limiting business disruption and gain practical insights to evaluate and implement robust backup solutions tailored for the Salesforce platform.

Technical requirements

There are no technical requirements for this chapter since the principles discussed here can be used with several Salesforce backup solutions on the market.

Why backups should be part of your DevOps process

Salesforce often serves as the critical system of engagement and operations for many organizations. The data within Salesforce provides a 360-degree view of customers and enables marketing, sales, and service activities. As a result, any prolonged downtime or data loss within Salesforce can cripple an organization's ability to do business. Customer relationships suffer, revenue-generating activities halt, and productivity grinds to a standstill.

According to multiple studies, the average cost of an hour of downtime for most companies exceeds $300,000. For some larger enterprises, this hourly cost can be in the millions. Extrapolated over several hours or days, major outages create substantial financial and reputational damage. In the worst cases, companies without adequate data protection and recovery plans can be forced completely out of business by catastrophic data loss.

However, viable and integrated data backups provide organizations with the capability to quickly restore service and limit disruption. Rather than permanently losing data and productivity, companies can restore from recent backups and continue operations with only a brief period of constrained activity during recovery. Sophisticated tools can automate backup processes and make restoration seamless.

Beyond just protecting against disasters, fully incorporating backup tools and procedures into the DevOps toolchain has additional benefits. Backups give developers more confidence to innovate and experiment rapidly, knowing their work is protected. Integrated backups also encourage using consistent processes and environments across development, testing, and production to minimize confusion when restoration is required.

Treating backups as an essential element of DevOps for Salesforce limits potential business disruption empowers developers, and assures organizations that their critical Salesforce data is fully protected.

The cost of data loss

The average hourly cost of critical system downtime can vary significantly depending on the size of the organization, industry, and specific systems affected. However, research indicates that large enterprises experience average downtime costs ranging from $300,000 to $400,000 per hour (source: `https://www.statista.com/statistics/753938/worldwide-enterprise-server-hourly-downtime-cost/`). For small and medium-sized businesses, hourly downtime costs typically range from $10,000 to $23,000.

These figures represent averages, but actual costs can be far higher for revenue-critical systems or in heavily regulated industries. Some key factors that contribute to downtime costs include the following:

- **Lost productivity and revenue**: Employees cannot work and revenue generation halts
- **Customer dissatisfaction**: Outages erode customer trust, satisfaction, and loyalty
- **Recovery and remediation costs**: Restoring systems and data recovery accrues sizable IT expenses
- **Regulatory non-compliance fines**: Healthcare, finance, and other regulated sectors carry steep penalties
- **Reputational damage**: Brand reputation suffers from extended outages, impacting future business

Given the enormous potential cost of critical system downtime, business continuity planning is imperative for minimizing impact. Strategies such as redundant systems, comprehensive disaster recovery plans, regular backups, testing, monitoring, and maintenance help reduce downtime costs. Investing in continuity helps organizations maintain operations and customer service during outages.

Backups limit disruption

While data loss and system outages cannot be prevented entirely, viable data backups provide organizations with the capability to quickly restore service and limit disruption. Rather than permanently losing data and enduring prolonged productivity losses, companies can restore from recent backups and resume operations after a brief period of constrained activity during recovery.

With proper backup systems in place, organizations can reduce the **recovery time objective (RTO)** to just hours or minutes for mission-critical systems such as Salesforce. For example, sophisticated backup tools optimized for the Salesforce platform enable administrators to roll back to a pre-outage state in under an hour in many cases.

Well-designed backup solutions incorporate a set of key capabilities to enable rapid yet secure restoration after outages, while also integrating seamlessly into day-to-day development workflows.

For example, external cloud-based backup storage is essential for ensuring access to data copies, even when primary systems are fully down. By storing backups in different locations than live data, businesses are protected against disasters impacting both systems simultaneously. Configuring automated, recurring backups on daily or intraday schedules also provides constant protection by capturing point-in-time snapshots consistently without manual oversight that could lead to gaps.

Backup solutions focused on aligning with modern development practices allow on-demand backups to be triggered right before risky release events, providing a failsafe restore point if issues emerge. Advanced analytics help identify anomalies by detecting unusual data changes across backups, enabling investigation of potential corruption or loss.

Integration with existing developer tools, environments, and workflows simplifies restoration when needed by utilizing familiar interfaces. This reduces confusion during incidents, which speeds up recovery. Robust restoration engines optimized over thousands of real-world recoveries ensure that pre-outage configurations can be recreated rapidly.

Enterprise-grade security, including access controls and strong encryption for data at rest and in transit, is essential for protecting highly sensitive backup copies. By incorporating these types of sophisticated capabilities, backup solutions can augment development outcomes while still delivering reliable protection.

By incorporating solutions with these types of capabilities into regular operations, teams can quickly diagnose issues, rapidly restore service, and limit the business disruption caused by data loss or system outages. The overall cost and reputational damage are contained to the brief recovery window required to restore from viable backups.

Backups complement development

Incorporating backup tools and procedures fully into the development life cycle and DevOps toolchain provides benefits far beyond just disaster recovery preparedness. When backups are treated as an integral part of the development process rather than an afterthought, it enhances developer agility, augments testing, and accelerates release cycles.

For developers, viable backups provide a safety net that enables increased innovation velocity and freedom. Rather than cautiously limiting changes due to fear of unintended consequences, developers can rapidly implement new features and evolve system architectures, knowing they have a backup snapshot to roll back to in case of issues. Backups shift developer mindsets from tentatively changing systems to boldly advancing them.

Backups also facilitate creating more realistic and reproducible test and staging environments. Capturing both data and configuration details allows you to refresh sandbox environments so that they match production more closely. This enables more accurate testing and training simulations. Backup data can also be used to generate masked test datasets for development and quality assurance testing without compromising security.

During daily development operations, integrated backups provide additional advantages. Anomaly detection algorithms help identify data issues that were introduced during coding cycles early for rapid remediation. Streamlined integration with **continuous integration/continuous delivery (CI/CD)** pipelines allows backups to be captured with ease with each new build for subsequent restoration if pipeline changes have unanticipated impacts.

In the case of applications where data (rather than metadata) determines business logic (such as Salesforce CPQ), the ability to roll back quickly after deployment for developers may well be more efficient than running large quantities of end-to-end automated tests pre-deployment on each change.

For developers building on scratch orgs, restoration capabilities keep them productive by reverting to previous known good states, when necessary, after aggressive customization experiments. Comprehensive backups that include code, configurations, and dependencies aid developer troubleshooting and debugging efforts.

For administrators and release managers, on-demand backups right before deployment provide an instant rollback point if new changes or upgrades cause problems in production environments. This safety net enables CD with reduced risk. Release managers gain confidence to incrementally improve systems on an ongoing basis knowing rollbacks are possible.

By facilitating developer freedom, augmenting testing, and accelerating release cycles, integrated backups enhance business agility and time-to-market for new innovations. Treating backups as complementary processes to development and operations, rather than just as disaster recovery tools, amplifies their value in modern DevOps practices.

Backups protect against errors

Even the most careful administrators and developers will inevitably make mistakes that impact data integrity. Accidental configuration changes or inadvertent code deployments happen at some point, despite best intentions. More concerning, malicious actions by compromised users also pose a threat to organizations. When human errors or intentional tampering occurs, viable backups serve as the last line of defense for rapid recovery.

On the development side, even extensively tested code changes may still have unanticipated downstream impacts when they're deployed to production, affecting data accuracy or availability. Backups allow for rapidly rolling back code changes to regain system stability and data reliability. Code-related incidents can be diagnosed properly by comparing backups before and after deployments to pinpoint root causes.

Data accidents can also occur, such as bulk record deletions or modifications executed against the wrong dataset. Without backups, re-entry of lost data can take many hours or days, if possible at all. Data retention policies may also legally require long-term backup of certain datasets if originals are lost. With regular backup schedules and storage, rapid restoration of information minimizes business disruption.

In cases of internal security threats and malicious actions, backups may be the only option for recovery after destructive events such as mass data deletion. While prevention is ideal, backups provide an insurance policy to counteract even worst-case scenarios. Forensic analysis of backups can also aid investigations into suspicious activities that compromised security in the first place.

Notable Salesforce-specific incidents such as the NA14 outage in 2016 and the **Permageddon** permission issue in 2019, in which Salesforce had to reset permissions for teams that integrated Pardot, to protect user data, ultimately requiring admins to rebuild profiles and permissions, highlight the need for viable backups, even when you're relying on a major cloud platform. Without accessible backups, companies can face massive costs and disruption.

Ultimately, even human errors and intentional misuse must be planned for as realities when managing large complex systems such as Salesforce. Maintaining viable backups, securing access appropriately, and implementing checks and alerts on changes can help organizations quickly undo the impacts of inevitable mistakes or malice. Having reliable data recovery capabilities provides greater peace of mind day-to-day for administrators and developers.

Backups verify releases

The rapid pace of change within modern development environments means new features and upgrades are constantly being released to users. While extensive testing occurs before releases, anticipating how all users will interact with changes is impossible within even large-scale test environments. As a result, unanticipated impacts inevitably occur over time as real-world usage differs from predicted patterns.

To enable the continuous delivery of incremental improvements in this dynamic environment, development teams need a way to swiftly diagnose and resolve issues introduced by new releases. Backups provide this capability by capturing a known good state immediately before any given release deployment. If users experience problems after a release, administrators can pinpoint whether the root cause stems from that release by rapidly restoring to the pre-deployment backup snapshot.

With this capability to roll back and conduct root cause analysis based on backups, development teams gain confidence in shipping changes frequently. There is less reluctance to continuously deliver incremental improvements, new features, and upgrades since they know that releases can be rolled back if substantial issues appear. Release velocity and innovation accelerate.

On-demand backups right before each deployment also create reproducible release testing environments. Release candidates can be deployed repeatedly to staging environments that have been restored from the same backup to verify all changes precisely. Automating on-demand backups as part of CI/CD pipelines further enhances release verification.

For users, rapid resolution of release-related defects based on backups maintains confidence and satisfaction. There is no need to wait for lengthy debugging and new patched versions when backups can be used to quickly restore the previous stable state. The overall quality and responsiveness of the development process improve.

Viable backups enable development teams to accelerate innovation and gain assurance that continuous delivery risks can be managed. Release changes can be made boldly knowing any adverse impacts are reversible.

Metadata backups

In today's digital age, data often holds the title of *new gold*. However, in the Salesforce realm, if data is considered gold, then metadata can be viewed as the intricate blueprint that illustrates how that gold is extracted, refined, and molded into valuable entities. This comparison underscores the immense significance of metadata in the elaborate world of Salesforce.

Metadata isn't just a solitary layer of information; it is a comprehensive mosaic of configurations, definitions, and automations that breathe life into data. Metadata determines how each object and field behaves, their interrelations, and their presentation to users. It acts as the DNA of a Salesforce org, controlling form and function.

The ability to interpret and make sense of data is inextricably linked to the contextual foundation that metadata establishes. Envision a scenario with millions of records that are devoid of any indication of their structure or interconnections. It's akin to attempting a complex billion-piece jigsaw puzzle without the guiding image on the box. Data, such as account records, only achieves its full potential value when coupled with its associated metadata. This fusion ensures that data isn't merely a cluster of numbers and characters but a coherent and impactful compilation driving decisions and operations. From a practical sense, this means that data restoration can often be entirely dependent on having the matching metadata state as well. Records, which include values for fields that no longer exist, such as picklist values, can be problematic, as can records stored before new required fields have been added.

Moreover, for Salesforce administrators and developers, the real concern isn't just the potential loss of data itself, but the possible erasure of months or years of meticulously crafted customizations. The prospect of reconstructing hundreds of custom objects, redefining thousands of page layout configurations, recalibrating complex user permissions, and redeveloping sophisticated flows and triggers is a daunting scenario. Such large-scale rebuilding represents substantial time, effort, and resources required to regain previous levels of business process automation. In this context, a robust metadata backup emerges as a crucial safety net, ensuring swift recovery from disruptions.

We cannot emphasize the pivotal role of metadata in safeguarding an organization's data security and access controls enough. While data may represent discrete records, it's the metadata that encapsulates the policies that dictate which users can view and modify those records and how. Metadata doesn't just dictate which raw data a user can access but also modulates how they interact with it and its relationship with other data components. In the absence of viable metadata backups, you might possess a treasure trove of data but lack the necessary mechanisms to properly secure and control access to it.

Furthermore, while data at rest provides tangible historical records, it's the metadata that propels it into dynamic action via automation. From streamlining routine tasks such as lead assignments to orchestrating complex multi-step processes crossing departments, metadata diligently operates behind the scenes enabling Salesforce's responsive nature. Rules, validations, and triggers encoded in metadata ensure data accuracy and consistency.

Within the vast framework of Salesforce, data and metadata are intertwined elements that paint a comprehensive tableau of an organization. Although backing up data is vital to preserve historical records and insights, the relevance, security, and actionable nature of this data is firmly anchored in the surrounding metadata. As enterprises continue to pour significant resources into tailoring Salesforce deployments to their unique requirements, the indispensable nature of comprehensive metadata backups becomes glaringly evident. A genuinely robust backup strategy must seamlessly integrate both data and metadata, ensuring that neither foundational element is left vulnerable.

Data backups

While metadata captures the structural blueprint and logic in Salesforce, organizations must also back up their data to fully protect business operations. Data consists of the actual records and content that users create, update, and manage within Salesforce as part of their daily work. This includes accounts, contacts, leads, opportunities, cases, and custom objects.

The data in Salesforce often represents the core customer information, sales transactions, service issue history, and other operational datasets on which organizations run their business. Losing access to current production data could set back operations by months or years, depending on the volume.

However, backing up data at scale within Salesforce introduces unique challenges. The flexible data model, when coupled with complex relationships spanning hundreds of objects and massive data volumes, requires backup techniques and tools that are specifically optimized for Salesforce.

For example, the declarative, configurable architecture of Salesforce allows interlinked multi-object data graphs to model business domains to be created. An account record could have hundreds of related child records across contacts, opportunities, cases, and other objects. Backup solutions designed for Salesforce can preserve these complex webs of object relationships when capturing and restoring data.

The volume of data also demands optimized backup performance and granular restore capabilities. Salesforce production instances often contain terabytes of data across billions of records. Full data backups and restores must be executed efficiently to fit within limited maintenance windows. Granular restore features help apply surgical changes by restoring only select records or fields that have been modified inadvertently.

Lastly, Salesforce's flexible schema requires maintaining data integrity when objects and fields mutate over time. Backup tools need to map backups to the current structure rather than forcing rigid schemas that break when data models evolve. Tracking field history helps properly align changing data types and attributes.

Backing up data is as important as metadata for fully protecting business continuity in Salesforce. But to be effective, data backup solutions must be tailored for Salesforce's unique data modeling, massive scale, and flexible schema capabilities. The nuances of the platform demand data backup tools designed for purpose.

At first glance, you might assume that backing up every element in your org is the most prudent approach. However, this isn't always the case and can sometimes be counterproductive. There are certain objects that, while frequently updated, don't hold significant value in backups. Objects such as `AuthSession`, `LoginGeo`, and `LoginIp`, for instance, undergo frequent changes and don't contain vital business data.

Similarly, if you're considering backing up a custom object such as `Case`, the associated `CaseFeed`, `CaseHistory`, and `CaseShare` objects may not provide much backup value for the same rationale. Omitting these objects can result in more compact backups, facilitating quicker backup and restoration processes – in the case of sharing tables, these are dynamically recreated once the records to which they relate are restored. Employing a backup solution that allows you to track and assess your data's modifications will be even more effective if you exclude high-churn objects. This exclusion streamlines your monitoring process, making it easier to identify impactful changes to essential data.

The recovery process

In the event of a crisis, when Salesforce data becomes compromised or lost, the immediate availability of backups is a lifeline. Yet, merely having backups at the ready isn't the entire solution for ensuring business continuity. An intricate architecture encompassing the recovery process, its validation, and the seamless restoration of data is paramount.

The initial step of this process is rooted in validating the backup's viability. It's a common pitfall to just assume the most recent backup is devoid of errors and ready for use. This assumption can lead to further complications, emphasizing the necessity for continuous monitoring of backup integrity. By automating and continuously monitoring backups, organizations can promptly detect anomalies, ensuring that a reliable and untainted backup is always at hand.

However, even before leaping into recovery mode, organizations must adopt a strategic stance. Analyzing the nature and extent of the data loss is critical. Delving into backup analytics can shed light on whether the data was corrupted or deleted entirely. It helps pin down which specific records and objects were affected, and when the anomaly occurred. This thorough examination ensures that the restoration process zeroes in on the affected areas, safeguarding any unaffected data from being inadvertently overwritten.

Once the scope of data requiring restoration is clear, the restoration process itself can be planned. For metadata, it is advisable to restore components incrementally in a logical order matching dependencies. Foundational elements such as core custom objects and fields should be addressed first, providing a base for permissions, business logic, and presentation layers to follow. Breaking restoration into smaller sections avoids error cascades and simplifies troubleshooting.

When substantial metadata volumes exist, a phased approach to restoring prioritized categories reduces risk. The recommended sequence is as follows:

1. **Data tier**: The core custom objects, fields, and schema that define the foundation of the org's data structure.

2. **Security**: Permission sets, profiles, and sharing rules that control user access and data isolation.

3. **Programmability**: Any Apex classes, triggers, components, and tests that enable custom business logic.

4. **Presentation**: Visualforce, Lightning, and layout metadata that constitute the UI presentation layer.

5. **Other**: Additional metadata such as emails, reports, and documents that customize and configure the org.

This workflow matches the platform's inherent hierarchy from raw data components up through complex overlays.

Similarly, when restoring large data volumes, core objects should be prioritized first, while still capturing related data dependencies. Salesforce's recommended priority is as follows:

1. Users

2. Accounts

3. Campaigns

4. Contacts

5. Opportunities

6. Cases

7. Price books

8. Products

9. Leads

10. Contracts

Such a division of object data is further encouraged by the Salesforce platform, depending on the restoration mechanism. If you're using Apex, the behavior around record chunking should be well understood by architects – be sure to read and consider the *Creating Records for Multiple Object Types* section of the Salesforce documentation at `https://developer.salesforce.com/docs/atlas.en-us.apexcode.meta/apexcode/langCon_apex_dml_limitations.htm#:~:text=Creating%20Records%20for%20Multiple%20Object%20Types`.

Robust backup solutions can restore interconnected data across multiple objects to maintain relationship integrity. Segmenting very large datasets by owner or timeframe helps avoid platform limits when restoring manually. Architects should also be aware of the concepts of lookup skew, ownership skew, and the platform's behavior around record locking when designing a restoration process.

Lookup skew in Salesforce refers to a situation where many records (usually tens of thousands or more) are associated with a single record through a lookup relationship. This can lead to performance issues and can negatively impact database operations such as queries, reports, and data loads. Ownership skew in Salesforce is a different but related concept to lookup skew. It occurs when many records in a Salesforce organization are owned by a single user or a small group of users. This can create performance issues and operational challenges, like those experienced with lookup skew.

By following a structured, phased restoration workflow specific to data loss circumstances, organizations can streamline recovery, troubleshoot issues early, and minimize errors caused by oversights in addressing interdependencies.

You might be wondering about the best way to perfect this restoration process. The answer lies in the utilization of Salesforce sandboxes. By conducting dry runs in these environments, teams can refine and optimize recovery procedures. Over time, these repeated practices forge a sort of *muscle memory*, enabling swift and efficient responses to real-time crises. Moreover, detailed documentation of this recovery blueprint serves a dual purpose: it's a valuable reference guide and an essential training tool for onboarding new team members.

For organizations that have integrated DevOps into their operations, the recovery process can be streamlined further. Harnessing familiar tools and environments expedites restoration efforts. When teams are equipped to use tools and interfaces they interact with daily, it diminishes the likelihood of errors borne out of unfamiliarity.

While the importance of robust backups cannot be understated, an organization's resilience in the face of data crises hinges on more than just backups. It requires a harmonious blend of meticulous planning, rigorous testing, comprehensive documentation, and continuous training. Only then can organizations be confident of a swift and effective response to data mishaps. Preparedness isn't just a strategy; it's the bedrock of data security in the Salesforce ecosystem.

Incident and disaster recovery planning

Robust backup solutions are an essential foundation for data protection, but organizations must also develop detailed plans for responding to and recovering from incidents. Preparing incident response and disaster recovery procedures alongside backup tools provides a comprehensive approach to minimizing business disruption.

Incident response plans

Incident response plans outline the immediate actions that are taken during a crisis such as a data breach or system outage. They establish a clear protocol for investigation, containment, communication, and initial recovery steps. Here are some of the key elements:

- Defining roles for assembling an incident response team with cross-functional expertise
- Checklists for evidence gathering, damage assessment, and root cause analysis of incidents

- Plans for internal and external communication with affected stakeholders
- Compliance protocols for reporting incidents to regulatory bodies
- Initial recovery workflows for restoring from backups safely
- Documentation for lessons learned and plan improvement after incidents

Having an incident response plan helps you avoid making rushed, stressed decisions during crises, instead enabling a deliberate, optimized reaction.

Disaster recovery plans

Disaster recovery plans focus on long-term processes for restoring normal business operations after major outages. They set policies and technology strategies for resilience, such as the following:

- Identifying maximum acceptable downtime thresholds for systems
- Architecting infrastructure redundancies and alternative sites
- Defining backup schedule frequency to limit potential data loss
- Calculating how long restoration from backups will take
- Creating procedures for orderly restoration backed by testing
- Training personnel and conducting simulations to refine recovery capabilities
- Ensuring compliance with regulatory requirements around availability
- Documenting plans, system diagrams, dependencies, and procedures

Careful disaster recovery planning reduces the operational, financial, legal, and reputational consequences of catastrophic system disruptions.

By developing coordinated incident response and disaster recovery plans alongside data backups, organizations can minimize business disruption, enhance resilience, and improve responsiveness.

Of course, we all know that Salesforce has considerations that may not always exist in other software systems. For example, architects should consider how to handle reinstating data that's further along the business process than the typical new record well in advance of any data restoration exercise. Think about a rule that Opportunity records cannot be created as Closed Won. However, if you're restoring a backup in the event of a data loss, you may very well want to do that.

Validation rules are another simple example here, and some DevOps solutions can deactivate these before restoration. However, more complex frameworks have grown around flows and triggers – and managed packages may have further custom solutions, given that managed flows and triggers cannot be deactivated. Therefore, when designing business logic to handle data validation, ensure there's also the ability to insert data in any state during a data restoration exercise.

Securing backup data

Backup data often contains sensitive information such as customer details, employee records, intellectual property, and other proprietary or regulated data types. As such, properly securing backup data is imperative for mitigating compliance, contractual, and cybersecurity risks.

For storage, cloud-based backups are common given Salesforce's cloud nature, but jurisdictional data sovereignty policies may dictate on-premises backups. In any case, backups should be stored separately from live data to limit exposure from single points of failure.

Managing access to backups is critical. This can be done with role-based controls, minimum privileges, and strict identity management. This ensures that only authorized individuals can view or modify backups. Encryption safeguards for data in transit and at rest using industry standards such as AES-256 are a must. Encryption keys should have robust life cycle management as well.

Monitoring backup operations, access, anomalies, and changes provides valuable activity audit logs to demonstrate compliance and support incident investigation if needed.

Backup platforms must assist with evolving compliance needs around retention policies, data residency, right-to-be-forgotten, and regulatory mandates. Providers should have rigorous cybersecurity programs that cover software development, incident response, vulnerability management, and business continuity.

By holistically addressing backup security and compliance requirements upfront, organizations can appropriately safeguard sensitive data while enabling streamlined recovery when needed.

Navigating GDPR and CCPA regulations for data backups

In an era marked by heightened sensitivity to data protection and privacy, businesses operating across Europe and the US are subject to two major regulatory frameworks: GDPR and CCPA. These regulations directly influence how organizations manage and store backup data.

GDPR overview

The **GDPR** empowers individuals within the **European Union** (**EU**) and **European Economic Area** (**EEA**) with expansive rights over their data. Among the many provisions, the right to erasure stands out prominently when considering backup strategies. As stipulated in Article 17 of the GDPR, individuals possess the authority to mandate virtually any company – even those outside the EU and EEA – to eliminate their data from the company's archives within a stipulated 30-day period. Consequently, businesses catering to EU and EEA clientele must have the proficiency to pinpoint and expunge specific records from their backups.

Insights into CCPA

Coming into force in 2020, the **California Consumer Privacy Act** (**CCPA**) bestows comparable rights to California's residents. While the CCPA's purview is somewhat narrower than the GDPR's, it imposes specific criteria that companies must fulfill before being accountable for CCPA-related requests. Notably, like its European counterpart, the CCPA empowers individuals to inquire about their held data and demand its removal. As these regulations become increasingly standard, businesses should anticipate the need to adhere to either or both the GDPR and CCPA. Thus, evaluating backup strategies for compliance with these data protection norms is indispensable.

Data retention considerations

An important decision in architecting backup solutions involves establishing data retention policies to govern how long backup data persists before deletion. Organizations take varied approaches to retention depending on business needs, legal factors, and budget constraints.

Many default to indefinite data retention to maximize the historical snapshots available for recovery. With no set deletion schedules, all backup data is perpetually available. This ensures confidence that even very old backup copies can be accessed if needed to restore lost production data or address a historical audit. However, indefinite retention leads to continuously expanding storage consumption and cost over time as new backups accumulate.

Other companies choose to implement limited data retention windows that automatically delete backups after a set period. Retention may be mandated by industry regulations requiring data to be kept only for a specific number of years due to privacy statutes. Contractual clauses with customers or partners may also dictate maximal retention timeframes. From a budget perspective, deleting backups periodically helps control the otherwise unlimited growth in storage expenses that's inevitable with indefinite retention approaches.

Some organizations align backup data retention schedules with their consumer data retention policies, which limit how long they persist personal information. This ensures backups reflect corporate deletion commitments. However, it can pose risks if valuable historical business data is deleted prematurely alongside expired consumer records. A better approach is to retain business data indefinitely while deleting only consumer data from backups based on data types.

The tradeoff with limited retention policies is that the availability of snapshots for historical recovery diminishes over time. While recent backup data is maintained, older backups eventually get deleted forever. So, retention schedules imply a tolerance for permanently losing access to dated records after the retention period elapses.

In regulated industries such as financial services and healthcare, retention minimums may be mandated for certain data types, allowing early deletion of other data past a specific age. Compliance factors should be incorporated when defining retention policies.

Ultimately, organizations need to weigh the pros and cons of varied retention approaches based on their unique business needs, data recovery requirements, growth constraints, and legal obligations. However, having explicit formal data retention policies for backups provides consistency, predictability, and alignment with corporate data governance standards. As with all data policies, retention guidelines should be reviewed regularly.

Options for Salesforce backup

When designing a backup strategy, organizations have several approaches to consider.

No backups

Inaction can itself be an intentional action, but when it comes to backing up your data, it's not recommended. The lack of any data protection exposes companies to major risks of business disruption, compliance violations, and even bankruptcy after data loss incidents. False confidence in native Salesforce recovery or recycling bin services leaves gaps that should not be left open.

Manual exports

Self-service data exports provide minimal protection at least, but require manual repetition, offer slow and limited restoration, and incur overhead for storage and compliance. A lack of metadata backups to complement the data backup and provide context only hinders full recovery.

Version control

The integration of **version control systems** (**VCSs**) as a mechanism for metadata and data backup represents a significant advancement over manual approaches. In scenarios where catastrophic failures occur, a VCS can act as a reliable source for disaster recovery, enabling teams to redeploy the entire metadata to a new Salesforce org, ensuring business continuity. Additionally, maintaining a detailed history of changes is crucial for audit trails and compliance requirements, which VCS facilitates by tracking changes in a structured and accessible manner.

However, the reliance on VCSs for backup in Salesforce DevOps is not without its challenges and limitations. The complexity of incorporating VCSs into Salesforce necessitates a deep understanding of both the Salesforce environment and version control practices, which can be daunting, especially for click-based admins who are not familiar with version control. The risk of overwriting existing code or introducing updates that conflict with the main repository is heightened when multiple developers work on the same project, even though VCSs offer a failsafe for overwrites.

The scope of VCSs is limited in capturing the nuances of Salesforce data, which might lead to incomplete backups and recovery challenges. The dependency on external tools introduces additional points of failure in the backup and recovery process, making it time and resource-intensive. VCSs might not be sufficient for full disaster recovery in cases of complete system failure or data corruption.

Achieving a seamless and efficient integration of VCS that is accessible and user-friendly for Salesforce admins presents a significant challenge. Ensuring compliance with data protection laws and security standards adds another layer of complexity to using a VCS as a backup solution. Inefficient use of a VCS can lead to increased technical debt, especially if deployments frequently encounter bugs and errors, and the potential for increased technical debt looms. Without a comprehensive VCS strategy, there may be a lack of complete visibility into the history and context of changes, hindering debugging, decision-making, and understanding the impact of specific changes in the Salesforce environment.

Native Salesforce tools

Salesforce's backup solution, which is now generally available, offers automated backups, effortless data restoration, and robust encryption to enhance data security. However, a notable limitation is the confinement of data within the Salesforce infrastructure. It lacks an off-platform backup option, which could be a setback for organizations seeking diversified data backup strategies. Initially, Salesforce had a data recovery service that was discontinued, but due to significant customer feedback, it was reinstated, which led to the creation of the new Backup and Restore service.

Purpose-built backup solutions

Robust third-party tools designed specifically for Salesforce provide automation, data monitoring, fast full restores, security integrations, and other advanced capabilities tailored to the platform's unique needs.

When evaluating options, the highest priorities are confidence in comprehensive and rapid recovery, minimal disruption during incidents, plus security and compliance. The budget must be weighed against the high costs of downtime. Integrated DevOps tools maximize value.

Many, if not all, of these solutions offer a free trial, which will allow you to ensure that they have coverage and ease of use – these two factors alone are critical decision points.

Restoring both data and metadata accurately can be very hard. Some metadata types and corresponding data in Salesforce cannot be restored. These considerations should be part of the architectural planning for backup and disaster recovery so that the business understands the limits of what can be restored. As a simple example, in most cases, you won't get the original Salesforce record IDs back after restoring a record, so other systems should not necessarily rely on record IDs.

Factoring in any limitations informs the choice of tools for backup. If certain aspects are hard to do and important to the business, that should be at the top of any vendor evaluation.

Summary

In this chapter, we explored the critical need for comprehensive data and metadata backups within Salesforce to minimize business disruption from data loss incidents.

We discussed the potentially catastrophic costs of data loss and system outages in terms of lost productivity, revenue, reputation, and regulatory compliance if recovery is not swift. Viable backups limit damage by enabling rapid restoration.

Key capabilities such as external storage, automation, integration, smart restoration, and enterprise-grade security are required elements of a robust Salesforce backup solution. Metadata must be backed up alongside raw data to provide structure, access controls, and automation. Effective techniques for large-scale Salesforce data backup were also covered.

Incident response plans outline immediate actions during crises, while disaster recovery plans focus on long-term restoration procedures. Testing and documentation are key. Carefully securing sensitive backup data is imperative as well.

Comprehensive data protection combining backups, planning, security, compliance, and purpose-built solutions designed for Salesforce enables organizations to minimize disruption, safeguard information assets, and maintain business continuity and customer trust.

Ultimately, your backups are only as effective as your ability to restore them. Equally, you can't restore what you haven't backed up, so they should be extensive and regular.

In the next chapter, we'll tackle another of the more operational aspects of DevOps, which is monitoring for changes. In Salesforce, changes can arrive from multiple sources, even production. Keeping tight control over these changes and ensuring all your environments are up to date and in sync through effective monitoring will be our next topic.

10

Monitoring for Changes

In this chapter, we will explore some vital aspects of managing your Salesforce environment. The key to maintaining a stable and smooth-running Salesforce environment lies in efficient change management and monitoring. However, with the increasing complexity and volume of data, manual change control becomes less feasible. Hence, the need for automation and comprehensive environment monitoring arises.

This chapter will delve into the importance of monitoring your Salesforce environment. We will examine how uncontrolled changes, even those made with good intentions, can lead to instability and disrupt the smooth functioning of your Salesforce environment. We will also discuss how monitoring tools can help us detect changes across our environments, giving us the ability to see the who, what, when, and where of all changes, both intentional and unintentional.

In addition to metadata monitoring, we will also explore how monitoring other factors, such as data metrics, can help us spot potential issues before they become user-impacting. We will discuss how monitoring changes can provide us with crucial insights into the health of our environments, and how this can boost our confidence that our environments align with the source of truth.

We will also learn about different types of monitoring, such as metadata monitoring, data monitoring, posture monitoring, and operational monitoring and observability. Each of these types of monitoring has its unique importance and role in maintaining a stable Salesforce environment.

We will cover the following topics in this chapter:

- How to manage your environments through different kinds of monitoring
- How metadata monitoring works
- How and why to monitor for relevant data changes in your environments

By the end of this chapter, you will have a comprehensive understanding of the importance of environment monitoring in Salesforce and how it can help you maintain a stable and efficient Salesforce environment. The knowledge you will gain from this chapter will be instrumental in helping you avoid instability and disruptions in your Salesforce environment.

How to manage your Salesforce environments

Managing your Salesforce environment is crucial for the stability and effectiveness of your organization's operations. The importance of this task cannot be overstated – a well-managed Salesforce environment ensures seamless workflows, data integrity, and optimal performance. The consequences of neglecting this aspect can be severe. You can experience a cascade of issues starting with minor data discrepancies, which can escalate into major workflow disruptions. Eventually, these problems can lead to a substantial loss in customer trust and a notable drop in revenue.

This underscores that, without vigilant management, the risk of operational disruptions, compromised data security, and, ultimately, financial and reputational damage increases significantly. In the following sections, we will delve into the different types of monitoring that are necessary for maintaining the health and alignment of your Salesforce environments, illustrating why proactive and comprehensive management is not just beneficial but essential for any enterprise leveraging Salesforce.

The need for monitoring

We strive to maintain stability and integrity across our Salesforce environments. But uncontrolled changes, no matter how well-intentioned, can undermine our efforts. A developer tweaks a validation rule directly in production. An admin deletes some ostensibly outdated fields in a sandbox. Changes occur outside the pipeline that cause environments to drift out of sync. Before we know it, we're battling instability instead of innovating.

Change management is non-negotiable for enterprise Salesforce development. However, manual change control has limitations. As environments and team sizes grow, we need automation to stay on top of changes. Comprehensive environment monitoring gives us that advantage.

In the context of DevOps and system monitoring, it is crucial to emphasize the significance of a robust deployment process as the primary line of defense against unforeseen system alterations. An efficient and straightforward deployment process minimizes the likelihood of circumventing source control, thereby reducing the risk of unexpected changes. While monitoring remains an essential aspect, refining the deployment process can substantially decrease the frequency and severity of anomalies detected during monitoring. This approach underlines the interdependence between deployment strategies and monitoring efficacy, illustrating that improvements in deployment procedures can lead to a more stable and predictable system behavior.

Robust monitoring goes beyond production and examines changes throughout our environments. Sandboxes, especially developer sandboxes, are hotbeds of experimentation. Changes here may intentionally fall outside the pipeline at first. But we still need visibility. Staging and testing sandboxes also require oversight to prevent unvalidated changes from proliferating.

With automated monitoring, we can detect changes across all our environments, not just production. The most advanced tools capture point-in-time snapshots of metadata and compare them to identify modifications. This allows us to see the who, what, when, and where of all changes, both intended and unintended.

Metadata monitoring focuses specifically on changes to components such as custom objects, fields, Apex classes, and Lightning pages. But keeping tabs on other environmental factors is also key. Data metrics can help us spot many problems before they impact the user.

Monitoring changes gives us crucial insights into the health of our environments. We gain confidence that environments align with the source of truth. We can validate that the intended changes propagate properly through the pipeline. We can also rapidly respond to unintended changes before they create stability issues.

By combining proactive monitoring with streamlined remediation, we can take control of changes in Salesforce. Our development teams gain the freedom to innovate without jeopardizing stability. Architects sleep easier knowing environments align with design, and our users enjoy maximum uptime and productivity. In the following sections, we'll dive into these topics in greater detail.

Exploring different kinds of monitoring

Effective monitoring is the cornerstone of maintaining and improving the performance, security, and reliability of systems. Different kinds of monitoring cater to diverse aspects of Salesforce environments, each serving a unique purpose and providing distinct insights. Understanding these varieties is not just about gathering data; it's about strategically utilizing this information to make informed decisions and proactively manage systems.

In this section, we'll delve into the various forms of monitoring – from metadata and data pattern monitoring to posture monitoring and operational observability. Each type plays a critical role in understanding and optimizing a Salesforce environment.

Metadata monitoring

Metadata monitoring refers to the practice of tracking changes made to Salesforce metadata components such as custom objects, fields, workflows, and Apex code. By monitoring metadata, admins can stay aware of configuration changes being made across their orgs with relatively low latency. This gives visibility into who made what changes and when, which is useful for troubleshooting, compliance, and change management. The goal of metadata monitoring is to maintain control and transparency over customizations as teams scale their Salesforce development. Rather than manual checks, automated tools can watch metadata around the clock and alert the required people on important updates.

Monitoring changes and patterns in Salesforce data

In addition to monitoring metadata, it's important to monitor changes and patterns in Salesforce data itself. Configuration data, such as CPQ configurations, should be tracked as though it were metadata. Data anomalies such as spikes, drops, or outliers should be monitored for potential data quality issues or business changes. Ongoing data behavior such as growth trends, usage patterns, and data flows should be analyzed to inform capacity planning and optimization. Automated tools can apply logic to surface insights from production data in real time. The goal is to gain visibility into both data stability and change to proactively identify and address potential problems.

Monitoring posture

Posture monitoring refers to evaluating the overall security health of a Salesforce org. This includes tracking configuration settings such as user permissions, credential policies, and sharing rules to detect risky settings that could enable access exposures or breaches. Posture monitoring also means analyzing usage patterns to identify abnormal end user or integration behavior that could signal compromised credentials or attacks. Tools can automatically check configurations against security benchmarks and alert when potential vulnerabilities are introduced. The goal is to achieve ongoing visibility into the security standing of Salesforce orgs and prompt notifications of changes that induce risk. Posture monitoring enables admins to proactively remediate issues before they can be exploited and maintain the secure posture of their instances.

Operational monitoring and observability

Operational monitoring refers to tracking the performance, availability, and overall health of applications and infrastructure in production environments. This includes monitoring metrics such as response times, error rates, and resource utilization to detect problems and optimize configurations. Observability builds on operational monitoring by incorporating additional signals such as logs, traces, and custom telemetry to gain deeper context and insights into system behavior.

Together, operational monitoring and observability provide the real-time visibility required to keep applications and services running smoothly. However, the focus is on monitoring the current state rather than changes over time. While important disciplines in their own right, operational monitoring and observability are distinct from the change monitoring we have covered. Change monitoring, for instance, might focus on how customizations evolve over time, while operational monitoring might focus on whether the deployed customizations keep functioning within their performance parameters and continue to meet their acceptance criteria.

The goal of change monitoring is tracking alterations to configurations, data, and security to identify risks, issues, and improvement opportunities proactively through alerts and audit trails. In contrast, operational monitoring and observability aim to facilitate rapid troubleshooting and optimization reactively when performance problems or outages occur in production. Since our focus is on change monitoring rather than current state visibility, we will not be covering the specifics of operational monitoring or observability practices in this book. However, they are complementary disciplines that are part of a comprehensive monitoring strategy.

In this section, we introduced an extensive range of topics, from the necessity of metadata and data pattern monitoring to the critical aspects of posture monitoring and operational observability. We learned that each form of monitoring plays a pivotal role in not only safeguarding the integrity and security of our Salesforce orgs but also in enhancing their performance and reliability. We will now move on to monitoring the changes to our organization's metadata.

Monitoring metadata

In this section, we'll delve into the pivotal role of metadata monitoring within the Salesforce platform, an aspect that stands as the cornerstone of environment control and management. Metadata, the underlying structure defining every component in your Salesforce org, undergoes constant evolution as your organization customizes and expands.

By providing a comprehensive overview of how and why metadata should be monitored, we aim to underscore the necessity of implementing robust metadata monitoring strategies, thus ensuring a more controlled, transparent, and efficient Salesforce environment.

Why monitor metadata?

Monitoring changes made to metadata is an essential discipline. As you customize and expand your org, the associated metadata evolves as well. This happens because everything in the core Salesforce platform exists as metadata, so any change you make results in changing that metadata. This also means your metadata gets more complex as your level of customization increases.

Tracking these metadata changes provides the following multifaceted benefits:

- **Enabling collaboration**: With visibility into metadata alterations, developers can avoid costly overwrites of parallel work in progress. Developers and admins share a common understanding of the current state across connected orgs, reducing misalignments.

- **Accelerating development**: Identifying misalignments early prevents cascading reworks. If a new field was added to a sandbox but not production, catching this early prevents wasted efforts building on top of the discrepant metadata.

- **Supporting compliance**: Detailed metadata change history satisfies governance processes requiring audit trails of modifications. On-demand reports can validate that proper protocols were followed.

Without comprehensive monitoring, metadata changes can accumulate in the shadows and go unchecked. Perhaps a developer adds a field in a sandbox but neglects to deploy it to production. An admin directly adjusts a validation rule in production to fix a bug. These small undetected misalignments slowly snowball into major headaches.

Manual tracking and loose version control workflows have blind spots. Metadata alterations inevitably slip by unnoticed. Automated solutions can close these gaps by regularly cataloging metadata state across all connected orgs down to the most granular components, but they come at a cost. Comparisons reveal precise differences, highlighting each metadata addition, deletion, or modification in any environment.

With a more comprehensive view, architects can gain more visibility into the shape and stability of their Salesforce environments. Developers proceed with confidence, assured parallel work will not be overwritten. Products and admins collaborate from a shared source of truth. Compliance teams have an audit trail of modifications.

As architects, we often work as stewards of the long-term health of the environments we work with, and diligently tracking changes to metadata can be an important part of that. Fortunately, solutions exist to fit robust metadata oversight seamlessly into modern development practices. We will explore this in the following sections.

Monitoring metadata in production

Monitoring metadata changes in production orgs is critical for maintaining transparency and control as environments scale and evolve. The main objective is to gain ongoing visibility into customizations being made across the org by various teams and individuals. Even if these components are deployed through a CI/CD pipeline, we still need the security of knowing that the metadata in production is as expected. By tracking all metadata component additions, edits, deletions, and deployments, admins can stay aware of new features and configurations entering the org in real time rather than manually piecing together change activity after the fact.

With metadata change visibility, admins can identify who made what changes, when to support auditing, when to troubleshoot, and change management processes. Monitoring metadata enables identifying consequences and tracing the causes back to a specific configuration change that introduced an issue. It also supports compliance by providing documentation of all customizations. Additionally, monitoring metadata changes helps surface unnecessary duplications that should be consolidated, as well as orphaned components that can be removed. The overarching goal is maintaining a well-managed, transparent organizational structure as complexity increases over time through ongoing visibility.

In addition, some minor metadata customizations, such as reports and documents, can safely be changed directly in production, but monitoring this metadata is still required to maintain visibility and control over changes being made across environments. Even for allowable production changes, tracking who made what changes and when is critical for auditing, troubleshooting, and governance.

A wide range of metadata components should be monitored to maintain full visibility into customizations in a Salesforce production org. At a high level, any configurable items built on the Salesforce platform to extend functionality or tailor the system to business needs should be tracked. This spans both declarative tools accessible to admins as well as programmatic components developed by engineers.

Specific examples include custom objects, fields, page layouts, validation and workflow rules, Visualforce pages, Lightning components, Apex triggers and classes, permissions sets, profiles, sharing rules, and more. Monitoring should also cover clicks-not-code configurations such as approval processes, assignment rules, email templates, and flows. Higher-level changes to the overall app structure via the Lightning App Builder, Experience Builder, and Community Builder are important to capture as well. Comprehensive metadata monitoring is not limited just to business logic and end user components, but also operational settings such as authentication, integration, and security configurations. The goal is to track all custom-defined metadata so that any changes are detected to maintain transparency over the evolving shape of production orgs.

You can monitor production metadata using a manual or semi-automated process, which can be viable given the typically small number of production orgs in a typical environment landscape. This work can involve several tools that you can combine to suit your particular needs:

- **Monitor deployments**: From this item in **Setup**, you can track all the change set and metadata API deployments to your org

- **Setup audit trail**: Here, you can see all the **Setup** changes that have been made to the org. This is usually a good starting point if you insist on a manual process

- **SOQL queries against metadata objects**: There are system objects representing different types of metadata that can be used by an admin via the developer console

- **Event Monitoring**: If you have Shield, the Event Monitoring module gives you very detailed logs that can be exported and analyzed in an analytics tool

If the manual process for monitoring seems daunting or impractical, there are a fairly large number of vendors that provide out-of-the-box solutions for this scenario, including Gearset, Panaya, Salto, and Elements.cloud.

Having now covered the process of monitoring metadata in production, let's look at how to monitor metadata in our sandbox environments.

Monitoring metadata in sandboxes

Sandboxes play a critical role in Salesforce development and testing workflows. The metadata that's monitored in sandboxes depends on its intended purpose.

Full-copy sandboxes contain a replica of the production metadata and data. All of the same metadata components monitored in production should be tracked here as well. Full-copy sandboxes allow the production environment to be emulated accurately for rigorous testing. Changes here should only be deployed to production after verification.

Developer and Developer Pro sandboxes only contain metadata with small data volumes. Monitoring should focus on code components such as Apex, Lightning, and key configuration components to facilitate development isolated from production data. As new features are built, metadata and behavior differences from production will emerge and require alignment before release.

Sandbox refreshes and deletions can wipe out configuration variations between environments. Ongoing metadata monitoring provides continuity through these events to maintain visibility into changes. The extent of monitoring coverage should align with the role of each sandbox. However, comprehensive visibility in both production and sandboxes is key to managing metadata seamlessly across the org landscape.

While manual methods may seem sufficient for small orgs and deployments, relying solely on ad hoc monitoring and scripts quickly becomes impractical as the Salesforce footprint grows. The diversity of metadata and configurations across sandboxes and production orgs makes manual tracking burdensome. Developers waste time piecing together changes rather than building, while admins lack visibility into the testing and release process.

Attempting to manually monitor metadata faces limitations at every step. Gathering metadata from multiple sandboxes and production requires repeatedly executing retrieve calls or downloads. Consolidating these results to compare across environments involves tedious parsing and analysis. Tracking changes over time forces manual versioning and change management. Even with rigorous discipline, gaps inevitably arise in capturing metadata snapshots. Source tracking via SFDX, where source changes are automatically flagged, can assist with this task and is a welcome addition to the DevOps toolkit, but when scaling, this isn't necessarily enough.

Building custom scripts and tools can automate portions of metadata collection and comparison. The various Salesforce APIs provide access to metadata for retrieval. However, robustly monitoring all metadata types involves carefully orchestrating API calls across the Metadata, Tooling, and REST APIs. However, objects and components may require specialized logic. Maintaining scripts also demands ongoing development, especially as APIs evolve.

The complexity quickly exceeds an admin or developer's bandwidth. The learning curve and overhead divert focus from critical tasks. Even if successful, a custom solution only automates metadata capture, not sophisticated monitoring and analytics. Edge cases will lead to blindspots in tracking metadata configurations. Instead, relying on an existing, proven third-party solution is a smart investment.

Purpose-built tools for metadata management are far better equipped for comprehensive monitoring. They provide out-of-the-box support for all metadata types across Salesforce APIs. Automated snapshot collection and comparison powers change tracking across environments. Usage analytics identify trends and hotspots to guide optimization. Integration with **integrated development environments (IDEs)** and release management systems enables end-to-end visibility from development through deployment.

A note on scratch orgs

Scratch orgs have a more transient and disposable nature than sandboxes. They are spun up on demand to facilitate development or testing and then deleted once work is complete. This ephemeral life cycle means comprehensive metadata monitoring in scratch orgs provides less long-term value. The focus should be tracking changes made during short-term usage of a given scratch org instance, rather than preserving history through refresh or deletion. Lightweight change awareness helps coordinate work within a scratch org across members of a development team. However, meticulous monitoring and governance practices for scratch orgs can hinder agility. While configuring and customizing scratch orgs should not go entirely unchecked, the monitoring objective is pragmatic change visibility rather than exhaustive audit trails. The ephemeral nature of scratch orgs shifts priorities toward agility over governance compared to production and sandbox environments.

Monitoring data behavior

Monitoring data behavior within Salesforce environments is not just a best practice, but a necessity for maintaining system health and ensuring business continuity. Therefore, it's crucial to understand why this aspect demands as much attention as metadata monitoring. Data in Salesforce isn't just a collection of numbers and text; it represents the real-time interaction of users and processes within your system. By closely monitoring these data changes and trends, we gain invaluable insights into the operational effectiveness and potential risks lurking within our environments.

In this section, we will explore the multi-faceted importance of data monitoring in Salesforce. We will discuss key reasons for monitoring data behavior, such as the following:

- The prevention of configuration drift

- Maintaining visibility as user needs evolve

- Identifying optimization opportunities

- Enabling audit trails for compliance

- Forecasting capacity requirements

Each of these elements plays a pivotal role in comprehensive environment management, ensuring that your Salesforce implementation remains robust, compliant, and aligned with your business objectives.

Why monitor your data?

Keeping close tabs on changes and trends in your Salesforce data is just as critical as monitoring metadata for comprehensive environment management. Metadata represents the structure and components of your implementation. However, data provides crucial visibility into how users and processes are utilizing Salesforce in reality.

Monitoring data alongside metadata gives a more complete picture of the environment's state. Without monitoring data in addition to metadata, blind spots exist that can allow issues to emerge gradually over time.

There are several key reasons why data change monitoring should be a priority:

- **Catch configuration drift**: Salesforce configuration data like those for CPQ require oversight. Data monitoring ensures configurations remain aligned accurately.

- **Maintain visibility as usage evolves**: Regular data loads, ongoing usage, and changing needs cause Salesforce data to continuously evolve. Monitoring helps ensure alignment as data changes. Often, data anomalies reveal underlying issues with the application.

- **Identify optimization opportunities**: Usage metrics reveal data access patterns to optimize indexing, storage, and more. Monitoring guides strategic optimization like archiving.

- **Enable audit trails**: Change monitoring provides audit trails required to demonstrate compliance with data governance policies and chains of custody.
- **Forecast capacity requirements**: Historical growth trends help accurately project future storage needs based on how data is used over time.

Without monitoring, small misalignments in configuration data can slowly compound over time. Settings can drift out of sync across orgs and out of compliance with governance policies. Proactive oversight prevents this by maintaining continuity and control as configurations change.

The volume and diversity of data can make manual inspections impractical over time. Automated ongoing monitoring provides administrators and architects with full traceability into both metadata and data. As always, this may come at a cost.

However, with comprehensive visibility enabling early optimization, planning, and issue resolution, environments can support growing complexity while delivering more successful business outcomes. Monitoring data alongside metadata provides a holistic view of the environment's state, which is key to managing Salesforce implementations at scale.

Monitoring configuration data

In addition to standard business data, Salesforce orgs contain configuration data that requires just as much oversight as metadata for environment management.

Configuration data encompasses custom settings, rules, and records that control behavior in Salesforce rather than just capturing business transactions. Here are some examples:

- CPQ quotes, products, price books, and discount schedules
- Billing charges, subscriptions, and payment methods
- Community membership types, moderation rules, and themes
- Einstein recommendation settings and usage metrics

This configuration data can be just as integral to environment stability as standard metadata. But unlike metadata, changes to configuration records are not captured in deployment logs or monitored by default.

Without oversight, configuration data can drift out of compliance with business rules. Critical settings may be altered that impact system behavior or contractual terms. Values can become inaccurate or outdated if they're not kept in sync across connected orgs.

Therefore, monitoring configuration data is essential for the following reasons:

- Maintaining alignment across environments as configuration data changes
- Providing transparency over modifications to critical settings

- Enabling audit trails for compliance requirements

- Preventing unwanted configuration drift

- Alerting on risky or improper adjustments

Full visibility into configuration data changes allows architects to ensure stability and integrity.

Certain types of configuration data may be subject to strict governance policies. For example, auditors may require reviewing all changes made to CPQ pricing and discounting rules that could affect revenue recognition.

Monitoring configuration data satisfies compliance needs by providing comprehensive audit trails. Queries can instantly validate that proper protocols were followed for config record modifications.

Without monitoring, configuration data gaps can lead to obscure errors or unchecked drift. The impacts often emerge slowly over time as small misalignments compound. Proactive oversight prevents these issues by providing continuity and control as configuration data changes.

While native Salesforce tools such as field history tracking provide limited insights, comprehensive monitoring requires purpose-built solutions. The diversity of configuration data demands automation for efficient collection, comparison, and alerting.

With the ability to track configuration records alongside standard metadata, architects gain a more complete picture of the environment's state. Monitoring configuration data closes blind spots that could otherwise allow critical settings to gradually drift out of compliance. Maintaining alignment of configurations and business rules throughout your Salesforce environments is key to stability.

Monitoring data anomalies

In addition to standard business data and configuration data, monitoring for irregularities and anomalies is key for identifying potential issues early. Unusual data behaviors could signify emerging problems that require intervention.

Here are some common data anomalies that warrant alerts:

- Sudden spikes or dips in record volumes

- Skewed data distributions or improbable outliers

- Bulk deletions or updates of records

- Bottlenecks around specific records or users

- Missing or invalid values in certain fields

- Slow processing for particular data types

Watching for statistically improbable outliers reveals potential data errors such as invalid entries or integrity issues before they propagate. Inconsistent data distributions can indicate quality problems needing remediation.

Sudden drops in record counts or storage could represent batch deletion scripts that inadvertently wipe out important data. Transactional spikes may signal integration errors that duplicate records.

Performance lags when loading specific record types could indicate flawed data models needing optimization. Bottlenecks updating particular records may reveal product catalog errors impacting order processing.

Proactive monitoring helps surface anomalous behaviors early before they disrupt processes and decisions. Setting expected baselines aids in detecting significant deviations.

Tools that automatically flag irregularities against historical norms such as DynaTrace or Odaseva allow rapid triage to determine appropriate responses. Alerts empower admins to quickly identify root causes and resolve potential data issues.

The volume and diversity of data make manual inspection for anomalies impractical. Automated solutions are necessary to baseline expected ranges and reliably detect outliers.

For example, monitoring data anomalies could alert on the following:

- Case volumes exceeding the 7-day average by 40%
- More than 10% of contact records missing phone or email
- Nightly batch processing taking over 50% longer than usual

By augmenting change monitoring with automated anomaly detection, administrators can catch problems before they impact end users. Hard-to-spot data issues can be surfaced through monitoring before causing operational disruptions.

In Salesforce, it is often quite easy to do a level of anomaly detection with standard reports. Event Monitoring also includes some anomaly detection built in. This means that the implementation challenges associated with data monitoring can, in some cases, be less than for metadata monitoring.

In general, it is critical to monitor data in production environments and full-copy sandboxes. Other environments may not require the same level of scrutiny, although you may have cases where it makes sense to do more comprehensive data monitoring, even in lower environments.

Handling incidents revealed through anomaly alerts may require collaboration across teams. However, identifying and resolving problems early helps maintain data integrity and health.

Watching for unusual data behaviors provides unique visibility that's unattainable through metadata monitoring alone. Combined with change tracking, anomaly detection produces a more complete view of the Salesforce environment state.

Monitoring data quality

In addition to tracking changes and anomalies, monitoring **Salesforce data quality** is important for maintaining the fidelity and integrity of environments. Data quality is a big topic, much of which is not directly relevant to monitoring for changes. Therefore, we will only cover a sliver here.

Allowing data quality issues to accumulate over time without oversight puts environment stability at risk. Some common data quality dimensions to monitor include the following:

- **Completeness**: Missing values in required fields
- **Validity**: Improper data formats or invalid entries
- **Accuracy**: Incorrect or outdated values
- **Consistency**: Contradictions across related records

Low data quality can lead to several compounding issues, including the following:

- Processing failures from invalid data, which may directly impact deployment
- Difficulty reporting on incomplete records
- Bad decisions due to inaccurate information
- Declining trust in data by business users
- Poor performance in reports or queries

Dedicated monitoring ensures data quality assurance is a part of ongoing operations. Data issues can be quickly detected and resolved as they emerge rather than after the fact.

For example, monitoring could alert if more than 5% of records in an object are missing essential fields such as phone, address, or correct owner. Failing to meet completeness thresholds triggers corrective processes.

Continuously tracking key quality metrics highlights areas needing improvement. Data stewards can be notified automatically to implement fixes and optimize entry workflows.

The Salesforce Labs Data Quality Dashboards provide a free starting point for monitoring key quality metrics across standard and custom objects. Architects can also build custom-quality dashboards suited to their specific needs.

Monitoring data volumes

Tracking storage consumption, record counts, and transaction volumes provides key insights into data growth trends over time. Historical metrics enable accurately forecasting infrastructure needs and licensing costs as data expands. Noticing surges in volume can also reveal potential processing issues worth investigating. Though simple, monitoring key volume metrics provides critical visibility that guides optimization and planning.

Salesforce provides native functionality to view current storage usage across your org, down to the per-user and per-record type level. From **Setup**, administrators can access storage usage reports showing available and used data space, top users by utilization, and largest files. Clicking on a user reveals a breakdown of their stored data by record type.

Storage totals are calculated asynchronously, so usage may not update immediately after large imports or file uploads. Individual users can also view personal storage utilization details in their account information.

In this section, we delved into key areas such as the prevention of configuration drift, maintaining visibility as user needs evolve, identifying optimization opportunities, enabling audit trails for compliance, and forecasting capacity requirements. These insights are not only critical for ensuring the operational effectiveness of your Salesforce system but also play a pivotal role in aligning it with your business objectives. Now, let's summarize what we've learned.

Summary

Managing your Salesforce environments, which include both metadata and data, is a crucial aspect of Salesforce DevOps. This chapter emphasized the importance of monitoring your environments, not only for the sake of maintaining stability and integrity but also for understanding and overseeing changes across every aspect of your Salesforce orgs.

We started by discussing the need for monitoring, detailing how uncontrolled changes can lead to instability and how automated change control can help maintain order. Then, we explored different types of monitoring, including metadata monitoring, data monitoring, posture monitoring, and operational monitoring.

We dove deep into the specifics of metadata monitoring, discussing the importance of monitoring metadata in production and sandbox environments, and the various tools and methods you can use to do so. We also touched upon the need for monitoring data behavior, including configuration data, data anomalies, data quality, and data volumes.

What we covered in this chapter emphasizes that monitoring in Salesforce is not just a tool but a necessary practice to ensure system stability, data integrity, and compliance with governance policies. It provides detailed visibility into the who, what, when, and where of changes, thus allowing for better control and prevention of issues.

In real-life scenarios, these monitoring strategies are pivotal. They prevent minor issues from escalating into significant workflow disruptions, enhance collaboration and compliance by providing real-time visibility into changes, and offer strategic decision-making insights for capacity planning, optimization, and identifying business trends.

In the next chapter, we will change track and begin exploring specific DevOps tools.

11

Data Seeding Your Development Environments

In this chapter, we delve into the importance and process of populating your development environments with realistic data, which is crucial for accurate development and testing. We will also explore data masking as a fundamental technique to ensure sensitive data remains protected throughout this process.

We will cover the following main topics:

- **The benefits of accurate data for development and testing**: We will look at how data in our development environments brings realism, improved error detection, opportunities for performance tuning, and helps meet compliance and validation needs.

- **Seeding data in your environments**: In this section, we explore practical steps for getting test data into your Salesforce orgs – from data generation to import – and discuss how these processes can be automated while being mindful of complex data relationships.

- **Protecting sensitive data with data masking**: Finally, we ensure we understand the importance of data masking, with a look at how to implement it. We'll discuss compliance best practices and some tools to help implement them.

By the end of this chapter, you will have garnered a comprehensive understanding of how to seed realistic data in your development environments while ensuring the protection of sensitive information through data masking.

Technical requirements

There are many ways to seed your Salesforce development environments with realistic data for testing, each with its own requirements. If you're not using a dedicated Salesforce DevOps solution that includes this capability, then you can use tools and APIs provided by Salesforce themselves.

While the Data Import Wizard is built into Salesforce, Data Loader is a separate download but does come with its own dependencies. You can find out more, including the download links, at `https://developer.salesforce.com/tools/data-loader`.

To make use of Bulk API, you would need to write a script in your programming language of choice, thus making the programming language itself a requirement. An example is given later for Python, but other languages that can make REST calls could be used instead. We will standardize Bulk API V2 for this chapter.

The benefits of accurate data for development and testing

Creating a realistic development environment is a cornerstone of effective system development, especially in complex and data-driven platforms such as Salesforce. One of the most critical aspects of establishing this realism is ensuring the accuracy and integrity of data used for development and testing purposes. High-quality, realistic data lays the essential groundwork for understanding how the system will truly behave once deployed in a live production environment. This is crucial for enabling developers to make informed design decisions and foresee potential pitfalls or issues early in the development life cycle.

The primary benefit of accurate, high-fidelity data is the sheer level of realism it brings into the development environment. When developers and **quality assurance** (**QA**) testers have access to data that mirrors real-world data, they gain invaluable perspective into how the system will function under live operational conditions. This realism permeates various facets of the development process, including the **user interface** (**UI**) and user experience design, core functionality testing, integration testing, performance testing, and more. Utilizing accurate data ensures the system is comprehensively evaluated and prepared for the intricacies and demands of production deployment.

Accurate test data also plays an indispensable role in effective error detection and debugging. Bugs, defects, and inconsistencies in system behavior tend to surface when subjected to real-world data conditions and usage patterns. Unlike synthetic datasets or placeholder data, high-fidelity test data carries the full complexity, diversity, and nuances of actual live data. This means issues that may go undetected with fabricated or sample data will be revealed when exercising the system with accurate datasets. Early detection of defects then allows issues to be addressed promptly before they cascade into bigger problems down the line.

Performance tuning and optimization is yet another area where accurate test data delivers immense value. The performance profile and system behavior under real-world data loads can deviate substantially from that observed using synthetic datasets. By leveraging accurate load-testing data, developers can simulate real-world usage patterns and data volumes, identifying any bottlenecks, slowdowns, or capacity limitations. This enables precise performance tuning to ensure optimal throughput and responsiveness when the system goes live.

Additionally, realistic test data plays a crucial role in compliance testing and validating adherence to regulatory requirements. In highly regulated industries where standards compliance is mandatory, comprehensive testing with precise, real-world data is essential. This confirms that the system consistently meets necessary compliance needs when running real workloads. Compliance testing with inaccurate data carries the risk of missing violations that could occur in production.

The many benefits of highly accurate test data in development and testing cannot be overstated. It brings realism to the entire development life cycle, enables proactive defect detection, allows performance optimization, and ensures compliance validation. In development teams, it can also help to reduce ramp time for new developers and/or new development environments, as rather than having to build up realistic data piece by piece over time, a consistent, known good dataset can be set up relatively quickly Making the effort to curate accurate test data pays dividends in building highly reliable systems that function smoothly in production environments. This makes it a foundational pillar of effective Salesforce development and **continuous delivery** (**CD**) workflows.

Seeding data in your environments

Seeding development and testing environments with large volumes of high-fidelity, realistic data is indispensable for emulating the behavior of live production systems on Salesforce's inherently data-centric platform. Thoroughly seeding sandboxes with representative data enables comprehensive validation under real-world conditions. However, accomplishing this efficiently at scale requires thoughtful implementation of robust tools, automation, and data modeling best practices.

There are several approaches to providing your environments with data, and we'll look at each of them in turn. We'll start with the decision to either mirror your production data or generate dummy data, then look at options available for loading that data. By the end of this section, you should be in a strong position to get your environment data ready.

Working with production data

Seeding development environments with data is a crucial task to ensure that the testing and development carried out in these environments are reflective of real-world scenarios. In Salesforce, this often involves populating environments such as sandboxes with sample data from production – something that isn't done by default by Salesforce and therefore falls upon developers, architects, and admins to carry out. This process not only furnishes the environments with realistic data but also fosters a better understanding of how the system will behave in production-like circumstances.

The initial step in this seeding process is the extraction of data from the production environment. Salesforce provides various tools and functionalities to aid in this task. The data extracted can be a replica of the production data or a subset thereof, depending on the needs of the development or testing scenario and the capacity of your target sandbox environment. It's imperative to select a representative sample of data that encapsulates different data scenarios likely to be encountered in production.

Once the data is extracted, the next step is to import this data into the development environment, such as a sandbox. Tools such as the Salesforce Data Loader, Import Wizard, and Bulk API come into play here. They facilitate the import of data at different scales, ensuring that development environments are populated with data in an efficient and streamlined manner. We'll look at each of these tools later in this chapter.

A critical consideration during this data seeding process is the potential presence of sensitive data, especially **personally identifiable information (PII)**. When transferring data from production to development environments, it's paramount to ensure that sensitive information is handled securely. This often requires the masking of sensitive data to prevent unauthorized access or exposure. As this topic is significant, we will delve into the details of data masking in a later section, focusing for now on the data seeding process.

The seeding of data from production to development environments is a meticulous process that necessitates a keen understanding of the tools and practices involved. By accurately replicating production-data scenarios in development environments, developers and testers are better equipped to understand, test, and fine-tune the system, thus significantly contributing to the development of robust and reliable changes.

Challenges and constraints in loading production data

Production data is not without its challenges and issues. Salesforce orgs typically have various validation rules and automated processes (such as workflows, process builders, or triggers) to maintain data integrity and automate business processes. These can become roadblocks when seeding data. For instance, an org might have a validation rule that prevents the insertion of Opportunities at the "Closed Won" stage, as real data is expected to progress through the entire sales process. This poses a significant challenge when you need to seed data that bypasses these usual stages for testing purposes.

One approach to overcome this challenge is to create complex scripts that simulate the actual life cycle of records. This means scripting the insertion of Opportunities at an initial stage and then programmatically moving them through the required stages to reach "Closed Won." This approach respects existing validation and automation but can be time-consuming and complex to implement.

Another strategy is to temporarily disable certain validation rules and automation during the data seeding process. This can be risky, as it involves altering the production environment's configuration, and should be done with extreme caution. It's crucial to ensure that these changes are well-documented and reversed post-seeding.

Salesforce offers tools and features that allow bypassing certain automation during data loads. For example, using Data Loader with the "Insert Null Values" option or specific API headers can help bypass some automation.

It's important to understand that bypassing standard processes for data seeding can have implications for testing. If the seeded data doesn't go through the usual business processes, it may not accurately represent real-world scenarios. Therefore, while bypassing validation and automation can make data seeding easier, it's crucial to balance this with the need for realistic testing environments.

Generating test data

If it is not possible for you to use copies of production data, whether because of policy or access, then an alternative is to generate realistic mock data. The starting point is generating sufficiently large and diverse synthetic datasets that mimic actual business data variability. High-quality data synthesis tools and libraries produce plausible objects, relationships, and volumes that mirror operational data. This far surpasses limited manual data entry for exercising system functionality.

For Salesforce environments, several tools and libraries are at the disposal of developers and testers to generate realistic data. Here are some notable ones:

- **Mockaroo**: Mockaroo is an online tool that allows you to generate custom datasets. It provides a user-friendly interface to design your data schema and can generate thousands of rows of realistic test data that can then be imported into Salesforce.

- **GenerateData.com**: As with Mockaroo, `GenerateData.com` is an online tool for creating large datasets of custom test data. It also provides flexibility to define a data structure that can be used within Salesforce.

- **Snowfakery**: Snowfakery is a tool designed by Salesforce.org for generating realistic, complex, and related data for testing purposes. It allows users to create "recipes," which are instructions for generating data.

- **Data Generation Toolkit**: This tool can help generate complex data in Salesforce, providing realistic test data based on a predefined schema.

Importing test data

Importing synthesized data securely into the target Salesforce org is a crucial step in preparing the environment for development and testing. Salesforce provides several tools to facilitate this task, each suited to different scales and complexities of data loading.

Import Wizard

The Salesforce Import Wizard offers an intuitive interface for importing smaller datasets into Salesforce. For example, to import a CSV file with 200 new leads, you would navigate to the **Leads** object in Salesforce, click on **Import Leads**, and then follow the steps to map the CSV columns to the appropriate Salesforce fields.

The Import Wizard allows you to easily map fields and initiate the import with just a few clicks, making it ideal for less complex data imports or smaller data volumes. Once the CSV columns are mapped to Salesforce fields, you simply click to import the data. With just a few clicks, the Import Wizard provides a user-friendly way to get CSV data into Salesforce. There are some limitations with this approach, though – you can only import one object at a time, and any lookup fields need to be mapped by their underlying ID values, as there is no lookup-by-name logic for this process.

Bulk API

The Salesforce Bulk API is designed for programmatically importing large volumes of data. For example, to import a CSV file with 2 million account records, you could write a script in Python or Java that leverages Bulk API. The script would read the CSV file, map the data to the appropriate Salesforce object fields, and then use Bulk API to load the records.

Bulk API V2 handles the complexities of large-scale data loading such as batching records and recovering from errors. So, for large or complex datasets, Bulk API is preferred over the Import Wizard. With a script to map fields and manage the import process, Bulk API enables efficient loading of millions of records into Salesforce.

Bulk API V2 is also capable of importing records for different objects in a single operation. This feature sets Bulk API V2 apart from more declarative, straightforward tools provided by Salesforce, but requires architects to prepare their datasets for success.

The foremost step in preparing your dataset for Bulk API V2 operations is to thoroughly understand the relationships between different objects you intend to import. Salesforce data models often involve intricate relationships such as lookups and master-detail links. Ensuring that these relationships are correctly represented in your dataset is crucial. This means carefully mapping out parent and child records and understanding how they interlink, which can significantly impact import order and data integrity.

Once the object relationships are clear, the next step is preparing and serializing the data for Bulk API V2. This process involves formatting the data into a compatible format (usually CSV or JSON). Special attention must be paid to the way relationships are represented in this data. For instance, external IDs can be used to link related records instead of Salesforce IDs, which may not be available prior to the import. This step often involves cleansing and transforming data to ensure it aligns with Salesforce's data standards and constraints.

Perhaps the most critical aspect of using Bulk API V2 for multiple objects is determining the order of operation. Since Salesforce enforces referential integrity, parent records must be imported before their children. Therefore, devising a strategic import sequence is essential. This might involve creating a dependency tree or hierarchy that clearly outlines the order in which different objects should be seeded.

While Bulk API V2 is capable of processing large volumes of data efficiently, with large datasets, there's always a risk of errors or partial successes due to data quality issues or Salesforce limits (such as governor limits). Preparing for these scenarios involves setting up appropriate error-handling and retry mechanisms. This could include parsing error responses from Bulk API and adjusting the dataset or the import process accordingly.

Successfully importing records for different objects using Salesforce's Bulk API V2 is a complex yet achievable task. It requires a deep understanding of the data model, meticulous preparation of the dataset, strategic planning of the import sequence, robust error handling, and thorough testing and validation.

An example Python script that imports records into the Account object is shown next. This script makes use of the `salesforce-bulk` library, which you can add to your Python project with `pip install salesforce-bulk`:

```python
from salesforce_bulk import SalesforceBulk
import csv

# Salesforce credentials
username = 'your_username'
password = 'your_password'
security_token = 'your_security_token'

# Create a new bulk API connection
bulk = SalesforceBulk(username=username, password=password, security_
token=security_token)

# Define the CSV file and the object in Salesforce
csv_file = 'accounts.csv'
sf_object = 'Account'

# Create a new job for the data import
job = bulk.create_insert_job(sf_object, contentType='CSV')

# Open the CSV file and read its contents
with open(csv_file, 'r') as f:
    reader = csv.reader(f)
    csv_data = [row for row in reader]

# Split the CSV data into batches (Salesforce Bulk API has a batch
size limit)
batch_size = 10000  # adjust this based on your needs
batches = [csv_data[i:i + batch_size] for i in range(0, len(csv_data),
batch_size)]

# Add each batch of data to the job
for batch in batches:
    csv_batch = '\n'.join([','.join(row) for row in batch])
    bulk.post_batch(job, csv_batch)

# Close the job
bulk.close_job(job)

# Check the results of the job
job_results = bulk.get_batch_results(job)
for result in job_results:
    print(result)
```

Data Loader

The Salesforce Data Loader provides a balance between the easy-to-use Import Wizard and the fully programmatic Bulk API. With both a **graphical UI (GUI)** and command-line options that support scripting integration, Data Loader can efficiently import datasets ranging from thousands to millions of records.

For example, to import 75,000 contact records with related account data from a CSV file, you would launch Data Loader, authenticate to your Salesforce org, select the Contact object, map the CSV columns to Salesforce fields, and start the import process.

Data Loader handles batching and mapping complex data relationships. So, for medium-sized datasets or imports requiring some customization, Data Loader strikes a useful middle ground between the simplicity of the Import Wizard and the scripting of Bulk API.

Data load automation

Automating the end-to-end seeding workflow through scripts or software is pivotal for efficiency, consistency, and reliability in preparing development environments for realistic testing and development. Manual processes tend to be slow, repetitive, and error-prone, making them less ideal for tasks that require precision and speed. In contrast, automation eradicates these issues by scripting the processes of data generation, transformation, validation, and loading into the Salesforce environment. This ensures identical datasets in each sandbox or scratch org without the need for manual intervention, thereby saving time and reducing the likelihood of errors.

A practical approach to this automation could involve scripting the data generation process to create a sizable and diverse dataset that closely mirrors actual business data. This script could be scheduled to run at specified intervals or triggered by certain events, ensuring a continuous supply of fresh data for development and testing activities.

Following data generation, an automated data transformation process could be implemented to ensure that the data aligns with the schema and business logic of the Salesforce environment it will be loaded into. This could include tasks such as field mapping, data type conversion, and data cleansing, all of which prepare the data for loading. Also consider data truncation – if the data generation is from production and the amount of data goes beyond the capacity of the target sandboxes, this will need attending to, of course.

Validation is a key step in this automated workflow, ensuring the accuracy and relevance of the data before it's loaded into the development environment. Automated validation scripts could be developed to check the data for consistency, completeness, and adherence to business rules, thus ensuring that the data is of high quality and representative of real-world scenarios.

The data loading process is the final step, where some of the tools we discussed earlier, such as Salesforce Data Loader or Bulk API, could be scripted to automate the data loading process. For instance, a script could be written to use Data Loader to import the data, handle any errors that arise during the import, and log the results of the import for review. This would ensure that the data is loaded into the Salesforce environment efficiently and reliably.

The overarching benefit of this automation is the assurance of consistency across different development environments. By scripting the entire data seeding workflow, close-to-identical datasets can be ensured in each environment, thus providing a uniform landscape for testing and development. This is particularly beneficial in agile or **continuous integration/continuous deployment (CI/CD)** setups, where consistency and speed are of the essence. We talk of "close to" identical because taking source data from prod (and transforming/masking) on request could mean different results when done a week apart.

A continuous data seeding setup could be established to keep development environments constantly updated with fresh data, which is beneficial for ongoing testing and development, especially in dynamic projects with frequently changing requirements.

Handling relationships

When extracting and seeding data into development environments, you should capture and recreate relational links and dependencies between different objects and records. Salesforce data has intricate, interconnected relationships between various entities such as Accounts, Contacts, Opportunities, and so on. If you don't maintain these relationships while seeding data, you can quickly break data integrity and cause cascading issues in the seeded datasets.

To maintain data integrity, you should study the object metadata and data model to gain a clear understanding of key relationships and dependencies between objects. For example, Contacts have a relationship to Accounts via the `AccountId` field. Opportunities have relationships to Accounts and Contacts.

When you move on to extracting this data, care should be taken to extract related parent and child records together. For example, Accounts should be extracted along with their child Contacts and Opportunities. The related `ContactId` and `OpportunityId` fields need to be populated correctly to link records.

Similarly, when importing datasets into target environments, these same dependencies need to be handled appropriately. This includes importing data in the correct order so that dependencies are in place in advance. Parent records such as Accounts must be inserted first before child records such as Contacts and Opportunities, and any external ID fields used for relationships should be mapped to field values from the target environment.

For advanced relationships such as junction objects and many-to-many relationships, mapping the relationship fields and inserting records in the right order is equally important. Testing the inserted datasets to validate relationships is highly recommended.

Considerations for test-data management

In each of these scenarios, it's paramount to ensure that data integrity is maintained and sensitive information is handled securely during the import process. Leveraging these tools responsibly and in accordance with the scale of data to be imported will streamline the data injection process, making the Salesforce org ready for development and testing activities.

Equally important is enforcing tight security protocols on generated data. Some steps toward achieving that are listed next:

- **Data sanitization**: Sensitive information should be anonymized or masked before use in sandboxes
- **Data protection**: Data security policies should be defined and implemented through encryption, tokenization, masking, and similar techniques
- **Data access**: Access controls on data loading tools should be properly configured

Data seeding creates representative Salesforce environments to enable authentic validation. Realistic datasets, bulk loading tools, automation, modeling relationships, and stringent security considerations are all best practices for seamless, efficient seeding. Investing in these techniques pays dividends through improved testing, fewer defects, and smoother production deployments.

Protecting sensitive data with data masking

Safeguarding sensitive data is a top priority when managing vast amounts of information, especially in Salesforce environments. Data masking has emerged as a vital technique to address privacy, compliance, security, and confidentiality concerns that come with handling sensitive data in test and development environments.

Understanding data masking

Data masking, also called **data obfuscation** or **anonymization**, protects sensitive details by replacing, encrypting, or altering the original data with modified, fictional versions. This retains the utility of the data for testing needs while eliminating the risks of exposing sensitive information.

Common data masking approaches include the following:

- **Static data masking (SDM)**: Masking the data at rest before transfer to testing environments
- **Dynamic data masking (DDM)**: Real-time masking as the data is accessed
- **Format-preserving encryption (FPE)**: Encrypting data while retaining the original data format

Privacy concerns

Data masking upholds privacy by ensuring personally identifiable and confidential data remains secure in testing environments with lower security controls compared to production. Individuals and organizations expect their data to be handled securely, and masking helps preserve that confidentiality. This can be especially important in a situation where third-party contractors are brought in to work on a project for a customer. Full-time employees might have access to the production environment and its data, but contractors are less likely to.

Compliance and regulatory requirements

Data masking also meets compliance needs by adhering to regulations that mandate data protection, such as the **General Data Protection Regulation (GDPR)** and the **Health Insurance Portability and Accountability Act (HIPAA)**. This builds trust with customers and stakeholders. Compliance is about more than just avoiding penalties – it maintains crucial trust.

Security and confidentiality

In addition, data masking reduces threats of unauthorized data access and breaches. It strengthens security by converting sensitive details into realistic but fictional data, reducing risk considerably.

Implementing data masking

Implementing data masking in Salesforce is critical to ensure the privacy and security of sensitive information, especially when transferring data from production to less secure development or testing environments. There are several approaches to enable data masking in Salesforce, and we'll look at a few of these in turn:

- **Programmatic masking**: You can write your own custom code to implement data masking programmatically. This gives full control over how data is masked to meet specific needs. However, it requires expertise in both the data structure and Salesforce platform and can be time-intensive to develop and maintain.

- **Salesforce Data Mask**: This is Salesforce's own managed data masking solution. It helps comply with data regulations by masking sensitive fields and objects, both standard and custom. Different masking levels can be configured based on data sensitivity, and once masked, the data cannot be unmasked or replicated in other environments in a readable form. Data Mask is installed and configured in a production org, and then masking is executed from sandboxes created from that production org. This helps protect regulated data such as PII in sandboxes mirroring production, enabling faster testing.

- **DevOps tools with masking**: Tools such as Gearset and DataMasker have built-in data masking capabilities. For example, Gearset can kick off a data deployment and then mask selected data according to configured settings before loading to the destination org. DataMasker quickly masks large datasets, prevents email and automation accidents, and aids compliance with regulations such as GDPR and HIPAA. It integrates with DevOps tools such as Copado and provides realistic masking formats.

These methods provide options to fit different technical skills, resources, and requirements. They ensure sensitive information remains protected while still enabling meaningful development and testing work on Salesforce environments – a crucial balance to strike. The right data masking approach is key to safeguarding privacy while allowing progress.

Compliance and best practices

Managing test data for your testing and development environments needs a meticulous approach to comply with data protection laws and follow best practices. Some key regulations related to sensitive data include GDPR, the **Children's Online Privacy Protection Act (COPPA)**, the **Personal Information Protection Law (PIPL)**, HIPAA, and the **California Consumer Privacy Act (CCPA)**, but this is not an exhaustive list. Here's an overview of the aforementioned regulations:

- GDPR imposes robust requirements for handling EU citizen data, requiring you to handle data responsibly and for clearly stated purposes

- COPPA protects children's online privacy, placing specific requirements on websites or services for children

- China's PIPL is like GDPR, focusing on safeguarding the personal information of Chinese citizens

- HIPAA is related to healthcare data and is primarily of note in that industry, as it requires the secure handling of patient health data, outlining protections for confidentiality, integrity, and availability

- CCPA underscores protecting California residents' personal information

Beyond these regulations, there are some best practices that it is important to follow. Using data masking to obscure sensitive details while keeping data's testing utility is recommended – some may choose to implement custom approaches to randomize data within specific ranges to maintain a degree of relevance. For example, take the `AnnualRevenue` field on Account – while a number, they'd never expect 1 or something and want to keep a similar sort of range to randomized data.

Encryption adds security during the storage and transmission of sensitive data. Applying strong access controls ensures only those with authorized access can view your data, with **role-based access control (RBAC)** enabling tiered access. Excluding sensitive data from source control repositories prevents unauthorized access and breaches, even inadvertently.

With masking or dummy data, maintaining data relationships and formats is key for realistic, meaningful testing. This includes preserving referential integrity and aligning with application logic so that your test data isn't the cause of any issues or errors, creating false negatives in your testing work.

Complying with regulations and following best practices in data management is vital for secure, effective testing. The goal with dummy or obfuscated real data is to ensure privacy and security while enabling productive testing and development. This careful data management greatly contributes to reliable, smooth DevOps processes, facilitating the transition from development to production with data integrity. A great best practice to start this process is to use the data classification metadata fields provided by Salesforce and ensure they're accurate and populated for new fields going forward. Accurate information here will help audits, masking, and third-party tools.

Tools and resources

Having the right tools and resources is critical when undertaking data seeding and masking in Salesforce. Assembling a robust toolkit and connecting with a network of resources can significantly enhance efficiency and enable effective data management practices for secure, productive testing environments.

Salesforce provides powerful native tools such as Data Mask for masking sensitive information in sandboxes, essential for data privacy compliance during testing. Data loaders such as Salesforce Data Loader and third parties are crucial for automating data import and export between environments and external systems.

Additional data masking tools such as DataMasker and DevOps tools with built-in masking functionality provide different techniques to protect data while retaining utility. Encryption tools add an extra layer of security for data at rest and in transit, helping keep it secure throughout its life cycle. Access control solutions such as role-based systems help manage authorized access to sensitive data, whether that is in Salesforce itself or in connected systems.

Tapping into online communities, forums, documentation, training materials, conferences, and experts provides invaluable insights on the latest tools, trends, and best practices for Salesforce data management, seeding, masking, and compliance.

Having a toolkit tailored to your needs and connecting with a network of resources enables successful navigation of the intricacies of Salesforce data management. This empowers organizations to boost efficiency, ensure compliance, and build secure, productive testing environments through effective data practices.

Summary

In this chapter, we discussed the importance of seeding development environments with accurate, realistic data to ensure robust testing and development within Salesforce.

We explored using sample data from production environments, as well as the alternative approach of data generation with the various tools available for generating and importing test data.

We covered the importance of data masking, to protect sensitive information to comply with global data protection regulations such as GDPR and HIPAA, and looked at best practices for managing data in non-production environments.

These techniques and strategies can be brought together as an approach to effective data management in your development and testing environments. You will then be well equipped to meet the security and compliance needs of your organization while having a working set of data to accelerate your development life cycle.

In the next chapter, we'll start to examine the dedicated Salesforce DevOps products available on the market, starting with an in-depth exploration of Gearset. We'll examine its capabilities and features and how it fits into the broader landscape of Salesforce DevOps tools.

12

Salesforce DevOps Tools – Gearset

In this chapter, we'll start our exploration of the marketplace for Salesforce DevOps solutions by taking a look at **Gearset**, a leading Salesforce DevOps platform widely used in the Salesforce ecosystem.

We will cover the following main topics:

- Gearset overview – An overview of Gearset and its key capabilities

- Gearset's strengths – A breakdown of the key strengths of the Gearset platform

- Gearset's weaknesses – A look at some of the potential weaknesses in Gearset's approach to DevOps

By the end of this chapter, you should be suitably informed about Gearset to be able to decide whether it is the right platform to adopt for your Salesforce DevOps needs.

Technical requirements

The obvious technical requirement for this chapter is, of course, a Gearset license if you wish to follow along. If you don't have a license, there is a 30-day fully featured free trial available at `gearset.com` so that you can try things out.

Gearset overview

Gearset emerged in 2015 as a specialized tool designed for release management within the Salesforce ecosystem. It was created by a team based in the Microsoft developer ecosystem, who found themselves surprised how Salesforce lacked comparable DevOps tools to those they were used to in the Microsoft world. As it has grown and matured, Gearset offers a comprehensive suite of features that cater to various aspects of deployment and data management.

Central to Gearset's functionality is its ability to deploy changes rapidly and reliably. By simplifying the deployment process, Gearset allows users to focus more on the strategic aspects of release management rather than being entangled in the complexities of the process.

The platform integrates multiple key features under one roof, facilitating a seamless and integrated experience. This integration not only streamlines the workflow but also ensures that users have access to a wide range of tools essential for effective release management. From automating release pipelines to offering advanced data management and backup capabilities, Gearset provides a robust and versatile solution to meet the diverse needs of Salesforce professionals.

Gearset's comprehensive feature set, coupled with an intuitive design, makes it an indispensable tool for professionals seeking to optimize their Salesforce deployment processes. Let's look at some of that feature set now, grouped by the area of DevOps that each feature best relates to:

Feature type	Features	Description
Deployment	Live metadata comparison	Allows users to see immediate comparison results with line-by-line diff viewing, highlighting changes in metadata, Apex, HTML, and more
	Version control support	Supports deploying to any Git-based version control repository, including on-premises options
	Deployment rollback	Enables users to easily roll back unwanted changes in their metadata
	Complete deployment history	Users can annotate deployments and view detailed reports for every change made
Automation	Deployment pipelines	Provides complete visibility and management of release pipelines with powerful integrations
	Continuous integration (CI)	Facilitates the most reliable CI on Salesforce, simplifying the delivery process
	Monitoring	Tracks daily org snapshots and changes, ensuring no overwrites
	Unit testing	Automates Apex tests, tracks code coverage and test status, and alerts users to failing tests

Feature type	Features	Description
Data management	Data seeding	Allows users to select specific data from their Salesforce orgs and deploy it to other environments, maintaining the integrity of relationships between objects
	Smart relationship handling	Automatically detects and handles parent-child relationships and circular references
	Data migration tools	Enables deploying records on multiple objects in a single run, viewing data deployment histories, and sharing deployment templates
	Support for alesforce **Configure, Price, Quote (CPQ)**	Deploys complex CPQ config data and CPQ records
	Data masking	Masks sensitive data for confidentiality and compliance
Backup	Automated backups	Frequent backups of both data and metadata minimize data loss
	Quick restores	Allows for easy restoration of lost records or entire orgs
	Analysis and alerts	Provides the ability to browse backups, track trends, and configure alerts for unusual changes
	Security and control	Offers management of encryption keys and secure data storage with **Amazon Web Services (AWS)**

Table 12.1 – Gearset capabilities in each key area of Salesforce DevOps

As you can see, Gearset is a comprehensive Salesforce DevOps platform, covering the core requirements of a mature solution. Next, we'll start looking at how it works in more detail, identifying key strengths and any weaknesses.

Gearset's strengths

At the heart of Gearset's technology is its metadata comparison engine, which can quickly identify net changes between a source and target set of metadata, whether that's in source control or in a Salesforce org, in both directions. This allows Salesforce practitioners to quickly see what has changed and build that into a deployment or a set of changes to commit to source control in an easy-to-understand user interface. In the following screenshot, we can see a line-by-line comparison of XML metadata:

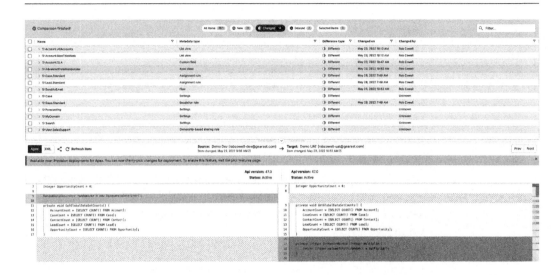

Figure 12.1 – Gearset's comparison of XML metadata.
The intent of this screenshot is to show the page layout; text readability is not essential.

By contrast, the next screenshot shows a richer user interface for managing picklist value metadata:

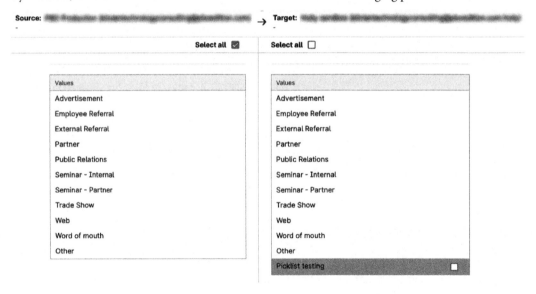

Figure 12.2 – Gearset's comparison of picklist values, with a custom user interface instead of XML

A core aspect of Gearset's appeal lies in its deep understanding of Salesforce metadata, allowing users to manage and deploy changes with a level of detail and insight that is rare in the realm of DevOps tools. This capability is especially critical when handling complex deployments, which can often be fraught with challenges and risks.

Gearset's metadata handling capability, therefore, is not just a feature; it represents a fundamental shift in how Salesforce deployments are managed, making them more accessible and less error-prone. This commitment to reducing errors is best evidenced in Gearset's problem analyzers, which check the artifacts in each deployment for potential issues that may prevent the deployment from being successful. By combining static code analysis with its knowledge of metadata dependencies and common issues, many issues are not only pre-empted but can be automatically resolved before actual deployment. The next screenshot shows how Gearset has identified some issues:

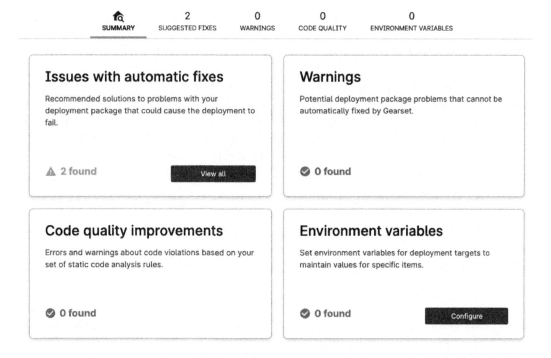

Figure 12.3 – The problem analyzer detecting issues

Clicking the **View all** button allows you to see the specific issues and resolve them, as shown in the next screenshot:

⌃ **Add** the following to the deployment

Items that are missing in the target

Missing dependencies selected: 0 **/** 1

Problem: Some items reference components that aren't in the target.

Solution: Adding these missing components to the package will make the deployment more likely to succeed.

☐ Add missing components
   ☐ Account.Target_Date__c
     ☐ Account.ExampleDate__c (CustomField)

New items found with permissions that are not included in the deployment

New items with permissions that are not included in the deployment selected: 0 **/** 1

Figure 12.4 – Problem detail and the option to automatically resolve it within Gearset

Beyond basic deployment, Gearset excels in CI and testing. In software development, maintaining high standards of code quality is essential, and Gearset's tools in this area ensure that these standards are not just met but consistently upheld. By automating key parts of the testing and integration process, Gearset helps teams focus on development rather than getting bogged down by the mechanics of testing and integration. This automation is a game-changer, particularly for teams working on large-scale or complex Salesforce projects, where the scope for errors is significant.

The flagship automation feature of Gearset is called **Pipelines**, a visual representation of the various environments and repositories that make up your continuous integration and continuous deployment CI/CD pipeline (hence the name), which enables teams to manage their entire release pipeline more efficiently. It integrates seamlessly with tools such as version control providers and Jira and features advanced branch management for handling multiple branches simultaneously:

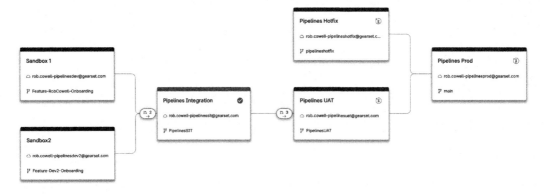

Figure 12.5 – An example Gearset pipeline view, showing Git commits waiting
to move between environments.
The intent of this screenshot is to show the page layout; text readability is not essential.

Gearset's data backup and recovery features address another critical need in Salesforce DevOps – data security. In an era where data is not just valuable but also vulnerable, having robust backup and recovery mechanisms is non-negotiable. Gearset's approach to data backup is comprehensive, ensuring that not only is data securely backed up but also easily recoverable in the event of loss or corruption. This level of data security and management is a significant strength, offering peace of mind and operational stability to Salesforce teams:

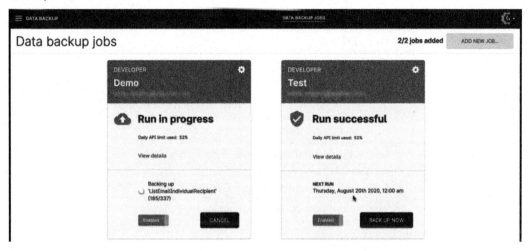

Figure 12.6 – Gearset data backup jobs

Gearset's strengths as a Salesforce DevOps platform are rooted in its holistic approach to Salesforce management. It's not just a tool; it's a solution that comprehensively addresses the multifaceted challenges of Salesforce DevOps. From deployment to testing, and data management to recovery, Gearset stands out as a platform that understands and effectively responds to the needs of the Salesforce DevOps community.

Gearset's weaknesses

Where some see strengths, others see weaknesses, and Gearset certainly isn't immune to this, particularly in comparison to other Salesforce DevOps solutions – something that happens often when organizations are starting their DevOps journey and determining which solution best fits their needs.

The flexibility to choose your approach to how you want to manage your DevOps process is often perceived as a weakness for teams that need a little more guidance and handholding with a specific approach. Equally, while some see strength in Gearset being an application outside of the Salesforce platform and integrating into it via APIs, others perceive it not being a Salesforce native application as a weakness.

Gearset is specifically tailored for the Salesforce core platform, with the additional support of features such as **CPQ** and Salesforce Industries (formerly known as **Vlocity**). For teams looking for an all-in-one DevOps solution that covers not only other Salesforce products (or "clouds") but other non-Salesforce platforms too, Gearset will not come across as the best choice. Some tech leaders prefer to invest in all-in-one solutions for their entire IT estate.

For more advanced DevOps practitioners, the lack of direct code-editing capabilities and API access is limiting, as it hinders integration with other tools and automation of certain processes in a more scripted fashion as other solutions provide.

Here's a recap of those points to aid your decision process:

Weakness	Description
Flexibility in DevOps management	Gearset's flexibility for users to choose their own DevOps approach is seen as a weakness by teams needing more guided, specific methodologies.
Not Salesforce-native	Being an external application and not a Salesforce-native app is perceived as a drawback, as it integrates via APIs rather than being integrated within the Salesforce platform.
Limited scope	Gearset is tailored for the Salesforce core platform and supports features such as CPQ and Salesforce Industries, but it's not an all-in-one solution for broader Salesforce products or non-Salesforce platforms.
Limited advanced DevOps capabilities	The lack of direct code editing and restricted API access is seen as a limitation for advanced DevOps users who require deeper integration and automation capabilities.

Table 12.2 - A summary of Gearset's weaknesses

Summary

Gearset has emerged as a leading DevOps solution tailored specifically for the Salesforce ecosystem. Its comprehensive feature set allows it to address a wide spectrum of needs related to deployment, testing, data management, and backup/recovery. Gearset simplifies and streamlines processes such as metadata deployment and CI, reducing manual effort and minimizing errors. This efficiency stems not just from automating rote tasks but also from Gearset's deep insight into Salesforce metadata.

While some may perceive Gearset's flexibility and Salesforce-focused approach as weaknesses compared to broader, all-in-one DevOps platforms, Gearset unquestionably excels at managing core Salesforce development and release processes. For teams looking to optimize their Salesforce DevOps workflows, few tools match Gearset's combination of robust functionality and intuitive usability. As Salesforce projects grow larger and more complex, Gearset provides the reliability and precision needed to ship updates with confidence. For most Salesforce teams, Gearset should be a strong contender as a DevOps solution.

In the next chapter, we move on to look at one of the other major players in Salesforce DevOps: Copado. In much the same way, we'll look at its key strengths and weaknesses as an out-of-the-box solution for Salesforce DevOps.

13
Copado

This chapter will delve into the key features and capabilities of Copado, covering its underlying data model and administration. We will examine how Copado addresses the challenges of Salesforce development by automating and simplifying tasks such as version control, build automation, testing, and deployment. We will also look at how Copado integrates with native Salesforce objects for centralized reporting and process monitoring.

In addition to exploring the technical capabilities of Copado, we will also discuss the platform's strengths and weaknesses; understanding these is crucial for organizations considering Copado implementation, as it helps them align their expectations and plan their resources effectively.

We will cover the following topics in this chapter:

- An overview of Copado
- Understanding the strengths of Copado
- Exploring the weaknesses of Copado

By the end of this chapter, you will have a comprehensive understanding of Copado and its role in Salesforce DevOps. The insights you gain will equip you to make informed decisions about leveraging Copado in your own Salesforce environment and help you navigate the complexities of Salesforce development with greater ease and efficiency.

An overview of Copado

Copado provides an end-to-end platform for developing in **Salesforce** using **DevOps** principles and practices. As a native app built on the Salesforce platform, Copado aims to address gaps in the core Salesforce product that inhibit effective **continuous integration and delivery (CI/CD)**. This overview will detail Copado's underlying data model, key technical capabilities, and administration based on its publicly available documentation.

Copado allows teams to implement DevOps workflows entirely within Salesforce without the extensive use of external tools. It integrates version control, build automation, testing, and deployment while retaining native reporting and process visibility. The platform centers around a core abstraction layer that handles much of the complexity of tasks, such as branch management, automatically.

Platform

Copado utilizes a **user-story-centered data model**, that is to say, a deployment model centered around user stories, to associate any requirements with specific metadata changes. The user story entity relates code to its business purpose and scopes for work for incremental delivery. Stories flow through predefined pipelines that span the lower development environments up through to production, as is the case with other configuration management databases. The following screenshot shows a sample pipeline:

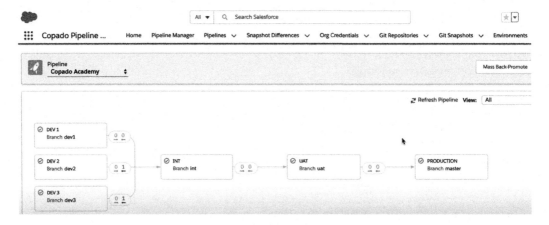

Figure 13.1 – An example of a Copado pipeline

The Copado platform layers abstraction on top of complex **Git** branching and merging operations through the use of a semantic conflict resolution engine. This prevents developers from needing to handle merge conflicts and Git commands manually. Instead, the platform handles branching in a declarative way by using the pipelines flowing from the lower to higher environments.

All user actions within Copado integrate with native Salesforce objects for centralized reporting and process monitoring. This retains auditability and visibility within the comfortable Salesforce interface that administrators already understand. No external dashboards or reports are needed to monitor the DevOps processes.

Copado's capabilities cover the entire DevOps lifecycle, from the initial requirements through to production deployment:

- Requirement management for user stories

- Automated version control

- Continuous integration, triggering quality gates

- Co-ordinated promotion through the environments

- Deployment pipeline configuration

- Org syncing through back promotion

- Built-in visibility and reporting

Together, these aim to provide a comprehensive system for development teams to implement agile, iterative DevOps patterns within Salesforce.

Version control

Copado integrates Git version control by automatically creating feature branches for each user story's committed metadata components. The exact branch structure mirrors the progression of user stories flowing between different Salesforce sandboxes and environments defined in the pipelines.

The following screenshot shows integration with version control:

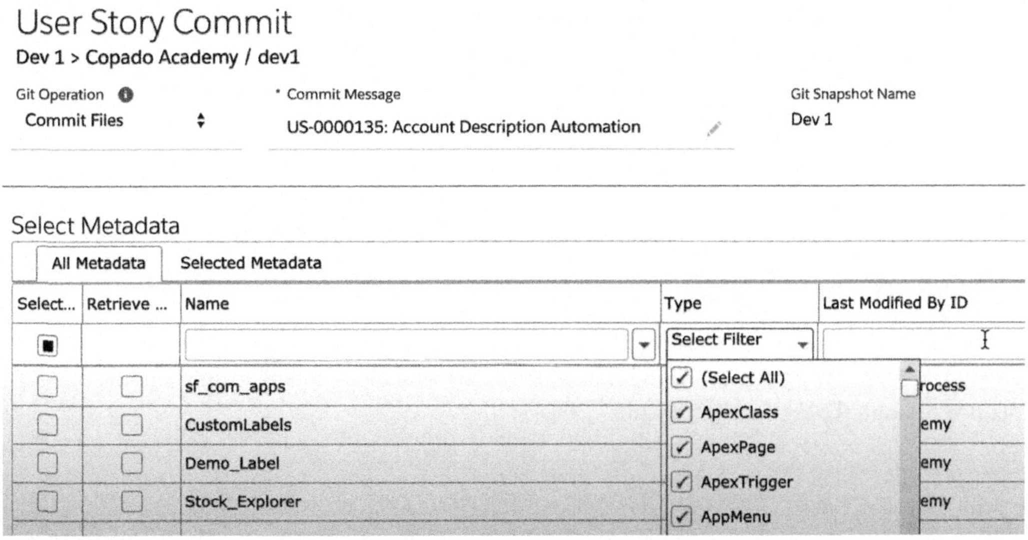

Figure 13.2 – Copado Git integration

Bi-directional deployment and the merging of branches keep all environments and sandboxes in sync as changes flow upstream and downstream through testing and production. No manual Git operations are required on the part of the developers or administrators.

Copado's conflict detection utilizes semantic analysis for metadata rather than just syntactic code reconciliation. This allows it to detect logical conflicts between components that may not be mergeable, such as conflicting field-level security rules. The platform alerts users to these conflicts early to avoid deployment failures.

An administrator can define an organization's branching strategy and environment topology through the pipelines in Copado without needing to know Git internals. The complexity is hidden below the abstraction layer.

Build integration

Continuous integration is a key capability of Copado. Upon each code check-in or commit action, the platform can automatically trigger configured tests, validations, and other quality gates. These may include Apex tests, linting, static analysis, or any other custom steps.

The output of tests and validations is recorded directly onto related user stories within Salesforce for traceability. Developers can see the results immediately without a separate CI server. You can retain compliance on code quality through native reporting.

Third-party tools, such as **Jira** and **Azure DevOps**, can integrate with Copado's CI pipeline via built-in webhooks or custom **Apex** adapters. Custom plugins allow admins to modify and customize Copado's standard CI/CD process to insert custom quality gates. For instance, you could configure a webhook to call out to your preferred security scanning tool via its API just before your code is deployed to your UAT or production environments.

Copado aims to promote shift-left testing and quality assurance by baking it into the commit process automatically. The mandatory gates keep all code checked in at a minimum quality bar through consistent, automated enforcement.

Deployment

Within deployment, Copado introduces the concept of promotions for moving user stories between environments in the pipelines. Promotions pull metadata changes downstream using the pipelines defined through the declarative Copado interface.

The following screenshot shows a sample user story:

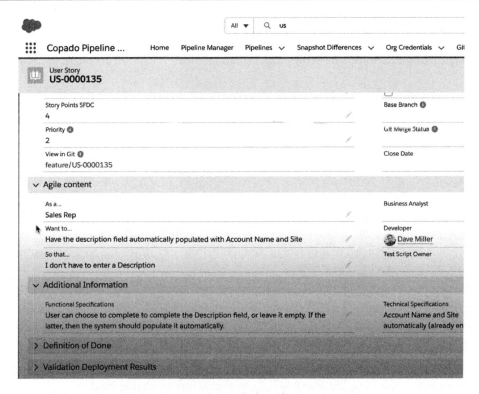

Figure 13.3 – A sample Copado user story

Permission schemes grant the approvals required for progression between pipeline stages. Mandatory manual approval gates can ensure that any changes are authorized. Copado's selective rollback capability can also redeploy previous metadata commitments (as needed) to rapidly revert production.

> **Important note**
>
> "Stages" are categorized as collections of environments fulfilling similar business roles, such as development, testing, production, etc. They provide release managers with the ability to organize their pipelines and environments visually and systematically. Additionally, stages facilitate the configuration and execution of various functionalities when actions are carried out within them. For instance, in scenarios involving quality gate rules or automation rules or when using Copado's **Continuous Delivery** and **Deployment** steps, one can choose particular stages at which to apply these processes.

Connection behaviors configure additional actions, such as automated email notifications, that execute on a per-stage basis in the pipelines. For example, you may want all production deployments to email a security auditor. Behaviors standardize these processes.

Promotions couple code movement with approval and notification policies to avoid *shadow IT*, the performance of IT tasks by non-IT staff, and implement compliance. Rollback mitigates risk by allowing unsafe changes to be removed from the environment automatically if they are found to cause issues.

Environments

Copado keeps Salesforce sandboxes in strict transactional sync without repetitive and manual refresh operations. Refreshing between lower environments creates significant friction in development workflows.

> **Important note**
>
> **Back promotion** is a process designed to transfer user stories from higher to lower environments, serving three main purposes: it ensures synchronization across environments by maintaining consistent changes, facilitates the propagation of hotfixes from production to the lower environments, and helps reduce merge conflicts by recommending the back promotion of changes for streamlined integration.

Instead, back promotions (see callout) automatically merge upstream code changes into lower environments on demand. The platform continuously monitors the state of each organization for deployment readiness before executing downstream distributions.

Limited canary releases introduce a subset of new metadata to a sandbox before complete distribution for incremental rollout. This limits risk and allows testing smaller change batches.

Together, these capabilities allow developers to access the latest shared changes without refreshing, even as updates continually flow to production. It provides a tight inner development loop.

Change management

Change management, in this context, refers to the ability to control any changes to user permissions and access; this poses challenges in Salesforce because permissions and access controls sit across interconnected metadata entities such as profiles, permission sets, and field-level security rules.

Full profile deployment in Copado encapsulates all associated metadata to deploy profiles as a single atomic unit. This avoids permissions drifting out of sync as changes spread. Similarly, permission sets maintain consistent field-level access between environments.

The platform tracks all modifications, attributing them to specific developers, user stories, and commitments for complete auditability. You can produce detailed reports on modifications to sensitive configurations or attributes, such as the record owner.

In summary, change tracking preserves security compliance and configuration integrity as changes flow bi-directionally between lower and higher levels. Dependent metadata is deployed in a single package, avoiding the fragmentation that can come from multiple deployments.

Administration

A key goal of Copado is enabling implementation without extensive training or specialization. All configurations leverage declarative, point-and-click customization similar to the core Salesforce interface. Users already familiar with Salesforce will find the tool intuitive.

Reporting integrates with Salesforce core objects, such as user stories and promotions, to generate process metrics and dashboards for visibility. Prebuilt templates ship out of the box.

Admins oversee access control, usage policies, and other platform governance by using the same tools as the core of Salesforce. Change sets can push policies between environments and profiles control access.

Ultimately, the declarative nature of Copado administration keeps the learning curve low. Organizations can iteratively refine roles and permissions as practices mature without disruption.

Copado provides an extensible platform for implementing the continuous deployment of Salesforce applications using practices such as immutable infrastructure and infrastructure as code. Its core value comes from the native integration and automated handling of deployment complexities inherent to the Salesforce platform.

Overall, Copado aims to eliminate many of the repetitive tasks and barriers to implementing modern DevOps practices within Salesforce development. By providing version control, CI/CD, and environment management, it allows teams to scale agile and iterative development. The consolidation within Salesforce UIs simplifies adoption.

Robotic testing

Designed to dramatically reduce the time and effort required for developing and deploying test cases, **Copado robotic testing (CRT)** offers detailed analyses of test cases, enhancing the effectiveness of testing processes. As a primarily cloud-based solution, it can be accessed via www.robotic. copado.com, and it also has the flexibility of being available as an on-premise service. To cater to a diverse user base, CRT offers a limited free version, which serves as an excellent resource for learning and understanding the framework.

One of the standout features of CRT is its versatility in writing test cases for a broad spectrum of applications. This includes web-based applications, mobile applications, Salesforce Apps, ServiceNow apps, SAP systems, simple websites, and REST APIs. Its dual nature as a low-code and pro-code platform makes it particularly accessible; users without extensive knowledge of test scripting languages or frameworks can still develop test cases efficiently, thanks to its keyword-driven development feature.

CRT further streamlines the testing process with its capability to live test and video-stream test case executions. This feature significantly expedites the debugging process, allowing for real-time issue identification and resolution. Additionally, the framework provides the flexibility to schedule test case executions in alignment with organizational policies.

In summary, Copado robotic testing stands out as a comprehensive, flexible, and efficient test automation framework suitable for a wide range of applications and user expertise levels. Its combination of live testing capabilities, integration options, and a structured approach to testing infrastructure makes it a valuable tool in the landscape of software development and quality assurance.

Understanding the strengths of Copado

Founded in 2013, Copado has emerged as a leading end-to-end DevOps platform tailored for Salesforce development and release management. With substantial growth capital from Salesforce Ventures and other investors, Copado offers a comprehensive suite of capabilities to support and accelerate Salesforce deployments.

A key strength of Copado is its deep native integration with the Salesforce platform. Copado was originally constructed to solve a big need in the market right now: to help underpin the Salesforce DevOps lifecycle.

By building natively on Salesforce, Copado inherits the security, authentication, and other advantages of the platform while maintaining tight integration between development and operations. This contrasts with other tools that operate outside of Salesforce, leading to potential integration challenges.

Relatedly, Copado's metadata intelligence gives it an edge in understanding dependencies, detecting conflicts, and merging changes within Salesforce environments. Copado's secret sauce is its ability to build (on your behalf) a feature-specific branch by converting the one-to-one relationship between your user story in that feature-specific branch.

> **Important note**
>
> A merge conflict happens when two changes are made in separate environments to the same metadata components in a way that can't be reconciled automatically.

Rather than operating on files, Copado works at the metadata API layer, giving it an advantage in merging and deploying changes. This helps address the merge conflicts that users commonly encounter with Salesforce metadata.

Copado also shines in providing end-to-end application lifecycle management, not just deployment. Its issue tracking, user stories, pipelines, and workflows support development teams in planning, co-ordinating, and tracking work from idea through to release. Jira tickets, for instance, become Copado user stories, connecting development work to downstream release processes. This can accelerate development by linking business requirements to developer efforts.

For larger development teams, Copado is difficult to match in terms of functionality and integration. It combines the advantages of Salesforce's platform with Heroku's scalable infrastructure for computationally intensive tasks, such as metadata processing. The Heroku architecture eases security audits while providing necessary performance. This allows Copado to offer **application lifecycle management (ALM)**, testing, compliance, and other tools not found in most deployment-focused solutions.

Exploring the weaknesses of Copado

Copado has emerged as a robust solution, offering a comprehensive suite of features that support all aspects of the Salesforce development lifecycle. However, as with any tool, it has its limitations and challenges. This section explores these potential weaknesses, providing a balanced view of the platform's capabilities and limitations.

One of the key challenges often mentioned in relation to Copado is its complexity. The tool offers a wide range of features and capabilities, which can be overwhelming for new users. The learning curve associated with effectively leveraging all of the tool's features can be steep, potentially slowing down implementation and adoption.

A related issue is the potential difficulty of integrating Copado into existing Salesforce and CI/CD ecosystems, particularly those with complex tech stacks. Compatibility and seamless integration with various tools may require additional configuration and effort, which can be a challenge for teams with limited resources.

Furthermore, Copado requires ongoing maintenance to keep it aligned with changes in Salesforce, your CI/CD pipeline, and your organization's evolving needs. Managing these continuous changes can be time-consuming and may strain resources, especially for smaller teams.

Another potential weakness of Copado is the way it handles backend processing. Although the use of Heroku for backend processing allows Copado to leverage Heroku's power and speed for metadata retrieval, processing, and deployments, it also has a startup cost. If Heroku is being used to deploy metadata from a code repository, it has to clone that metadata first, leading to some performance cost for each job.

However, it is worth noting that Copado claims to have optimized this process, fetching only the minimal amount of history to enable the merge. But even with this optimization, the startup cost can still be a potential bottleneck, especially for larger deployments.

Additionally, while Copado's use of Salesforce as its user interface and for data storage offers some benefits, it also presents some challenges. For instance, all logs and other files are stored as attachments in the Salesforce package, which can make them difficult to read. Moreover, the UI, being built on Salesforce, can look slightly awkward to some users and may not always provide the most intuitive user experience.

Moreover, Copado's notifications about job results are not always obvious, which can lead to confusion or missed notifications. This can be particularly problematic in a DevOps environment, where timely notifications about deployments, tests, and other processes are crucial. See, for instance, the following screenshot of a notification that hasn't been updated properly and, therefore, is marked as done but is neither finished nor successful:

Figure 13.4 – A stalled Copado notification

Ultimately, while Copado is undoubtedly a powerful and comprehensive DevOps tool for Salesforce, it is not without its challenges. Understanding these potential weaknesses is crucial for organizations considering Copado implementation, as it allows them to plan for these challenges and ensure they have the necessary resources and strategies in place to overcome them.

Summary

In conclusion, Copado offers a robust and comprehensive suite of DevOps tools specifically designed for Salesforce. By offering deep, native integration with Salesforce, it effectively addresses gaps in the platform, automating complex tasks such as version control, CI/CD, and environment management.

Its user-story-centered data model and seamless integration with third-party tools make it a valuable asset for agile and iterative development. However, like any tool, it has its limitations. The complexity and steep learning curve might pose challenges for new users. Additionally, the backend processing via Heroku, while being powerful, may introduce performance costs for larger deployments.

Despite these potential hurdles, with the right planning and resources, Copado can significantly streamline Salesforce development and release management, making it a noteworthy consideration for organizations looking to enhance their Salesforce DevOps lifecycle.

To address the challenges posed by Copado's complexity and learning curve, a strategic approach involving thorough training and resource allocation is essential. Organizations can invest in comprehensive training programs for their teams, focusing on hands-on experience and real-world scenarios to build proficiency. Utilizing Copado's extensive documentation and community resources can also aid in this learning process. Moreover, phased implementation strategies can help teams gradually adapt to the tool's intricacies, starting with basic functionalities and progressively moving to more advanced features.

Regarding the performance costs associated with backend processing via Heroku for larger deployments, optimizing the configuration and scaling strategies within Heroku can mitigate these issues. This might involve leveraging more efficient resource allocation, optimizing workflows for better performance, and ensuring that the Heroku environment is tailored to the specific needs of the deployment. Additionally, regularly monitoring and reviewing the performance metrics can help in identifying and addressing any inefficiencies promptly. By tackling these aspects, organizations can harness the full potential of Copado, making it a powerful asset in their Salesforce DevOps toolkit.

With these measures in place, Copado's strengths can be fully realized, overcoming its initial barriers to offer a streamlined and efficient solution for Salesforce development and release management. In moving forward, the next chapter will introduce Flosum, another tool in the Salesforce DevOps landscape, and explore its features and capabilities.

14
Salesforce DevOps Tools – Flosum

Flosum is another of the major players in the Salesforce DevOps ecosystem, offering a suite of tools designed to enhance and streamline the development process. This chapter delves into the multifaceted nature of Flosum, exploring its modules, integration capabilities, and unique position in the Salesforce landscape.

Our journey will uncover how Flosum's native Salesforce platform construction not only aids in seamless integration but also allows for remarkable customization and extensibility.

We will cover the following main topics:

- Flosum overview – an overview of Flosum and its key capabilities
- Flosum's strengths – a breakdown of the key strengths of the Flosum platform
- Flosum's weaknesses – a look at some of the potential weaknesses in Flosum's approach to DevOps

By the end of this chapter, you should be suitably informed about Flosum to be able to decide whether it is the right platform to adopt for your Salesforce DevOps needs.

Technical requirements

If you wish to explore Flosum further, as well as the offer of a product demo via their website at `flosum.com`, you can get access to a trial Flosum instance by starting their Flosum Expert certification at `success.flosum.com`.

A Flosum overview

As you would expect of a modern, Salesforce-specific DevOps solution, Flosum provides a broad spectrum of capabilities that cover the main facets of Salesforce DevOps. In this section, we'll take a look at these core elements and see how Flosum addresses them.

Deployments

The core of Flosum's offering is its DevOps module, a comprehensive suite designed to facilitate the entire development life cycle. It offers an integrated environment for managing code, configurations, and continuous integration, thereby streamlining the delivery process.

Flosum's approach to deployment and change management is both innovative and practical. It handles pre- and post-deployment changes effectively, treating modifications as delta branches. This granularity ensures that only relevant changes are deployed, minimizing the risk of errors and enhancing deployment efficiency.

The Domains feature in Flosum revolutionizes the management of multiple production orgs, offering a structured and unified approach. Alongside this, the Deployment Manager serves as a key tool to orchestrate deployments across various Salesforce Orgs, simplifying what would otherwise be a complex task.

Flosum's advanced features, such as the pre-deploy fix capability and overwrite protection, demonstrate its sophistication. These tools proactively identify and resolve common issues such as API version mismatches, offering a more streamlined deployment process. The peer review process, akin to Git's pull requests, further underscores Flosum's commitment to collaborative and error-free development.

Unique to Flosum is its approach to managing profiles and permission sets. It enables partial retrieval and deployment, focusing only on components relevant to the current branch. This specificity not only saves time but also reduces the complexity of deployments.

Flosum's DevOps workflow is characterized by versatility, offering two primary operational methods – **source tracking via the Salesforce Tooling API** and **snapshot-based difference tracking**. The source tracking capability makes use of Salesforce's own source tracking functionality, which was introduced for Salesforce DX and works in the same way in Flosum, whereas the snapshot feature not only aids in identifying changes but also facilitates efficient rollbacks, enhancing the overall robustness of the development process. An example snapshot in Flosum is shown here:

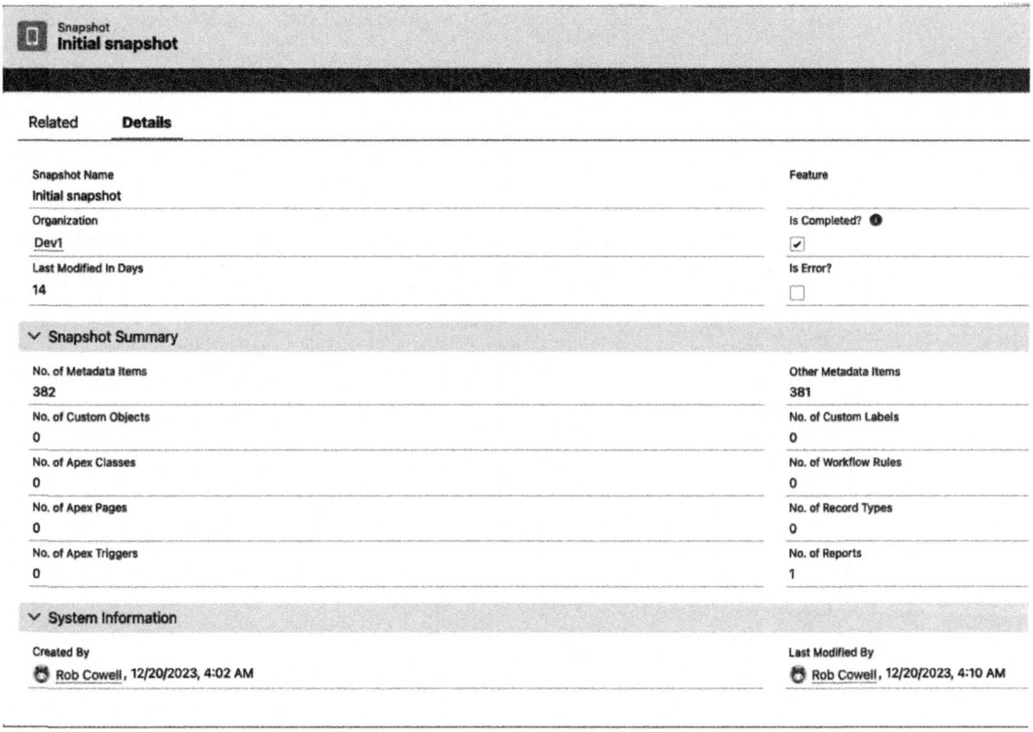

Figure 14.1 – A Flosum org snapshot

> **Note**
> The textual detail in the above figure is minimized and is not directly relevant for the display of the graphic. Please refer to the Free eBook download to access the detail in the graphic.

The process of deployment validation in Flosum is meticulous, resulting in a comprehensive metadata log. This log serves as a crucial record, providing insights into each deployment's history and aiding in future audits and analyses. The following screenshot shows an example of the extensive metadata logs attached to a deployment.

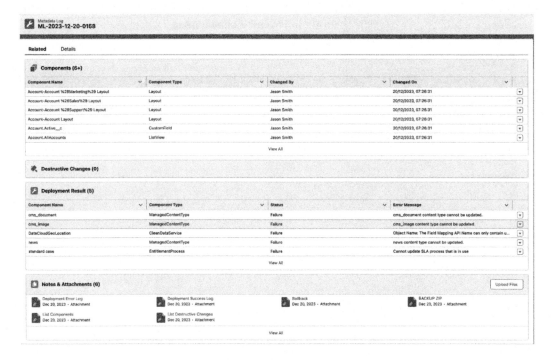

Figure 14.2 – A recent deployment showing the autogenerated metadata log

> **Note**
> The textual detail in the above figure is minimized and is not directly relevant for the display of the graphic. Please refer to the Free eBook download to access the detail in the graphic.

Flosum's approach to pipelines and automation is both flexible and powerful. Users can create individual automations and orchestrate them as needed, without being constrained to a fixed sequence. This flexibility allows teams to tailor their DevOps processes to their specific project needs. The following screenshot shows an example pipeline, complete with a visual representation of the flow of the automation.

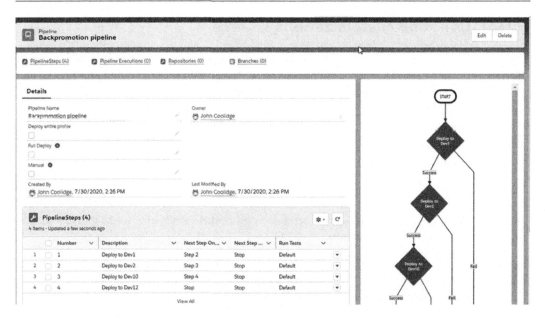

Figure 14.3 – An example automation pipeline

> **Note**
>
> The textual detail in the above figure is minimized and is not directly relevant for the display of the graphic. Please refer to the Free eBook download to access the detail in the graphic.

The Deployment Manager is Flosum's answer to CI/CD orchestration. It allows for the stacking of automation pipelines, offering a centralized and efficient way to manage continuous integration and delivery across multiple projects and environments.

The Trust Center

The Trust Center serves as the cornerstone of security within Flosum, offering robust tools for monitoring and ensuring compliance. This module periodically scans Salesforce Orgs, generating alerts for any detected security breaches or policy violations, and is a testament to Flosum's commitment to security and compliance. It not only monitors Salesforce Orgs for potential security breaches but also automates the generation of violation alerts and remediation changes. This proactive approach to security ensures that Orgs remain compliant and secure.

Backup and Data Migrator

Recognizing the critical nature of data integrity, Flosum's Backup and Data Migrator module provides robust solutions for both full and incremental backups. This module stands out for its support of big objects and binary data, ensuring comprehensive data protection.

Integrations and customizations

Flosum's integration capabilities are a testament to its flexibility. While it offers built-in source control and ticket tracking workflows, it can additionally connect with external applications, such as Jira and Azure DevOps, add flexibility, while Flosum Scan and AccelQ cover the spectrum of code scanning and regression testing. Branch management features such as permissioning, peer review, and merge tracking further attest to Flosum's commitment to a streamlined and secure DevOps process. This interoperability enables teams to leverage Flosum within their existing workflows, enhancing productivity without disrupting established processes.

Built natively on the Salesforce platform, Flosum offers unprecedented extensibility. Users can tailor reports, dashboards, and layouts to their specific needs, ensuring a highly personalized and efficient DevOps experience. This customization extends beyond aesthetics, allowing teams to adapt the tool to their unique workflow requirements.

By using Salesforce's comprehensive reporting and dashboard capabilities, Flosum provides vital insights into deployment metrics. These tools are indispensable for tracking progress, identifying bottlenecks, and making data-driven decisions.

Let's summarize that feature set now, grouped by the area of DevOps that each feature best relates to.

Feature type	Feature	Description
Source control management	Built-in source control	Offers an integrated source control system, allowing for effective management of code changes, versioning, and collaboration within the Salesforce environment.
	Integration with external tools	Supports integration with external source control tools such as GitHub, enabling teams to maintain their existing workflows while leveraging Flosum's capabilities.
Deployment management	The Deployment Manager	A key tool for orchestrating complex deployments across multiple Salesforce Orgs, streamlining the deployment process.
	Snapshot-based difference tracking	Tracks changes using regular snapshots of the Salesforce Org, aiding in identifying differences and facilitating rollbacks when needed.
Security and compliance	The Trust Center	Monitors Salesforce Orgs for security breaches and policy violations, providing alerts and automated remediation changes to ensure compliance.
	Overwrite protection	Includes merge conflict management with a built-in merge editor/diff viewer, enhancing the safety and accuracy of code integrations.

Feature type	Feature	Description
Backup and recovery	Backup and Data Migrator	Offers solutions for both full and incremental backups of Salesforce data, ensuring data integrity and availability for disaster recovery.
Code quality and testing	Flosum Scan	A built-in code scanner that helps maintain high code quality and identifies potential issues early in the development process.
	Integration with AccelQ	Supports integration with AccelQ for comprehensive regression testing, ensuring the reliability and stability of Salesforce applications.
Collaboration and review	Peer review framework	Facilitates a collaborative code review process, similar to Git's pull requests, allowing for per-line commenting and thorough review.
	Branch permissioning and Merge tracking	Enables effective management of branch permissions and tracks merges, ensuring controlled and secure development practices.
Automation and efficiency	Custom pipelines and automation	Allows the creation and orchestration of custom pipelines and automations, tailoring the DevOps process to specific project needs.
	Partial retrieval of profiles and permission sets	Enables selective retrieval and deployment of profiles and permission sets relevant to the components in the branch, enhancing efficiency.
Reporting and insights	Reports and dashboards on deployment metrics	Provides comprehensive reports and dashboards, offering vital insights into deployment metrics and aiding in data-driven decision-making.

Table 14.1 – A summary of Flosum's DevOps capabilities

Now that we've seen the range of DevOps features that Flosum offers, let's dig a little deeper and identify where the product's strengths and weaknesses lie.

Flosum's strengths

Flosum is strong in a great many areas and will certainly meet the needs of most Salesforce teams. Here are some of the key strengths of this platform:

- **Native integration with Salesforce**: It offers seamless compatibility and an intuitive user experience for those accustomed to Salesforce, simplifying operations and enhancing user experience

- **A comprehensive toolset**: It includes features for source control management, deployment automation, backup and recovery, and security and compliance monitoring, addressing a broad spectrum of DevOps processes

- **Customization and extensibility**: It allows extensive customization of reports, dashboards, and layouts to meet specific workflow requirements, adaptable to diverse team needs

- **Advanced deployment management**: The Deployment Manager is capable of handling complex scenarios, including managing multiple Salesforce Orgs, streamlining the deployment life cycle

- **Security and compliance**: It features a Trust Center module and other security functionalities for robust security monitoring and compliance, maintaining data integrity and adhering to regulatory standards

- **Integration with external tools**: It's compatible with tools such as GitHub and Jira, offering flexibility in using built-in or preferred external source control and ticket tracking workflows

- **Quality assurance**: It includes built-in code scanning capabilities and support for external code quality tools, focusing on high code quality and early issue identification

- **Backup and data migration**: It provides robust solutions for data integrity and availability, crucial for disaster recovery and business continuity

- **Branch and merge management**: It offers features such as branch permissioning and peer review frameworks, fostering collaborative and efficient development workflows

- **A user-friendly Interface**: It features an intuitive and accessible user interface, suitable for a wide range of users and reducing the learning curve.

- **Pipeline and automation flexibility**: It enables teams to create and orchestrate custom pipelines, automating processes to increase efficiency and meet dynamic DevOps needs

Flosum's weaknesses

Flosum, while a robust Salesforce DevOps solution, comes with certain limitations that might impact its suitability for some organizations. One of the primary constraints is its platform-specific focus. Designed exclusively for Salesforce, Flosum excels in this environment but may not be the ideal solution for companies looking for a more platform-agnostic DevOps tool. This specialization, while a boon for Salesforce-centric operations, limits its utility in more diverse technological landscapes where multiple platforms are in use.

For teams not deeply entrenched in the Salesforce ecosystem, Flosum presents a noticeable learning curve. Its functionalities and operations are tightly woven into the Salesforce platform, which can be challenging for those unfamiliar with Salesforce's nuances. This aspect could potentially slow the adoption and efficient utilization of Flosum in a non-Salesforce proficient environment.

Cost is another consideration that cannot be overlooked. Flosum's specialized nature and extensive features come with a price tag that could be prohibitive for smaller organizations or start-ups operating with constrained budgets. This aspect makes it less accessible for smaller teams seeking cost-effective DevOps solutions, but it is worth noting that this is true of all paid vendor-provided solutions, not just Flosum.

Integration with non-Salesforce tools, while supported for a considerable number of solutions, is not always seamless, requiring additional plugins or manual setup and installations. This limitation can be a significant drawback for teams that rely on a diverse array of tools and systems outside the Salesforce sphere. The need for broader integration capabilities might be more pronounced in environments where Salesforce is just one of many platforms in use.

Flosum's dependency on the Salesforce platform means that its performance and capabilities are subject to Salesforce's own performance levels and governor limits. Such a dependency could potentially lead to bottlenecks, as was observed with some slow page load times during testing. This reliance on Salesforce's infrastructure and limitations might impact Flosum's efficiency and scalability, particularly in complex or large-scale operations.

The comprehensive nature of Flosum, while a strength, also carries the risk of over-complexity. Some teams might find themselves overwhelmed by its extensive features, many of which may go unused in simpler deployment scenarios. This complexity could lead to inefficiencies, especially for teams that prefer a more streamlined toolset.

As per previous chapters on major Salesforce DevOps platforms, here's a quick summary table to aid your decisioning process.

Weakness	Description
A platform-specific focus	Designed exclusively for Salesforce, limiting its utility in multi-platform environments. Not ideal for companies seeking a platform-agnostic DevOps solution.
A learning curve for non-Salesforce users	Challenging for teams unfamiliar with Salesforce, due to its deep integration, potentially slowing adoption and efficiency.
Cost considerations	May be prohibitively expensive for smaller organizations or start-ups, affecting accessibility for teams with limited budgets.
Non-Salesforce integrations	While it supports some external tools, integrations with non-Salesforce tools may not be as easy to configure, impacting teams reliant on a diverse set of external systems.
Dependency on a Salesforce ecosystem	Performance and capabilities are closely tied to Salesforce, including its performance levels and governor limits. Issues within Salesforce directly impact Flosum's effectiveness, with observed slow page load times in some instances.
Potential for over-complexity	Extensive features can lead to complexity, which may be overwhelming and underutilized in simpler deployment scenarios.

Table 14.2 – An overview of Flosum's weaknesses

Summary

Flosum differentiates itself in the market through its flexibility and sophistication. It challenges the conventional DevOps approaches, notably distancing itself from the "Git orthodoxy." This stance, coupled with its strong emphasis on security and compliance inherent in its Salesforce platform foundation, positions Flosum as a unique and compelling option in the Salesforce DevOps arena.

Its range of features, from advanced deployment options to robust security measures, positions it as an essential tool for any Salesforce architect looking to streamline their DevOps processes. As we have explored in this chapter, Flosum's integration capabilities, customizability, and sophisticated toolset make it a standout choice in the realm of Salesforce DevOps.

In the next chapter, we'll move on to look at another of the popular choices of Salesforce DevOps tools, AutoRABIT.

15
AutoRABIT

In this chapter, we will take a deep dive into AutoRABIT's platform, examining how its core modules for release management, data protection, and code quality provide end-to-end orchestration optimized for the Salesforce ecosystem. We will explore key capabilities such as metadata handling, test automation, compliance guardrails, **continuous integration/continuous delivery (CI/CD)** pipelines, and more.

The goal is to provide readers with an overview of AutoRABIT and how it aims to solve common pain points that Salesforce teams encounter when adopting DevOps practices. You will gain a clear understanding of AutoRABIT's strengths and weaknesses based on real-world usage, helping you to determine if it is the right DevOps solution for your projects.

We will cover the following topics in this chapter:

- An overview of AutoRABIT
- Understanding the strengths of AutoRABIT
- Exploring weaknesses of AutoRABIT

By the end of this chapter, you will have a good understanding of AutoRABIT's purpose-built solutions for enterprise-scale Salesforce DevOps.

An overview of AutoRABIT

In the dynamic world of Salesforce development, organizations often grapple with challenges such as fragmented processes, testing bottlenecks, and stringent compliance controls. AutoRABIT, with its comprehensive suite of DevOps tools, emerges as a pivotal solution for these challenges. This section delves deeper into the AutoRABIT platform, elucidating how its integrated components – **Automated Release Management** (**ARM**), data protection (AutoRABIT Vault), and code quality (AutoRABIT CodeScan) – collectively enhance Salesforce DevOps processes.

We will not only explore the technical aspects of these solutions but also illustrate how they can have a real impact; for instance, reducing deployment time while enhancing compliance adherence or streamlining Salesforce development, ensuring data integrity and security in line with complex regulations. These practical insights underscore the transformative effect of AutoRABIT in diverse organizational contexts, offering readers a comprehensive understanding of its capabilities and applications in real-world scenarios.

AutoRABIT platform overview

The AutoRABIT platform comprises three pillars:

- **ARM**: AutoRABIT ARM provides end-to-end orchestration of the release process for development teams. It seamlessly integrates version control, CI testing, compliance controls, and deployment pipelines.

- **Data protection**: AutoRABIT Vault delivers backup and recovery capabilities for Salesforce data and metadata. It enables teams to protect information integrity and meet data privacy regulations.

- **Code quality**: AutoRABIT CodeScan performs static analysis of Apex and Lightning code to identify vulnerabilities and enforce secure coding standards.

Together, these solutions offer unified visibility and control over the entire **software development life cycle** (**SDLC**). Let's explore each one in more detail.

ARM

AutoRABIT's ARM platform tackles frustrations that come from not having robust processes as you scale development and configuration on Salesforce, such as conflicting changes or lack of visibility.

For teams suffering deployment headaches, ARM brings order to the chaos by providing a robust toolset for managing and monitoring releases. Integration-testing bottlenecks disappear through test automation, executing tests automatically during the deployment. Code progression follows a consistent, predictable path from commit to production, which means you can visually see where things are in the process. Comprehensive controls and metrics provide further guardrails and visibility that check the state of your code on an ongoing basis. The following screenshot gives an example of the **user interface** (**UI**):

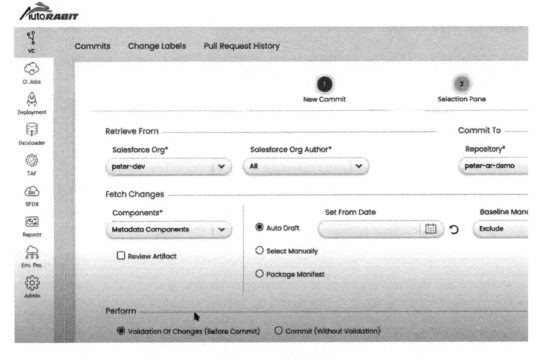

Figure 15.1 – AutoRABIT ARM UI

> **Note**
>
> The textual detail in the above figure is minimized and is not directly relevant for the display of the graphic. Please refer to the Free eBook download to access the detail in the graphic.

With ARM, releases become a non-event. Code flows rapidly from dev to deployment without surprises. Let's examine the key capabilities.

AutoRABIT offers advanced versioning, merging, and dependency management for intricate Salesforce metadata relationships. Specifically, it does the following:

- It detects granular differences between metadata and components across branches. AutoRABIT retrieves only changed elements needed for deployment. This *delta deployment* approach avoids the repetitive processing of unrelated files.

- The merging engine integrates concurrent changes from multiple streams. Customizable rules resolve conflicts without impacting unrelated components.

These features eliminate the headaches of tracking metadata changes across feature branches. AutoRABIT merges code cleanly without modifying unrelated elements. Deployments contain only relevant changes.

Another source of deployment delays is inadequate testing. AutoRABIT bakes robust test automation into the pipeline in the following ways:

- It runs Apex tests during validations, commits, and deployments with configurable pass rate rules. Making testing a mandatory step prevents unexpected regressions.

- AutoRABIT resolves test class dependencies on the fly based on components in change packages. Only relevant tests execute for speed.

- It integrates with test automation frameworks such as Selenium for UI testing.

By shifting testing left, issues surface earlier before reaching production. Testing becomes a daily activity rather than a release bottleneck. AutoRABIT enables reliable automation at all stages of delivery.

In regulated sectors such as healthcare and finance, releases demand rigorous compliance controls for security and access. AutoRABIT automates capabilities such as the following:

- Pre-deployment reviews of access changes. Adding a field requires checking permissions.

- Immutable audit logs of all deployment events provide trailing proof.

- Static code analysis integration exposes vulnerabilities before deployment.

- Backup and recovery protect data integrity.

These features ensure deployments are able to adhere to standards such as **System and Organization Controls 2 (SOC 2)**, the **International Organization for Standardization (ISO)** *27001*, the **General Data Protection Regulation (GDPR)**, and the **Health Insurance Portability and Accountability Act (HIPAA)**.

AutoRABIT supports CI/CD pipelines out of the box with the following benefits:

- Validation against target environments after commits surfaces issues early before merging

- Automated workflows promote code through the pipeline upon passing checks

- Chained jobs connect deployment events for release orchestration

- Deployments can trigger further steps such as testing

- The rollback console helps restore the pre-deployment state upon failures

With AutoRABIT, teams can set up structured pipelines, ensuring that each stage transitions seamlessly to the next without unnecessary delays.

> **Parameterization**
>
> Parameterization in a DevOps context typically refers to the practice of making configurations and deployments more reusable, maintainable, and standardized by externalizing configurable values into parameters rather than hardcoding them.

A major benefit of AutoRABIT is the flexibility to model intricate release processes. For teams hesitant to adopt highly structured pipelines, AutoRABIT allows them to move at their own pace:

- It supports complex Git workflows such as GitFlow with extensive branching capabilities.

- Parameterization enables configuring deployment steps once and reusing everywhere. Pipeline stages become **Plug and Play (PnP)**.

- AutoRABIT allows the creation of custom roles such as developers, admins, and package managers. Permissions are customized to needs through centralized identity- and context-based policies that can restrict data and features on a per-user/group basis.

- Scripting extends built-in functionalities without touching core code. Quick customizations augment the platform.

AutoRABIT allows starting simple and evolving release automation as needed through the expansion of pipeline capabilities.

AutoRABIT optimizes core deployment processes for performance, using mechanisms such as incremental deployments that push only component deltas between environments. This avoids the repetitive overhead of full redeployments. There is also an option to ignore non-essential metadata components to prevent churn without value. These optimizations maximize deployment throughput and reliability even for large, complex packages.

AutoRABIT offers extensive capabilities tailored to Salesforce's unique platform approach; for example, comprehensive metadata type support including Lightning Components, handling of managed package namespaces, and ISV partner solution support for products such as CloudSense and Conga.

AutoRABIT ARM is intended to provide a control tower over the entire DevOps toolchain. Let's next explore how it manages and protects Salesforce data.

AutoRABIT Vault for data protection

AutoRABIT Vault provides a robust solution for the backup and recovery of Salesforce environments, effectively serving developers, administrators, and release managers. This tool enables these professionals to safeguard their information assets confidently, offering a convenient self-service model. Organizations concerned about data integrity will find that Vault offers the required protection. It allows teams to run backups either on demand or on a predetermined schedule, effectively creating a safeguard against potential data loss. It has comparison and recovery options that enable users to compare the current state of data in their vault to what's in the live system, assuring users that their information is secure. The following screenshot shows an example of the Vault UI:

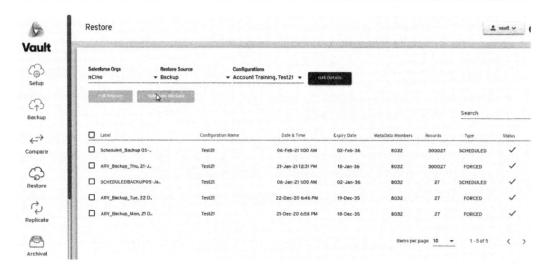

Figure 15.2 – AutoRABIT Vault UI

> **Note**
>
> The textual detail in the above figure is minimized and is not directly relevant for the display of the graphic. Please refer to the Free eBook download to access the detail in the graphic.

Key features of this tool include scheduled backups that ensure regular, automatic preservation of Salesforce data and metadata. These backups can be tailored to suit various needs, including daily, weekly, or incremental backups, and they cope well with high data volumes thanks to their batching process, which reduces the risk of partial failures. Organizations are not limited to full backups as incremental options are also available, which only capture changes since the last backup, making the process more efficient. For additional peace of mind, on-demand backups can be initiated at any moment with a simple click.

Efficient storage is another benefit, as Vault provides the flexibility to secure backups in different locations, including prominent cloud services such as **Amazon Web Services Simple Storage Service** (**AWS S3**), Azure Blob, or **Google Cloud Storage** (**GCS**), and on-premises solutions such as a **storage area network** (**SAN**) or **network-attached storage** (**NAS**). It accommodates **Bring Your Own Key** (**BYOK**) encryption methods, allowing for a secure backup strategy that caters to an organization's specific budgetary, security, and data jurisdiction requirements.

In terms of recovery, Vault offers good granularity for specific restoration requirements. For instance, users can delve into backups to conduct forensic analysis, easing audit processes. They have the option to restore individual records, groups of records, or entire objects. Moreover, in cases where only certain fields are affected, Vault provides the capability to restore just those impacted fields, preventing more extensive recovery actions. This type of precision ensures both data integrity and the preservation of the metadata and relationships, which helps avoid subsequent technical issues.

Sandbox seeding is another significant feature, enabling faster testing cycles by populating sandboxes and scratch organizations with representative data subsets. Vault allows users to replicate production data in smaller environments while offering the option to filter records, mask sensitive fields, and maintain referential integrity, which are all crucial for effective testing.

Compliance is also a key consideration, and Vault comprises features that help adhere to privacy laws and standards. These include data encryption both at rest and during transfer, IP restriction for backup access, automated retention policies for data life-cycle management, and anonymization tools that support regulations such as GDPR and the **California Consumer Privacy Act (CCPA)**. These integrated compliance measures provide organizations with the necessary tools to maintain high standards of data security and privacy.

Let's now move on to discussing AutoRABIT's solution for static code analysis.

AutoRABIT CodeScan for static analysis

AutoRABIT CodeScan offers a comprehensive static analysis tool designed to evaluate Salesforce code, highlighting potential defects and security issues at an early stage, where they can be addressed in a more cost-effective manner. The tool encourages a continuous inspection approach, allowing for proactive rather than reactive issue resolution, which can enhance the robustness and integrity of code.

For organizations facing challenges with technical debt and security vulnerabilities, CodeScan, as with other static code analysis tools, serves as a valuable asset to impose consistent standards across various projects and teams. It firmly applies an objective approach to code quality, thus contributing to the development of more resilient applications. The following screenshot shows an example of the CodeScan UI:

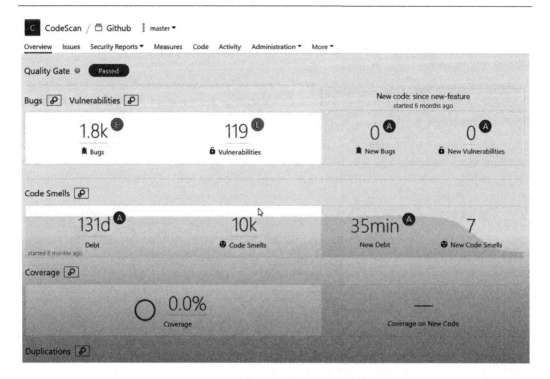

Figure 15.3 – Example of the CodeScan UI

> **Note**
> The textual detail in the above figure is minimized and is not directly relevant for the display of the graphic. Please refer to the Free eBook download to access the detail in the graphic.

Diving into CodeScan's primary features, the tool boasts extensive support for a variety of programming elements within Salesforce, including Apex, Visualforce, Lightning Components, and Flow. It comes equipped with over 600 predefined rules that encompass best practices for security, performance, and style, while also adhering to industry-wide standards such as the **Open Worldwide Application Security Project (OWASP)** Top 10 and the **Common Weakness Enumeration (CWE)** Top 25.

Moreover, CodeScan integrates effortlessly with CI/CD pipelines, helping promote security earlier in the development process, also known as *shift-left* security. Scanning commits and analyzing pull requests safeguards against the merger of suboptimal code. Builds can be configured to fail upon policy breaches, preventing unverified deployments, and developers receive quick feedback through incremental analyses of recently modified components.

Another feature is the ability for teams to create custom rules that reflect their unique organizational policies. While leveraging core rulesets such as the OWASP Top 10, teams can also encapsulate their specific coding guidelines and set severity levels for rule breaches, hence differentiating between critical issues and warnings.

AutoRABIT's CodeScan enforces security standards uniformly, providing developers with immediate feedback aimed at cultivating secure and resilient code bases.

Having covered the basics of the product, we will now discuss the strengths and weaknesses of AutoRABIT.

Understanding the strengths of AutoRABIT

AutoRABIT stands out as a sophisticated solution for large Salesforce customers, offering a comprehensive suite of tools designed to enhance the efficiency and effectiveness of their operations. Its platform transcends the limitations typically observed in point solutions, providing a cohesive end-to-end DevOps environment. Each of AutoRABIT's tools, including ARM for deployments, Vault to secure data, and CodeScan for quality analysis, are precisely tuned to work in harmony. This coherence affords users overarching visibility and governance, eliminating operational blind spots and negating the need for integrating disparate tools, thus positioning AutoRABIT as the epicenter of DevOps workflows tailored for the Salesforce ecosystem.

The approach AutoRABIT adopts toward testing is quite thorough. Embodied within the development process, testing is a continual activity, present at every stage, from code commits to deployment phases. By preemptively flagging issues early and frequently, AutoRABIT ensures that code meets stringent quality standards prior to progression. The emphasis on frequent, systematic testing circumvents the accumulation of technical debt by preventing defects from progressing downstream, and such consistency instills a deep-rooted assurance in the modifications being introduced.

For organizations operating under stringent regulatory frameworks, particularly in sectors such as healthcare, finance, and insurance, AutoRABIT offers a robust set of compliance and security measures. The arsenal of tools at their disposal, such as static code analysis, comprehensive access reviews, tamper-proof audit logs, and secure data encryption, fortifies companies against risk. AutoRABIT's comprehensive solution introduces a discipline in release management that is difficult to achieve with manual methods, ensuring adherence to the **principle of least privilege (PoLP)** through **role-based access control (RBAC)** and rigorous enforcement of code scans and backups.

By incorporating redundancy across multiple data centers and maintaining comprehensive **disaster recovery (DR)** protocols, the platform reassures its users of **high availability (HA)** and **business continuity (BC)**. This reliability is further underpinned by a commitment to stringent **service-level agreements (SLAs)**.

AutoRABIT is also strong in automation, which is applied to avoid unnecessary manual tasks. By intelligently discerning the context, such as disregarding irrelevant components during metadata comparisons, AutoRABIT streamlines operations. The automation is purposefully selective, encouraging human intervention only where necessary, hence allowing teams to dedicate more of their time to innovation rather than mundane repetition.

Having covered some areas where AutoRABIT is comparatively strong, we'll move on to look at some comparatively weaker points.

Exploring the weaknesses of AutoRABIT

AutoRABIT has established itself as a robust provider of DevOps solutions, yet feedback from customers has highlighted certain areas that could be refined. A closer examination of user reviews and feedback brings to light a spectrum of concerns, particularly focusing on aspects of performance, the inherent complexity of the system, the level of customer support, and various limitations that can impact user experience.

Regarding performance, there have been instances reported by users where AutoRABIT encounters delays, especially when handling large volumes of complex metadata. When committing substantial packages or executing significant deployment changes, the system appears to occasionally experience lag. This performance drop is frequently attributed to an elaborate web of dependencies within metadata, which the platform must navigate. As the level of complexity escalates, these slowdowns become increasingly evident, suggesting that performance tuning and optimization are aspects ripe for development.

In addition to performance issues, AutoRABIT's depth of customization, while powerful, brings a degree of complexity that can be daunting. For those less experienced, such as new developers, the extensive array of administrative settings and options can be overwhelming. The interface presents a myriad of parameters and adjustments that, while granting considerable control, can also lead to confusion. Even for seasoned administrators, there is a steep learning curve to master the full extent of AutoRABIT's capabilities. See the following screenshot for an example of a complex UI:

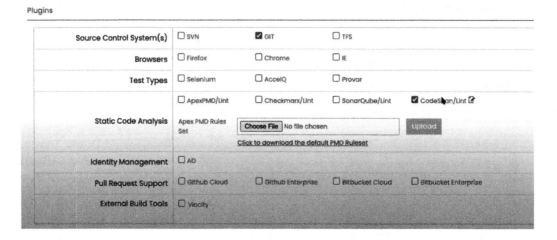

Figure 15.4 – Configuring plugins – a large number of choices

> **Note**
> The textual detail in the above figure is minimized and is not directly relevant for the display of the graphic. Please refer to the Free eBook download to access the detail in the graphic.

In addition to these usability concerns, there is a somewhat negative sentiment among users regarding the quality of AutoRABIT's supporting materials. Documentation, often the first resource for troubleshooting and learning, has been described as lacking essential details, leading to a tedious problem-solving process.

Customer support responsiveness is another critical area highlighted by users. Reports of long wait times when seeking help indicate a need for a more prompt and expansive support network. Moreover, transparent communication about potential delays could help set proper expectations and mitigate user frustration.

The platform's Salesforce DX integration has been tailored predominantly toward a GUI approach, which, while elegant, does not fully satisfy those who prefer using **command-line interfaces** (**CLIs**) for their automation and tooling needs. For teams that rely on CLIs, the current emphasis on the GUI feels insufficient, suggesting that a more robust CLI-based DX integration would be beneficial.

Lastly, some clients have expressed difficulty in predicting long-term costs associated with AutoRABIT's consumption-based pricing model. The challenge of forecasting resources for expanding teams and increasing usage adds to the complexity. A more transparent pricing structure, along with tools to assist in budget projection, would greatly assist teams in managing their finances and could prevent the strain of unexpected cost increases that risk souring customer relations.

To navigate AutoRABIT successfully despite these limitations, customers should take care to stay within documented platform constraints to avoid performance issues. Additionally, while AutoRABIT presents a highly customizable environment, clients should resist over-configuring initially before establishing familiarity with standard workflows. Learning the basics before tuning advanced parameters will yield better outcomes. Leveraging available training paired with a gradual ramp-up in configuration changes is advisable over attempting to master complete platform complexity out of the gate.

Though deficiencies exist in certain aspects of AutoRABIT, customers can take proactive measures to ensure successful adoption. With judicious platform usage leveraging available documentation and support channels, clients can achieve their objectives while base functionality matures over subsequent releases.

Summary

In closing, AutoRABIT offers an impressive breadth of capabilities tailored for Salesforce DevOps, with strengths in sophisticated metadata handling, embedded testing, compliance controls, and cross-module integration. However, as with any complex platform, there are also areas for continued improvement based on customer feedback around performance, usability, documentation, and support responsiveness.

Overall, AutoRABIT is well positioned as a leader in release automation, data protection, and code analysis for Salesforce teams seeking an integrated DevOps solution. While not a perfect fit for every organization, AutoRABIT provides robust options for those requiring advanced oversight and governance.

We will now change gears slightly and look at a whole range of other tools related to Salesforce DevOps in the following chapter.

16

Other Salesforce DevOps Tools

In this chapter, we explore an array of tools that complement and enhance the Salesforce DevOps landscape. These tools offer different features and cater to various aspects of the DevOps cycle, from planning and development to deployment and monitoring. Understanding the capabilities and applications of these tools will help you select the most suitable ones for your Salesforce implementation.

We will cover the following topics in this chapter:

- Salesforce DevOps Center

- Other commercial tools

- Open source tools

By the end of this chapter, you will have a comprehensive understanding of the Salesforce DevOps ecosystem, including insights into how each tool fits into your DevOps strategy. You will also be equipped to make informed decisions about which tools can best address the specific needs of your Salesforce projects.

Salesforce DevOps Center

The Salesforce DevOps ecosystem is vast and continuously evolving, with numerous tools emerging to cater to different needs within the development life cycle. In this section, we delve into an overview of some prominent tools and platforms that integrate with Salesforce, offering enhanced efficiency, collaboration, and automation for development teams. First, we will cover a new significant player, Salesforce's own DevOps offering: DevOps Center.

DevOps Center is a Salesforce solution designed to enhance change and release management processes by incorporating DevOps best practices into Salesforce development teams, irrespective of their position on the low-code to pro-code spectrum. This platform was developed in response to feedback from the Salesforce community seeking an alternative to change sets. While change sets remain available, DevOps Center is posited as a more advanced and efficient tool for managing changes within Salesforce environments.

DevOps Center has the following key capabilities:

- **Automated change tracking**: DevOps Center eliminates the need for manual tracking of changes, such as using spreadsheets or sticky notes, by automatically tracking alterations within the development environment

- **Source control integration**: It uses source control repositories, such as GitHub, as the **single source of truth (SSOT)** for project changes, ensuring consistency across all team members' work

- **Branch management**: The platform simplifies branch creation and management, facilitating the progression of changes through the release pipeline with a simple click-based interface

- **Tool flexibility**: Developers can use their preferred tools outside of DevOps Center and still maintain visibility of changes across the team due to the centralized source control system

- **Salesforce DX compatibility**: Under the hood, DevOps Center leverages Salesforce DX, including compatibility with the Salesforce CLI, Metadata API, and source control, without requiring users to be familiar with these tools

- **User interface (UI)**: A click-based UI allows users to interact with the DevOps process without needing to engage directly with underlying technologies such as the Salesforce CLI or GitHub

With DevOps Center, different types of developers can work together more effectively. For instance, a declarative developer can create work items, pull changes, and commit them to the source control repository, while a programmatic developer can review those changes before promotion. Release managers can deploy changes through the release pipeline within DevOps Center or by using the Salesforce CLI, thus improving the release management process. See the following diagram for different workflows that are supported:

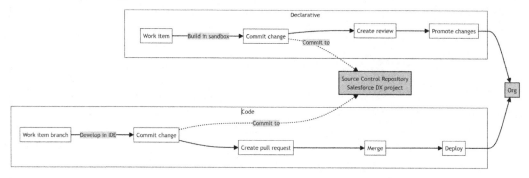

Figure 16.1 – Development flows for DevOps Center

The platform also includes features to identify conflicts between work items and provides information to help resolve them, which is particularly useful in teams with multiple parallel developments. DevOps Center can detect when a development environment is out of sync with the SOT and provides tools to synchronize environments, reducing the chance of conflicts or errors during deployment.

The platform offers enhanced visibility into the change and release process, including an activity history for auditing and error tracking. Features such as work items, conflict management, and validation-only deployments can contribute to increased productivity and smoother workflows.

Initially, DevOps Center only supports GitHub as the source control system. Users of other systems such as Bitbucket may need to switch to GitHub or wait for future updates. DevOps Center also currently supports org-based development rather than package based development (2GP), which may not align with the workflows of all development teams. Finally, while a number of external integrations are planned, at the moment, the number of external systems to which it can be connected is limited.

Overall, DevOps Center offers a simple platform for Salesforce development teams to manage change and release processes more effectively.

Other commercial tools

Commercial tools offer a range of functionalities tailored to Salesforce development and operations. These platforms often provide specialized features such as deployment management, impact analysis, and automation capabilities. They can be particularly beneficial for organizations seeking to streamline their development processes and enhance collaboration among team members. In this section, we will examine several commercial tools that have made significant contributions to the Salesforce DevOps ecosystem.

Salto

Salto is a DevOps platform designed to streamline and enhance the development and operational processes for Salesforce environments. As a SaaS product, Salto manages Salesforce configurations and metadata, aiming to provide a more efficient route for handling deployment, version control, and dependency tracking across various Salesforce instances.

The core capabilities of Salto include the following:

- **Exploration of configurations and metadata**: Salto provides users with tools to examine and understand the impact of changes in Salesforce configurations before they are made. This is facilitated by a user-friendly interface that abstracts the underlying XML data into a more readable format, using Salto's proprietary **Not Another Configuration Language** (**NaCl**).

- **Deployment management**: Salto allows users to move changes from one Salesforce environment to another with ease. The platform supports a pre-deployment validation process that identifies potential deployment issues such as missing dependencies, aiming to reduce the frequency of failed deployments.

- **Automation and continuous integration/continuous deployment (CI/CD)**: Salto has introduced CI/CD automation capabilities, enabling users to integrate the platform into their existing CI/CD pipelines. This allows for automated testing, building, and deployment processes, thereby helping teams implement DevOps best practices.

- **Version control integration**: Salto integrates with **version control systems** (**VCS**) such as Git, generally containing NaCL metadata, allowing users to create an audit trail for changes deployed to Salesforce environments. This integration also supports compliance with regulatory requirements by maintaining a record of changes for auditing purposes.

Salto is suitable for various use cases, such as simplifying the deployment process across multiple Salesforce sandboxes and production environments or managing complex Salesforce environments where interdependencies between configurations are common.

It provides a user-friendly interface that abstracts complex XML data into a more accessible format. This helps proactive identification of configuration dependencies, which helps prevent deployment issues. However, there is a need for users to learn Salto's proprietary NaCl language, which may present a learning curve.

In summary, Salto positions itself as a robust DevOps tool for Salesforce, aiming to streamline deployment processes, enhance change intelligence, and improve overall efficiency.

Panaya

Panaya ForeSight is a change intelligence platform designed to assist organizations in managing, maintaining, and debugging their Salesforce orgs. The platform offers a suite of tools aimed at providing visibility and control over the complex ecosystem of a Salesforce environment.

ForeSight equips users with the ability to perform in-depth analysis of their Salesforce org's metadata, which results in a detailed mapping of dependencies within the org's structure. This mapping is important for understanding the interconnections between various components, which is essential when planning changes or additions to the system. A key feature of ForeSight is its Discovery Chrome Extension, which enables users to obtain insights directly from any Salesforce page, helping to anticipate the impact on related components such as Apex classes, Process Builders, flows, and fields.

ForeSight ExplAIn, an AI-driven extension of the platform, adds another layer of intelligence by providing explanations in a human-readable format for customizations and automations within Salesforce. This feature assists in troubleshooting errors and automatically generates documentation, which can drastically reduce time spent on these tasks.

ForeSight is used for a variety of Salesforce management tasks, including release planning, reduction of technical debt, **root cause analysis** (**RCA**), and optimization of testing efforts. It is particularly useful for organizations that are migrating to new Salesforce features or managing the transition from workflow rules to flows. The platform enables organizations to plan changes with a clear understanding of their impact, automate impact analysis, and efficiently onboard new team members by providing them with comprehensive org insights.

One of the primary strengths of Panaya ForeSight is the platform's ability to reduce the manual effort associated with understanding and managing Salesforce orgs, thus allowing for more accurate and faster impact analysis. The AI-powered documentation and human-friendly explanations enhance the onboarding process for new hires and provide a quick reference for org functionalities. By enabling proactive management, ForeSight helps organizations shift from a reactive to a strategic approach, potentially leading to innovation and optimized workflows.

While the platform offers a comprehensive set of tools for Salesforce org management, the degree of its effectiveness can be contingent on the complexity of the org and the user's familiarity with the platform. Additionally, as with any AI-driven tool, the quality of the output is dependent on the data input, and the AI's output may not always be exactly what one would be looking for.

Prodly

Prodly aims to streamline the development and operations process, particularly for business users such as Salesforce admins and low-code developers. The product suite includes tools for environment management, work management integration, release automation, and compliance and security controls.

Prodly provides a user-friendly interface within Salesforce to manage various development environments, including the ability to spin up scratch orgs without the need for command-line tools. This capability leverages Salesforce DX's features but simplifies the process for non-developers. Prodly's environment management also includes a sandbox seeding feature, which allows users to populate environments with sample or specific sets of data. This feature supports automated data migration between environments, adhering to dependencies and order of insertion, preventing duplication, and saving time on manual configuration.

In terms of work management, Prodly integrates with Salesforce's Agile Accelerator and DevOps Center, enabling users to create and manage projects and work items and associate them with metadata changes detected by DevOps Center. This integration ensures a seamless process for managing both the application life cycle and the associated metadata.

Release automation within Prodly allows for the comparison of metadata between source and target environments, offering a preview of changes and a guided deployment process. This can help prevent deployment errors by providing insights before the deployment is executed. Furthermore, Prodly supports metadata deployments from org to org or from org to branch and vice versa, accommodating different development workflows, including those using source control systems.

Prodly suits organizations using Salesforce where there is a need to empower admins and low-code developers with DevOps capabilities. It is particularly useful for businesses managing complex applications such as Salesforce CPQ or B2B Commerce, where configuration data is as critical as metadata.

Elements.cloud

Elements.cloud is a DevOps platform designed to enhance the management and documentation of Salesforce environments. Its primary capabilities include capturing feedback, managing requirements, defining work items such as releases and user stories, and linking these to Salesforce metadata for impact analysis. The platform is integrated with Salesforce, allowing users to embed process diagrams into Salesforce record pages and providing context-sensitive help.

One of the key use cases for Elements.cloud is to streamline the process of documenting and analyzing changes within a Salesforce org. By automating the creation of metadata dictionaries and synchronizing them nightly with both production and sandbox environments, Elements.cloud facilitates a more efficient impact analysis process. This capability helps developers and administrators understand the relationships and dependencies between Salesforce metadata components, reducing the time and effort required for impact analysis by up to 50%.

Elements.cloud's strengths lie in its ability to provide a visual, hierarchical process mapping tool that is version-controlled and can be directly embedded within Salesforce. This enhances the user's ability to validate business process requirements, and the platform's risk assessment features help track the potential impact of changes from both a compliance and technical perspective. Additionally, the platform automates the documentation of metadata items, supports cleanup by identifying low-impact fields, and offers multi-level dependency analysis for in-depth impact assessment.

The platform also empowers users to drive process improvement savings by mapping out business processes and identifying areas for optimization. By linking process steps to user stories or requirements and attaching relevant documentation, Elements.cloud promotes an understanding of why certain changes were made, thereby fostering institutional knowledge and future-proofing developments.

Opsera

Opsera is a continuous orchestration platform designed to address issues in the DevOps field, particularly the challenges of connecting various tools in the delivery assembly line and creating visibility over this assembly line. It aims to provide insights into the speed, quality, and security vulnerabilities of product deliveries. Opsera combines the management of these tools within a **single pane of glass** (**SPOG**), enabling orchestration and visibility for different toolsets and processes.

Opsera offers toolchain automation, declarative pipelines, and insights modules. The toolchain automation module allows users to manage and deploy the necessary tools for application deployment, supporting both SaaS and traditional applications. It includes integrations to a variety of tools such as Jenkins, Argo CD, Artifactory, and SonarQube, with the flexibility to add others as needed. Opsera operates on a SaaS platform, where customers are set up with a single-tenant VPC and a personalized portal.

The declarative pipelines module provides a low-code environment where users can create workflows for deploying applications, including Salesforce and containerized applications designed for Kubernetes. It caters to both low coders and high coders by offering task-driven operations, which enable users to push changes directly from an organization to a Git branch, facilitating GitOps without requiring command-line Git knowledge.

Opsera's insights module delivers comprehensive dashboards with over 100 KPIs aligned with **DevOps Research and Assessment** (**DORA**), **Definition of Done** (**DoD**), and the **National Institute of Standards and Technology** (**NIST**) metrics. It provides visibility into the software delivery life cycle, including successful deployments, pipeline statuses, and unit testing metrics. This observability extends to Salesforce-specific metrics, offering insights into backups, rollbacks, migrations, and Jira lead time.

Opsera's use cases include the deployment of Salesforce applications, where it can handle both code and low-code elements, and the delivery of containerized applications to Kubernetes. It supports various environments and can manage the movement of applications from sandbox to production. Additionally, it provides visibility into application life-cycle management tools through direct integrations, API interactions, and command-line steps.

Opsera's primary strength lies in its ability to bring together disparate tools and processes under one orchestration platform, offering a unified approach to DevOps. Its SaaS-based approach with a single-tenant VPC ensures security and isolation. The platform's low-code environment is accessible to users with varying technical expertise, promoting collaboration between different team members.

Open source tools

Open source tools play a crucial role in the Salesforce DevOps ecosystem. They provide the community with flexible, adaptable, and often no-cost solutions that can be customized to fit specific requirements. These tools are developed and maintained by a community of users and contributors who work collaboratively to improve and update them. In this section, we explore several open source tools that have garnered attention for their utility and impact on Salesforce DevOps practices.

Happy Soup

Happy Soup is an open source project designed to perform impact and dependency analysis within Salesforce environments. The tool is built on JavaScript and Node.js, and its source code is publicly available on GitHub for transparency and collaboration. It is primarily aimed at Salesforce administrators and developers who need to understand the complex web of dependencies that exist within their Salesforce orgs.

The core functionalities of Happy Soup include the capability to analyze the impact of changes made to a Salesforce org and to understand the dependencies across various components. This is particularly useful when modifying elements such as custom fields, as it can help identify potential issues that such changes might cause across the system.

For example, if a custom field is modified, Happy Soup can quickly identify all the components within the org that rely on that field. This includes dependencies in report filters, Apex classes, JavaScript controllers in **Lightning Web Components** (**LWC**), workflow rules, and more. The tool provides a visual representation of these dependencies, making it easier to understand the breadth and depth of the potential impact.

Use cases for Happy Soup include the following:

- **Impact analysis**: Before changing a custom field, Happy Soup can be used to determine the dependencies and potential risks, allowing for informed decision-making
- **Dependency analysis**: The tool is useful for independent consultants or new team members to quickly understand how specific components or objects are used within an unfamiliar Salesforce org

- **Page layout optimization**: Happy Soup can export the fields of a page layout into an Excel sheet, facilitating discussions with business users regarding the relevance and necessity of each field

Happy Soup is a valuable tool for Salesforce professionals seeking to manage the complexities of their org's metadata dependencies and minimize the risks associated with changes to the Salesforce environment.

SFDX-Hardis

SFDX-Hardis is a Salesforce DX plugin designed to enhance the DevOps process for Salesforce development teams. It aims to offer a modular, scriptable approach to DevOps, encapsulating standard execution sequences or scripts of Salesforce DX commands into single, more accessible commands.

SFDX-Hardis serves as both a Salesforce DX plugin and a Visual Studio Code extension, providing a user-friendly interface for initiating DevOps tasks. It allows users to start new tasks, create fields, and manage branch merging through a guided wizard, which abstracts complex command-line interactions into simple UI-driven actions. The plugin facilitates operations such as branch creation, sandbox initialization, metadata retrieval, and commit preparation. It also includes a Visual Studio Code extension that offers a graphical interface for executing commands, aimed at users who may not be comfortable with command-line tools.

The plugin is particularly useful for Salesforce development teams that require a structured yet flexible approach to managing their DevOps pipelines. It supports both scratch orgs and sandboxes, making it suitable for various development workflows. Its capabilities extend to automated metadata retrieval, deployment simulations, and quality checks, including Apex test coverage validation. SFDX-Hardis can be integrated with CI servers such as GitLab, GitHub Actions, and Azure DevOps, thereby automating the deployment process upon successful merge requests.

SFDX-Hardis' integration with popular CI/CD systems and its focus on user experience make it a valuable tool for Salesforce development teams looking to adopt or enhance their DevOps practices.

DX@Scale

DX@Scale is a DevOps solution designed for Salesforce implementations. It aims to address the complexities and challenges associated with managing large-scale Salesforce projects by leveraging Salesforce DX principles and custom tooling. The solution is built around several core principles, including modular design, automation, and CI/CD practices.

DX@Scale allows for the creation of multiple artifacts, such as unlocked packages and source packages, that can be independently developed, tested, and deployed. It utilizes scratch org pools to reduce the time needed to provision development environments, enabling instantaneous access for developers. The solution implements a simplified branch model, with the master branch serving as the production branch, and feature branches used for development work. It also includes custom libraries, SF PowerScripts, and SF PowerKit, which are open source tools that provide additional functionalities such as package versioning, build optimization, and profile reconciliation.

DX@Scale is particularly useful for large-scale Salesforce projects with multiple teams and complex deployment requirements. It streamlines the development process by allowing for efficient management of dependencies and facilitating the creation of smaller, more manageable packages. The solution is also applicable in scenarios where rapid environment provisioning is required and where there is a need for a fast feedback loop between code changes and deployment validation.

One of the primary strengths of DX@Scale is its ability to deliver deployments rapidly, with full builds taking less than 25 minutes and unit tests executing between 2 and 5 minutes. Its use of CI/CD pipelines and artifact repositories ensures traceability and control over the deployment process.

CumulusCI

CumulusCI is a toolchain developed by Salesforce.org aimed at automating the application life cycle for Salesforce projects. It is designed to facilitate the development, testing, and deployment of Salesforce applications by providing a suite of automation tools that work together to create a cohesive development process.

CumulusCI integrates with VCS, utilizing Salesforce DX scratch orgs as the basis for all development work. It automates the creation of these scratch orgs, handling dependencies, package installations, metadata deployment, org configuration, and data seeding. CumulusCI orchestrates these processes through flows and tasks, which are composable blocks of automation defined in a project's repository. Tasks are individual operations in a Salesforce org, while flows are sequences of these tasks that achieve specific outcomes. These are configurable in YAML and can be extended with Python.

CumulusCI is used to build sophisticated environments tailored to various roles in the application life cycle, from developers and admins to end users. It supports immediate and independent environment creation, ensuring teams can work without infrastructure constraints. CumulusCI's portability means automation is not limited to CI servers but extends to local machines and web interfaces such as MetaCI and MetaDeploy.

The toolchain increases development velocity by allowing each team member to work in their orgs, significantly reducing conflicts and dependencies on shared environments. It embeds modern best practices such as source control and Salesforce DX into the development workflow. CumulusCI is open source, which aligns with Salesforce's community-driven initiatives and encourages contribution and collaboration.

Summary

As we conclude this chapter, it is clear that the Salesforce DevOps ecosystem offers a diverse array of tools that cater to a wide range of development scenarios. From Salesforce's own DevOps Center to third-party offerings and community-driven open source projects, the landscape is rich with options that can be tailored to fit the unique needs of any organization.

Each tool we have discussed brings its strengths and areas of specialization. By selecting the right combination of these tools, a Salesforce team can create a DevOps environment that not only streamlines the development and deployment processes but also fosters a culture of continuous improvement and collaboration.

Salesforce DevOps Center, for example, is a powerful Salesforce-native solution that integrates seamlessly with the platform, offering automated change tracking and source control integration. It is an ideal choice for teams looking for a tool that is closely aligned with Salesforce's own best practices and future developments.

Commercial tools such as Salto, Panaya, Prodly, and Elements.cloud offer a blend of features such as impact analysis, deployment management, and process documentation. These tools are typically well suited for organizations that require robust support, advanced functionalities, and a guided user experience.

Open source tools, including Happy Soup, SFDX-Hardis, DX@Scale, and CumulusCI, empower teams with flexibility and the ability to customize their DevOps processes. The collaborative nature of open source projects often means these tools are at the forefront of innovation, incorporating the latest ideas and techniques from the community.

When selecting tools for your Salesforce DevOps toolkit, consider the complexity of your org, the size of your development team, and the specific challenges you face. For instance, if rapid environment provisioning is a priority, tools such as DX@Scale and CumulusCI may be particularly useful. If impact analysis and dependency management are critical, then Salto and Panaya could offer the necessary insights.

It is also important to consider the future direction of your DevOps practices. As Salesforce continues to evolve, so too will the tools that support it. Keeping an eye on emerging technologies and updates to existing tools will help ensure your DevOps strategy remains current and effective.

In the end, the goal of any DevOps tool is to support the team in delivering high-quality software efficiently and reliably. By carefully evaluating the options and understanding how each tool fits within the broader ecosystem, you can create a DevOps environment that not only meets today's demands but is also ready to adapt to tomorrow's challenges.

With the knowledge gained from this chapter, you are well equipped to navigate the Salesforce DevOps ecosystem, making informed choices that will drive your organization's success. As the Salesforce platform continues to grow and evolve, so will the tools and practices surrounding it, offering new opportunities for innovation and excellence in the world of Salesforce DevOps. We will now move on to the final chapter of the book, where we summarize our main findings and map out where you can go from here.

17
Conclusion

In this chapter, we will summarize the key points and takeaways from our discussions on Salesforce DevOps, encapsulate the journey we have taken, and look ahead to the future of Salesforce DevOps practices.

We will cover the following topics in this chapter:

- A summary of Salesforce DevOps
- Common pitfalls to avoid
- Steps and best practices for implementing Salesforce DevOps

By the end of this chapter, you will have completed your learning journey and be ready to venture further into the exciting world of Salesforce DevOps.

A summary of Salesforce DevOps

In this final chapter, we'll take a moment to consolidate our learnings from the preceding chapters, providing a comprehensive summary of Salesforce DevOps. This reflection not only reaffirms the principles and practices discussed but also sets the stage for continuous growth in the dynamic field of Salesforce.

The field of Salesforce DevOps

Salesforce DevOps emerged as a response to the growing complexities and demands of managing the Salesforce platform's development and operational aspects. It represents a confluence of software development (Dev) and information-technology operations (Ops), aiming to shorten the development life cycle while delivering features, fixes, and updates in alignment with business objectives.

The journey began with understanding the Salesforce environment's evolution, from a CRM-focused tool to a comprehensive development platform. This transformation necessitated an adoption of true development best practices and the need for an effective delivery mechanism – enter Salesforce DevOps. DevOps introduces a culture of collaboration, integration, and automation, streamlining processes and fostering a more proactive approach to change management.

Key to this transition was recognizing the importance of a DevOps culture. It's not merely about the tools and technologies; it's about the mindset. By fostering a DevOps culture, teams can break down silos, encourage open communication, and ensure shared responsibility for the Salesforce lifecycle. This cultural shift is pivotal in driving the successful adoption and implementation of DevOps practices.

Throughout this book, we examined various aspects of Salesforce DevOps, including deployment strategies, version control, CI/CD, and the role of testing. Deploying changes effectively is at the heart of DevOps. We explored the Salesforce platform's built-in tools and the limitations that led to the emergence of third-party tools designed to augment Salesforce's capabilities.

One such area of focus was the importance of version control – a cornerstone of any DevOps practice. We discussed how it enables teams to track changes, collaborate on code, and maintain a single source of truth. This is complemented by CI/CD pipelines, which automate the process of integrating changes and delivering them to production, thereby streamlining deployments and minimizing the risk of errors.

Testing is another critical component of Salesforce DevOps. By automating tests and integrating them into the CI/CD pipeline, teams can ensure that changes are not only deployed quickly but are also reliable and meet quality standards. This proactive approach to error detection and debugging helps maintain the stability and integrity of the Salesforce environment.

We also delved into the complexities of managing Salesforce environments, emphasizing the need for monitoring and controlling changes. Unchecked changes, even those made with the best intentions, can lead to instability and disrupt the smooth functioning of the platform. Automated monitoring tools provide visibility into changes, enabling teams to act swiftly in response to any deviations from expected behavior.

Data management, including data backup and security, was another area we covered in depth. Data is the lifeblood of the Salesforce platform, and ensuring its integrity and security is paramount. We discussed strategies for data backup and recovery, data masking, and compliance with data protection regulations. These practices not only protect the organization's data assets but also ensure that development and testing environments have access to realistic, high-quality data for effective testing.

Key learnings from Salesforce DevOps tools

Salesforce DevOps represents an ecosystem teeming with diverse tools, each designed to cater to the nuances of development and operations within the Salesforce platform. Throughout this book, we dissected the functionalities of several leading DevOps tools, examining their strengths and weaknesses, and their impact on the efficiency and success of Salesforce development and operations. In this section, we'll bring together the insights we've gained from these discussions, offering a synthesis of the key learnings from Salesforce DevOps tools.

Salesforce DevOps tools span a broad spectrum, from metadata management solutions to continuous integration platforms, release automation, version control, and testing utilities. Each tool is tailored to address specific challenges inherent in Salesforce development. For instance, Gearset excels in metadata deployment and comparison, Copado thrives in managing complex deployment pipelines, and AutoRABIT shines with its code analysis and data backup capabilities.

Through our exploration, we have learned that no single tool is a panacea for all DevOps needs. Instead, organizations must carefully assess each tool's strengths concerning their specific requirements. A tool that offers exceptional metadata management may not necessarily provide the best testing framework, and vice versa. The key takeaway here is the importance of a nuanced approach to tool selection, ensuring that the chosen set of tools complements the organization's workflow and enhances productivity.

A crucial takeaway from our exploration of Salesforce DevOps tools is the significance of integration and automation. Tools that seamlessly integrate with Salesforce and other third-party applications create a cohesive development environment that minimizes manual effort and reduces the potential for errors. Automation, a core principle of DevOps, has been a recurring theme in our discussions. Tools that automate repetitive tasks, such as deployments and testing, allow teams to focus on innovation and problem-solving, rather than getting bogged down in operational minutiae.

For instance, the ability to automate the movement of metadata and code between environments, as well as the execution of tests, significantly accelerates the development cycle. We have learned that automation not only speeds up the process but also brings consistency and reliability to deployments. Consistency in executing tasks ensures that each deployment adheres to the same quality standards, reducing the likelihood of defects slipping into production.

Salesforce DevOps tools underscore the importance of collaboration and visibility across the development life cycle. Tools that provide a clear view of the pipeline, from development to production, foster a collaborative environment where all stakeholders have insight into the progress of projects. This transparency is essential in a DevOps culture as it ensures that everyone, from developers to release managers, operates from a shared understanding of the project's status.

Visibility across the DevOps pipeline also aids in identifying bottlenecks and areas needing improvement. For example, a tool that offers detailed logs and analytics can help pinpoint stages in the pipeline where delays commonly occur, guiding teams to implement targeted optimizations. Furthermore, collaboration features, such as the ability to comment on and review changes within the tool, enhance team communication and facilitate knowledge sharing.

Looking ahead – the future of Salesforce DevOps

As we close this comprehensive exploration of Salesforce DevOps, it is crucial to not only reflect on the journey thus far but also to cast our gaze forward, anticipating emerging trends and staying prepared for the continuous evolution of this field. In this section, we will consider the future trajectory of Salesforce DevOps, drawing insights on forthcoming developments, and discussing strategies for Salesforce practitioners to thrive in the ever-changing landscape.

The Salesforce platform has consistently demonstrated a commitment to innovation, regularly introducing new features and enhancements that empower organizations to connect with their customers in more meaningful ways. This ongoing evolution naturally extends to the realm of Salesforce DevOps, where new tools, practices, and challenges emerge alongside the platform's advancements.

One of the key future trends in Salesforce DevOps is the increasing emphasis on **artificial intelligence** (**AI**) and **machine learning** (**ML**). These technologies have the potential to revolutionize the way we approach development and operations, offering predictive insights, automating routine tasks, and optimizing workflows. As AI and ML become more integrated into the Salesforce ecosystem, DevOps practices will need to adapt to harness these capabilities effectively.

Another significant trend is the growing importance of security and compliance within the DevOps process. With data breaches and privacy concerns on the rise, organizations are placing a higher priority on securing their Salesforce environments. This focus on security will likely lead to the development of more advanced tools and methodologies designed to ensure that DevOps practices align with stringent security standards.

The Salesforce DevOps community is expected to become more collaborative and interconnected. As the platform's user base expands, sharing best practices, experiences, and innovations will become increasingly vital. This collective intelligence will drive the advancement of DevOps practices, fostering a more dynamic and resilient ecosystem.

To stay ahead in the Salesforce DevOps field, practitioners must embrace a mindset of continuous learning and improvement. This involves staying informed about the latest platform updates, engaging with the community, and being open to experimenting with new tools and techniques.

The Salesforce DevOps community is a vibrant and collaborative ecosystem, where sharing knowledge and best practices is highly encouraged. As the field evolves, the community's role becomes even more critical in shaping the future of DevOps practices.

One of the key benefits of community engagement is the collective problem-solving that it fosters. By sharing experiences and solutions, the community can address common challenges more efficiently and effectively. This collaborative approach accelerates learning and innovation, benefiting the entire ecosystem.

Community-driven initiatives such as open source projects and collaborative tool development can lead to the creation of powerful resources that enhance Salesforce DevOps practices. These initiatives leverage the diverse skills and perspectives of the community, resulting in tools and solutions that are robust, versatile, and widely applicable. The community plays a vital role in advocating for best practices and standards within Salesforce DevOps. Through discussions, forums, and thought leadership, the community helps establish guidelines that promote quality, security, and efficiency in DevOps processes.

Common pitfalls to avoid

If you're looking to implement DevOps to improve your Salesforce delivery process, or perhaps enhance an existing process, there are some key mistakes to avoid. We'll try to guide you on these, to help drive your DevOps success.

One of the most significant pitfalls in implementing Salesforce DevOps is the inadequacy of automation. Automation, when done right, can streamline processes, reduce manual errors, and enhance productivity. However, many organizations either underutilize automation or implement it without a clear strategy. For instance, automating a flawed process only leads to faster production of poor results. It is vital to ensure that processes are optimized before they are automated. This requires a thorough understanding of the existing workflows, identifying bottlenecks, and then applying automation to enhance these processes.

Another critical mistake is the lack of cross-team collaboration. Salesforce DevOps is not just a set of tools and practices but also a culture that encourages collaboration between different teams, including development, operations, and business units. Without this collaboration, there's a risk of working in silos, leading to misaligned goals, duplicated efforts, and delays in project timelines. Effective communication channels and regular cross-functional meetings are crucial in fostering a collaborative environment. This ensures that everyone is on the same page and working toward a common goal.

Many organizations fail to institute metrics and monitoring early enough in their Salesforce DevOps journey. Metrics and monitoring are not just about identifying issues; they provide critical insights into the effectiveness of DevOps practices. They help in understanding the impact of changes, detecting areas for improvement, and making data-driven decisions. Implementing these from the onset allows teams to track progress, benchmark against industry standards, and continuously improve their DevOps practices.

Underestimating the importance of training and skills development is a common oversight. Salesforce DevOps involves a range of tools and technologies that are continuously evolving. Teams must stay updated with the latest trends and best practices. Investing in regular training and skill development sessions ensures that the team is competent and confident in utilizing DevOps methodologies effectively.

Finally, ignoring the cultural aspect of DevOps can be detrimental. The success of DevOps depends not just on tools and processes but also on the mindset of the people involved. Encouraging a culture of openness, experimentation, and continuous learning is as crucial as any technical implementation. Resistance to change is natural, but creating a supportive environment where risks are encouraged and failures are seen as learning opportunities can significantly enhance the success of Salesforce DevOps initiatives.

Implementing a successful Salesforce DevOps strategy

As we bring our exploration of Salesforce DevOps to a close, it is essential to consolidate our understanding into actionable strategies. The journey through the various facets of Salesforce DevOps has equipped us with the knowledge to implement a robust and successful strategy within our organizations. This section is dedicated to synthesizing the wealth of information we've gathered into a practical roadmap for Salesforce professionals.

The foundation of any successful Salesforce DevOps strategy lies in establishing a strong culture that embraces the principles of collaboration, continuous improvement, and shared responsibility. Throughout this book, we have emphasized the importance of cultivating an environment where transparency, communication, and learning are valued.

A successful Salesforce DevOps strategy is underpinned by a culture that encourages team members to work together toward common goals. Collaboration should not be confined to developers alone; it must extend across all roles involved in the Salesforce life cycle, including administrators, QA testers, release managers, and stakeholders. Tools that facilitate communication and collaboration, such as shared repositories, integrated chat applications, and collaborative planning software, can significantly enhance team dynamics.

Continuous improvement should be a guiding tenet for teams looking to refine and enhance their Salesforce DevOps practices. This involves regularly reviewing processes, tools, and outcomes to identify areas for optimization. Encouraging a mindset that sees every challenge as an opportunity for growth will lead to a more resilient and adaptable organization.

In a DevOps culture, the responsibility for the success of the Salesforce platform is shared among all team members. This collective ownership not only ensures accountability but also empowers individuals to take initiative and contribute to the platform's overall health and performance.

The heart of Salesforce DevOps lies in the deployment process. Efficient and reliable deployments are critical for delivering features and updates that meet business needs. Our exploration has highlighted several key practices that contribute to successful deployment management.

Automation is key to achieving smooth and consistent deployments. Automating the deployment pipeline reduces manual errors, speeds up the delivery process, and ensures that every change is subjected to the same rigorous testing and validation procedures.

Effective change management ensures that every modification to the Salesforce environment is tracked, reviewed, and approved. This not only enhances security and compliance but also provides a clear audit trail for all changes.

Optimizing the release process involves balancing the need for speed with the imperative for quality. Teams must work to establish release cadences that align with business needs while ensuring that each release is thoroughly tested and validated. With DevOps, there is an additional advantage that soon becomes apparent – if you have quality, you can go faster, especially in the long run.

The greatest value to be extracted from a DevOps implementation is when it is firmly connected to business outcomes. For example, businesses can drive greater success by responding to ever-changing customer and market needs, enabled by a robust DevOps process that means new features can be released quickly. Alternatively, another measure of success could be reduced downtime due to DevOps, resulting in better product quality and perception in the market, as well as less time spent fixing issues and more time meeting customer expectations.

DevOps succeeds when everyone aligns with the approach and goals of the process. By everyone, we encourage you to think beyond just Dev and Ops teams and think across the entire software delivery life cycle, end to end. This mindset should become part of the planning phase, with business analysts and project managers already thinking about breaking requests into smaller chunks that can be incrementally delivered. At the other end of that pipeline, QA resources and even end users can be brought into a culture of DevOps and become accustomed to regular but incremental delivery.

With these ideas and thoughts in mind, let's look at a potential checklist for getting your Salesforce DevOps implementation off the ground.

A DevOps implementation checklist

Getting started with Salesforce DevOps involves several key steps to ensure a successful implementation. Throughout this book, while we've stressed the fact that there is no one way to do Salesforce, some common themes are applicable across the board. Here's a summarized list of best practices:

- **Understand your requirements**: Before diving into DevOps, assess your current process. Identify what's working well and areas that need improvement. This step helps in pinpointing the resources and support needed for DevOps success.

- **Start small and ramp up**: Implementing Salesforce DevOps doesn't mean overhauling everything at once. Begin with a solid foundation, focusing on successful deployments and version control. Gradually build up your DevOps processes. This approach has been more successful than trying to introduce everything simultaneously.

- **Build a DevOps culture**: DevOps is not just about tools but also about culture. A strong DevOps culture emphasizes collaboration, continuous improvement, and team buy-in. Involving the entire team in DevOps training and development is crucial for nurturing this culture.

- **Iterate and optimize**: Continuously learn from and optimize your processes. Encourage team members to come forward with ideas and suggestions to improve existing systems.

- **Measure success**: Regularly review your DevOps adoption to ensure you're working towards your goals. Utilize metrics such as Google's DORA to assess the velocity and resilience of your DevOps workflow.

- **Choose and set up the right tools**: The choice of tools for Salesforce DevOps should align with your organization's specific needs and existing systems. Assess tools based on their capabilities to support your workflow, integration with other systems (such as JIRA or your Git provider), and ease of use. Look for tools that offer automated change tracking, easy management of development pipelines, and seamless integration with source control systems. Consider tools that are known for their robustness in Salesforce environments, such as Gearset, Copado, Prodly, or AutoRABIT. It's important to choose a tool that not only fits your current way of working but also scales with your growth and evolving DevOps practices.

- **Create a project and set up a pipeline**: Once you've selected a tool, the next step is to create and manage your development pipeline. This involves setting up environments (such as development, testing, and production) and defining the processes for moving changes between these environments. The pipeline should allow for CI/CD, enabling you to automate testing and deployment processes. The tool should provide visibility into each stage of development, from code commits to deployment, and facilitate collaboration among team members.

- **Work item management and version control**: Implement a system for managing work items and tracking changes. This step is crucial for maintaining a clear history of changes, understanding the impact of each modification, and facilitating rollbacks if necessary. Your chosen tool should support version control practices, allowing you to keep a comprehensive history of all metadata changes. This ensures traceability and accountability, enabling teams to collaborate effectively and maintain high standards of quality and consistency in the development process.

Remember, Salesforce DevOps is an ongoing process that requires continuous learning and adaptation. Each step you take should be geared toward creating more efficient and collaborative development processes. For a more detailed guide and additional information, refer to the sources provided.

Final thoughts and recommendations

As we conclude our in-depth exploration of Salesforce DevOps, we reflect on the journey we've undertaken, and the comprehensive skill set we've developed. The world of Salesforce DevOps is complex and ever-evolving, but it is also one of immense opportunity and growth. In this final section, we'll distill the essence of what we've learned into actionable insights and offer recommendations for Salesforce professionals to continue to excel in their DevOps journey.

Salesforce DevOps is a domain that intersects technology, processes, and people. It includes many practices, from CI/CD to monitoring, testing, and collaboration. Our journey throughout this book has highlighted the importance of understanding the Salesforce ecosystem's unique challenges and leveraging specialized tools and techniques to address these challenges effectively.

Throughout this book, we've seen how DevOps practices can transform the way Salesforce development teams operate. By automating repetitive tasks, enforcing quality standards, and fostering a culture of continuous improvement, teams can deliver higher-quality software more quickly and with fewer errors. Moreover, the emphasis on collaboration and communication within DevOps aligns perfectly with the collaborative nature of Salesforce itself, where cross-functional teams often work together to deliver solutions that drive business success.

As Salesforce continues to grow and introduce new features, the importance of staying abreast of the latest developments cannot be overstated. For Salesforce professionals looking to continue their growth in DevOps, the following recommendations serve as a guide for ongoing professional development:

- **Invest in continuous learning**: The Salesforce ecosystem is dynamic, with new releases and updates introduced regularly. To stay current, professionals should invest time in continuous learning through Salesforce Trailhead, webinars, certifications, and other educational resources.

- **Engage with the community**: The Salesforce community is a rich source of knowledge and support. Engaging with this community through forums, user groups, and events can provide valuable insights and opportunities for networking and collaboration.

- **Embrace new tools and technologies**: As new tools and technologies emerge, being open to exploring and adopting them can provide a competitive edge. Innovations in AI, ML, and other areas are poised to change the landscape of Salesforce DevOps.

- **Focus on security and compliance**: With increasing concerns around data security and privacy, professionals should prioritize acquiring skills in these areas. Understanding how to implement secure DevOps practices is becoming increasingly important.

- **Encourage a culture of experimentation**: Encourage teams to experiment with new approaches and technologies. This culture of experimentation can lead to innovative solutions and improvements in DevOps practices.

- **Develop soft skills**: Technical skills are crucial, but so are soft skills such as communication, leadership, and problem-solving. Developing these skills can enhance collaboration and effectiveness in a DevOps environment.

As we part ways, we offer the following advice to Salesforce DevOps practitioners:

- **Stay agile**: The principles of agility – flexibility, responsiveness to change, and incremental delivery – are at the heart of DevOps. Embrace these principles in your daily work.

- **Prioritize quality**: Never compromise on the quality of your work. Quality is the cornerstone of trust in software delivery.

- **Collaborate and share**: DevOps is as much about people as it is about processes and tools. Share your knowledge, learn from others, and collaborate to achieve common goals.

- **Keep the end user in mind**: Ultimately, the software you deliver through DevOps practices is for the benefit of the end user. Keep their needs and experiences at the forefront of your decision-making.

- **Reflect and improve**: Regularly take the time to reflect on your practices, tools, and outcomes. Look for opportunities to improve and innovate.

Salesforce DevOps is an exciting and challenging field that requires a blend of technical expertise, process understanding, and collaborative skills. As practitioners, our journey is one of constant learning and adaptation. By embracing the principles discussed in this book and staying engaged with the Salesforce community, we can continue to grow and contribute to the success of our organizations. Salesforce DevOps is not just about deploying software; it's about creating a culture that values quality, efficiency, and continuous improvement. With the right mindset and tools, the possibilities for innovation and success in Salesforce DevOps are limitless.

Index

Other Books You May Enjoy

If you enjoyed this book, you may be interested in these other books by Packt:

Salesforce End-to-End Implementation Handbook

Kristian Margaryan Jorgensen

ISBN: 978-1-80461-322-1

- Explore the end-to-end Salesforce implementation lifecycle with templates and practical examples
- Discover common issues and strategies for mitigation and prevention
- Work with checklists to assess the state of your Salesforce implementation in each phase
- Purchase of the print or Kindle book includes a free PDF eBook

Becoming a Salesforce Certified Technical Architect – Second Edition

Tameem Bahri

ISBN: 978-1-80323-943-9

- Explore core architectural concepts essential for any Salesforce architect
- Understand Salesforce knowledge domains using practical examples
- Practice creating solutions using scenarios focusing on particular knowledge domains
- Discover key artifacts needed to document and explain an end-to-end solution
- Apply data life cycle management effectively in the Salesforce ecosystem
- Design appropriate enterprise integration interfaces to build your connected solution
- Know what to expect on the day of the review board along with valuable tips and tricks

Packt is searching for authors like you

If you're interested in becoming an author for Packt, please visit authors.packtpub.com and apply today. We have worked with thousands of developers and tech professionals, just like you, to help them share their insight with the global tech community. You can make a general application, apply for a specific hot topic that we are recruiting an author for, or submit your own idea.

Share Your Thoughts

Now you've finished *Salesforce DevOps for Architects*, we'd love to hear your thoughts! Scan the QR code below to go straight to the Amazon review page for this book and share your feedback or leave a review on the site that you purchased it from.

https://packt.link/r/1837636052

Your review is important to us and the tech community and will help us make sure we're delivering excellent quality content.

Download a free PDF copy of this book

Thanks for purchasing this book!

Do you like to read on the go but are unable to carry your print books everywhere?

Is your eBook purchase not compatible with the device of your choice?

Don't worry, now with every Packt book you get a DRM-free PDF version of that book at no cost.

Read anywhere, any place, on any device. Search, copy, and paste code from your favorite technical books directly into your application.

The perks don't stop there, you can get exclusive access to discounts, newsletters, and great free content in your inbox daily

Follow these simple steps to get the benefits:

1. Scan the QR code or visit the link below

https://packt.link/free-ebook/9781837636051

2. Submit your proof of purchase
3. That's it! We'll send your free PDF and other benefits to your email directly

Printed in Great Britain
by Amazon